Evaluation of Digital Libraries

CHANDOS
INFORMATION PROFESSIONAL SERIES

Series Editor: Ruth Rikowski
(email: Rikowskigr@aol.com)

Chandos' new series of books are aimed at the busy information professional. They have been specially commissioned to provide the reader with an authoritative view of current thinking. They are designed to provide easy-to-read and (most importantly) practical coverage of topics that are of interest to librarians and other information professionals. If you would like a full listing of current and forthcoming titles, please visit our website www.chandospublishing.com or email info@chandospublishing.com or telephone +44 (0) 1223 891358.

New authors: we are always pleased to receive ideas for new titles; if you would like to write a book for Chandos, please contact Dr Glyn Jones on email gjones@chandospublishing.com or telephone number +44 (0) 1993 848726.

Bulk orders: some organisations buy a number of copies of our books. If you are interested in doing this, we would be pleased to discuss a discount. Please email info@chandospublishing.com or telephone +44(0) 1223 891358.

Evaluation of Digital Libraries

An insight into useful applications and methods

EDITED BY
GIANNIS TSAKONAS
AND
CHRISTOS PAPATHEODOROU

Chandos Publishing
Oxford • Cambridge • New Delhi

Chandos Publishing
TBAC Business Centre
Avenue 4
Station Lane
Witney
Oxford OX28 4BN
UK
Tel: +44 (0) 1993 848726
Email: info@chandospublishing.com
www.chandospublishing.com

Chandos Publishing is an imprint of Woodhead Publishing Limited

Woodhead Publishing Limited
Abington Hall
Granta Park
Great Abington
Cambridge CB21 6AH
UK
www.woodheadpublishing.com

First published in 2009

ISBN:
978 1 84334 484 1

British Library Cataloguing-in-Publication Data.
A catalogue record for this book is available from the British Library.

Typeset by Domex e-Data Pvt. Ltd.
Printed in the UK and USA.

Printed in the UK by 4edge Limited - www.4edge.co.uk

Contents

List of figures and tables

Figures

Tables

About the contributors

Maristella Agosti is Professor of Computer Science, Department of Information Engineering and Faculty of Humanities, University of Padova. She is also group leader of the department's Information Management Systems Research Group. Her research interests include digital library management systems, digital library architectures, information retrieval, search engines, analysis of log data in digital libraries and search engines, annotation of digital contents, information retrieval (IR) across networks, web-link analysis for IR, and the design and development of advanced services for archives and digital libraries. She has been a programme committee member and chair for numerous conferences, and an editorial board member of the journals *Information Processing & Management* and *International Journal on Digital Libraries*. She is group leader in several European Union funded research projects, including the DELOS Network of Excellence on Digital Libraries and TELplus, which aims to strengthen, extend and improve the European Digital Library service.

David Bainbridge received his BSc in computer science from the University of Edinburgh in 1991 (class medallist). He was awarded a Commonwealth scholarship to undertake a PhD to study the problem of optical music recognition. He joined the Department of Computer Science at Waikato, New Zealand, where he completed his PhD in 1997. His research interests include digital media, with a particular emphasis on music. He is an active member of the Greenstone Digital Library Project, receiving the Namur Award in 2004 for its IT development for humanitarian aid. He has developed CANTOR, a software application that accepts scanned images of music and returns them in a variety of musically processed computer formats; and MELDEX, a melody indexing application, where a database of tunes can be searched using a sung melody rather than text constraints such as song title and author. At the New Zealand Digital Library, he has also been involved with metadata extraction, the women's history collection, video handling support and musical theme extraction.

Ann Blanford is Professor of Human–Computer Interaction and Director of the UCL Interaction Centre, University College London, where she teaches usability evaluation methods and organisational informatics. The main focus of her research is on ways of answering the question 'How well does your system fit?', in terms of cognition, interaction and work. Broad themes of her research include: working with information and the use of electronic resources (digital libraries etc.); human capabilities (cognitive resilience, sense-making, decision-making, problem-solving, communication and conceptualisation), and how to design to support these capabilities better; human error; understanding individual and small team interactions with technology; and models, methods and theories for evaluating interactive systems. She has been programme chair, programme committee member and workshop organiser at several conferences on human–computer interaction.

Colleen Cook is Dean of the Texas A&M University Libraries and holder of the Sterling C. Evans Endowed Chair. She received the 'Dissertation of the Year Award', in 2001 from the College of Education and Human Development at Texas A&M where she earned her PhD in higher education administration. She also holds BA and MLS degrees from the University of Texas at Austin and an MA from Texas A&M University. Dr Cook helped develop and promote LibQUAL+®, the premier assessment tool for measuring library service quality internationally. She was co-principal investigator of a three-year grant for the initial LibQUAL+® project supported by the Fund for the Improvement of Post-Secondary Education and managed by the Association of Research Libraries and Texas A&M University. She has written extensively on library management and information service issues. Her work appears in performance measurement and library journals including *Educational and Psychological Measurement, Library Trends, Library Quarterly, College and Research Libraries* and *Journal of Academic Librarianship*.

Nicola Ferro is Assistant Professor of Computer Science at the Information Management Systems Research Group, Department of Information Engineering, University of Padova. He holds an engineering degree in telecommunications from University of Padova and a PhD in computer science from the same university. The main topic of his research is digital document annotation in the context of digital libraries, in particular, the design and development of an advanced annotation service to search and retrieve documents by exploiting the annotations linked to them. Other relevant topics of interest are multilingual information retrieval and the evaluation of information retrieval systems. Concerning the evaluation of retrieval systems, he focuses on both the organisation and management of experimental evaluation forums and the design and development of advanced computational services for the collected data, such as cross-comparison and statistical analysis tools for the submitted experiments. He has written several articles on the abovementioned fields and was programme committee member of the European Conference on Digital Libraries series.

Brinley Franklin is Vice Provost at the University of Connecticut. He has served as Chair of the Association of Research Libraries (ARL) Statistics and Assessment Committee, Committee Member of the International Federation of Library Associations Statistics, and currently Board Liaison to the ARL Statistics and Assessment Committee. Together with Terry Plum, he developed the MINES for Libraries® protocol used in over 40 libraries over the last five years. He has written journal articles and book chapters and made numerous presentations.

Emmanouel Garoufallou is Lecturer at the Department of Library Science and Information Systems at the Alexander Technological Educational Institution of Thessaloniki. He also works as a library and information science (LIS) expert for the Public Library of Veria and as a consultant in academic and public libraries, museums and archives. He is a member of the DELTOS Research Group. He has been involved in various EU projects, such as Light, and currently in ENTITLE and EDLocal. He holds a PhD in digital libraries and an MA in LIS from the Manchester Metropolitan University, UK.

Sarah Giersch has consulted in the area of education technology since 2003, specifically on implementing, evaluating, conducting outreach for and promoting the sustainability of education in digital libraries. She has developed surveys to measure the use of networked electronic resources in and user satisfaction with digital libraries; an annotated bibliography on evaluating the educational impact of digital libraries; a business-plan review of models to sustain digital libraries; and has been involved in numerous workshops exploring topics on evaluating, sustaining and involving participants in building digital libraries. Giersch currently consults for the National Science Digital Library (NSDL), as the Director of Development and Special Projects. In this position, she helped NSDL obtain funding from the National Science Foundation to develop a professional development curriculum that supports K12 educators to incorporate science, technology, engineering and mathematics digital learning objects into their teaching practice and that promotes reflective dialogue through a community of practice. Prior to establishing a consulting practice, Giersch worked in the private sector conducting market analyses and assessments related to deploying technology in higher education.

Richard J. Hartley is Head of the Department of Information and Communications and Director of the Information Research Institute at Manchester Metropolitan University, UK. He teaches the areas of information retrieval and digital libraries. He is joint author of several textbooks including *Information Seeking in the Online Age* (2000) and *Organizing Knowledge* (2008). He is joint editor of the journal *Education for Information* and has been published widely in the field.

Judy Jeng received a PhD from Rutgers University, School of Communication, Information, and Library Studies. She proposed an evaluation model that takes into consideration effectiveness, efficiency, satisfaction and learnability. She has served as evaluation consultant for three digital libraries – the Moving Image Collections, the New Jersey Digital Highway, and the NJVid, in addition to her cross-institutional doctoral study of two library websites – Rutgers University and Queens College. She has written and presented widely on local, state, national and international levels. She is currently the Head of Collection Services at the New Jersey City University.

Michael Khoo is Assistant Professor at the College of Information Science and Technology (the iSchool) at Drexel University, Philadelphia. His research focuses on the sociotechnical dimensions of information technology use, with a focus on digital library evaluation, and understanding the different mental models and practices that users bring to their interactions with these systems. He has a background in communication and anthropology, and has worked in field sites ranging from the Indian Himalayas to customer call centres for a wireless phone company. He has studied and worked with a number of digital libraries, including the Digital Water Education Library, the Digital Library for Earth Systems Education, the National Science Digital Library, and the Internet Public Library.

Martha Kyrillidou is Director of ARL's statistics and service quality programmes, Martha is the editor of the ARL Statistics and the ARL Annual Salary Survey and one of the principal investigators in the development of LibQUAL+®. She has been involved in projects regarding the evaluation of electronic resources such as MINES for Libraries®, DigiQUAL® and E-metrics. She has written numerous journal articles and book chapters, and is a leader in library assessment.

Yvonna Lincoln is Distinguished Professor and Ruth Harrington Chair of Higher Education at the Department of Educational Administration and Human Resource Development, Texas A&M University. She has been Section Editor of 'Qualitative and Quantitative Methods' in the *Encyclopedia of Sociology*, co-editor of the *American Educational Research Journal* and *Qualitative Inquiry*, as well as editorial board member of the *Educational Researcher*. She has organised many conferences on qualitative research and has received many awards for her scientific and professional activities.

Dave McArthur works at GoH, following a position at the US National Science Foundation (NSF). As a visiting scientist, he worked in the NSF's Division of Undergraduate Education and helped manage several programmes including the National Science Digital Library. Prior to his appointment at NSF, he was a visiting professor at North Carolina Central University. He has also conducted research in information technology and educational technology at the RAND Corporation, Collegies and UNC Wilmington. In the past several years he has led NSF-sponsored grants in the area of digital libraries, initiating the project that developed iLumina, a digital library of faculty-contributed resources for online and web-enhanced courses. In October 2008, he became Director of Research in the School of Education at the University of North Carolina at Chapel Hill. Dave received a PhD in cognitive psychology from the University of Michigan and a BA from the University of Toronto.

Maria Monopoli has been awarded a PhD and an MSc in information science from City University, London. She also holds a bachelor's degree from the Technological Education Institute of Athens, where she is currently a visiting assistant professor in the Department of Librarianship & Information Systems, School of Management and Economics. She also works as a librarian at the library of the Bank of Greece. She has previously worked as a librarian in academic libraries in the UK and Greece and as a library administrator for the Library and Archive Department of the Organising Committee of the Olympic Games, Athens 2004. She has been an analyst of user studies for South Bank University Library's Learning and Information Services and a field researcher on the NHS Direct Online Research Project conducted by the Department of Information Science at City University, London. Her research interests lie within the area of evaluating digital libraries from the user's point of view (user thinking behaviour, usability studies and evaluation processes).

David Nicholas is Head of the School of Library Archive and Information Studies, University College London and also Director of the Centre for Information Behaviour and the Evaluation of Research. He has over 30 years' experience as an information researcher. He has been the principal researcher on several projects funded by such organisations as the NHS, the Department of Health, the Economic and Social Research Council and Nokia. He also provides consultancy services to a number of organisations including BBC World News Service, News International and the Volunteers Centre UK. His chief research interests include the digital consumer, the digital transition, scholarly communication, weblog analysis, information needs analysis, online and digital libraries – use and evaluation, and mobile phones as information retrieval platforms. He is the editor of *Aslib Proceedings: New Information Perspectives* and a referee for *Journal of Documentation, Journal of Information Science, Information Processing & Management* and *JASIST*.

Christos Papatheodorou is Associate Professor at the Department of Archives and Library Sciences, Ionian University, Corfu, where he teaches information systems, information retrieval and metadata. He holds a BSc and a PhD in computer science from the Department of Informatics, Athens University of Economics and Business. His research interests include digital library evaluation, metadata interoperability, user modelling, personalisation and web-mining. He has participated as a project proposals evaluator for the European Union Information Society Technologies research programme (Action Line Cultural Heritage) and has been involved as a researcher in several national and international research and development projects, such as the DELOS Network of Excellence on Digital Libraries. He has participated in the programme committee of various international conferences and workshops and was General Co-Chair of the 13th European Conference on Digital Libraries.

Terry Plum is Assistant Dean at Simmons Graduate School of Library and Information Science, and is responsible for technology and a satellite site campus at Mount Holyoke College in South Hadley, MA. He teaches courses in reference and information technology. He co-developed MINES for Libraries® protocol with Brinley Franklin. He has consulted internationally in library development, library science education, and information technology training in Georgia, Kosova and Vietnam.

Tefko Saracevic is Professor II (the highest university academic rank) at the School of Communication & Information, Rutgers University. He has been President of the American Society for Information Science and received the society's Award of Merit. He also received the Gerard Salton Award for Excellence in Research, from the Association for Computing Machinery's Special Interest Group on Information Retrieval. In a histogram of citations from papers in the *Journal of the American*

Society for Information Science and Technology for years 1956–2004 and involving 3,575 authors, he ranked first in citations to his work.

Rania Siatri is Visiting Lecturer at the Department of Library Science and Information Systems at the Alexander Technological Educational Institution of Thessaloniki. She also works as a library and information science (LIS) expert for the Public Library of Veria and is currently involved in the ENTITLE project. She is a member of the DELTOS Research Group. She holds a PhD and an MA in LIS from the Manchester Metropolitan University. Some of her main interests are information seeking, information retrieval, virtual learning environments, academic libraries and electronic information resources.

Yin-Leng Theng is Associate Professor at Wee Kim Wee School of Communication and Information, Nanyang Technological University (NTU). She jointed Nanyang Technological University in 2001. Between 1998 and 2001, she was a senior lecturer at Middlesex University (London) and taught human–computer interaction (HCI) and educational multimedia. Her research interests include user-interface design (interactive systems) – culture, ethics, security, privacy and trust in digital libraries; hypertext and the web; e-learning and learning objects; education and information literacy; and healthcare informatics. Her research in HCI and digital libraries led to the award of two research grants from the UK Engineering and Physical Science Research Council, and an academic research fund grant from NTU in 2003. She is also a co-investigator and a collaborator on a couple of collaborative research projects on geospatial digital libraries and reusable learning objects.

Giannis Tsakonas holds a BSc and a PhD in librarianship from the Department of Archives and Library Sciences, Ionian University, Corfu. Currently he works as a librarian in the Library & Information Center, University of Patras. His role in the development of the centre's digital library services has provided an opportunity for research into the role of the digital library as information infrastructure in the academic environment. He has been actively involved in the DELOS Network of Excellence Working Group on Digital Library Evaluation, while he also works on behalf of E-LIS, the international subject repository on librarianship and information science, as national editor for Greece. His research interests include digital library development in information contexts, such as the fields of academia and museums; user-centred digital library evaluation; information behaviour; aspects of information services integration; and visual communication.

Lee Zia is Program Officer in the Division of Undergraduate Education at the National Science Foundation (NSF) where he serves as the Lead Program Director for the National Science Digital Library (NSDL) programme. His involvement with NSDL is a natural extension of his longstanding interest in the application of information technology to education, which began when he started as a faculty member in the Department of Mathematics at the University of New Hampshire in the mid-1980s. While serving at NSF as a visiting scientist (1995–96), Zia helped develop the concept and vision for a digital library programme to support education. When the current NSDL programme officially came into being, he returned to NSF and became a permanent member of the staff in late 2000. Zia has written numerous articles about digital libraries and educational applications of information technology, and he participates both in intra-agency working groups at NSF that deal with NSF's emerging emphasis on cyberinfrastructure and in cross-agency interactions in this area.

The contributors may be contacted via the editors at:

Christos Papatheodorou
Department of Archives and Library Sciences
Ionian University
72 Ioannou Theotoki Street
Corfu 49100
Greece
E-mail: *papatheodor@ionio.gr*

Giannis Tsakonas
Library and Information Center
University of Patras
Rio 26504
Patras
Greece
E-mail: *john@lis.upatras.gr*

List of abbreviations

ACM	Association for Computing Machinery
ARL	Association of Research Libraries
ASIS	American Society for Information Science
CIBER	Centre for Information Behaviour and the Evaluation of Research
CLEF	Cross Language Evaluation Forum
CLIR	Council on Library and Information Resources
COUNTER	Counting Online Usage of Networked Electronic Resources
DIRECT	Distributed Information Retrieval Evaluation Campaign Tool
DLESE	Digital Library for Earth Systems Education
DLF	Digital Library Federation
DLI	Digital Library Initiative
DUE	Division of Undergraduate Education
EDNER	Formative Evaluation of the Distributed National Electronic Resource
EIESC	Educational Impact and Evaluation Standing Committee
eLIB	Electronic Library Programme
ICIAM	International Council of Industrial and Applied Mathematics
IMS	Institute of Mathematical Statistics
IMU	International Mathematical Union
IRS	Interoperable Repository Statistics
ISO	International Standards Organization
mEDRA	Multilingual European Registration Agency of DOI
MESUR	Metrics from Scholarly Usage of Resources
MINES for Libraries	Measuring the Impact of Networked Electronic Services
NISO	National Information Standards Organization

NIST	National Institute of Standards and Technology
NSB	National Science Board
NSDL	National Science Digital Library
NSF	National Science Foundation
OAI	Open Access Initiative
OARiNZ	Open Access Repositories in New Zealand
OCUL	Ontario Council of University Libraries
OhioLINK	Ohio Library and Information Network
PEAK	Pricing Electronic Access to Knowledge
PMH	Protocol for Metadata Harvesting (OAI)
SMART	Statistical Measures Available Real Time
SUSHI	Standardized Usage Statistics Harvesting Initiatives
TREC	Text Retrieval Conference
UPA	Usability Professionals' Association

Preface

After 20 years of major developments, shifts and transformations, the digital library domain has matured. Yet, despite reaching a satisfying level of consciousness, it still seeks new avenues of advancement. One of the most important vehicles to promote further advances is evaluation. Despite the various meanings of this term, the underlying need is imperative, if one wants to develop and provide useful and usable digital library services. After many years of development, digital library systems have acquired a user-friendly orientation, while the system-centric approach for their development still dominates. This is evident from a quick look at the proposed topics of the major digital library scientific events, whether generic or specialised. Evaluation areas can be easily traced as a reflection of the community's need to explore and learn the potential of these systems, the margins for improvement and the further steps they have to tread. Evaluation is thus closely related to the definition and the components of digital library systems. No one can ignore the strength of formal models, such as the 5S model (streams, structures, spaces, scenarios and societies) developed by Goncalves et al. (2004). The 5S model is indicative of the need for a unified conception about digital libraries and how this descriptive language can be integrated in evaluation activities, as it was exhibited in further publications. However, due to transformations and advances, our understanding of digital libraries remains challenged. The creators of the 5S model have thus refined it to create the minimum set of concepts necessary to classify a system as a digital library: catalogue, collection, digital object, metadata specification, repository and services. Moreover in this refined model, a set of quality dimensions for each concept has been defined formally (such as accessibility, preservability, pertinence, relevance, etc. for the digital object; accuracy and completeness for the metadata; efficiency, effectiveness and reliability for services, etc.) as well as a set of numerical indicators for these quality dimensions.

In putting together the present book, we sought to compile a team of authors who could share their knowledge and experience in a way that is both academically rigorous and accessible to the uninitiated. The selection of the authors was thus based on the solid expertise and knowledge of scholars representing the various classes in the digital library domain. As a consequence, the book is multidisciplinary in its nature, addressing many research and practical fields. It discusses many issues, both theoretical and practical, such as reasons for evaluation, processes, tools and methodologies. The book structure and the methodology for the presentation of its content are articulated on four main evaluation questions: who, what, why and how. This approach, proposed by Saracevic (2004), is quite integrated, as it covers all the theoretical and practical issues concerning digital library evaluation. These questions seem logical and elementary only if they are asked and answered with sincerity and upright research documentation. If certain points of the answers to these questions remain obscure, then the whole initiative has unclear direction, misses important data and produces ambiguous results. The book makes explicit the views and perspectives of researchers and digital library developers, librarians, curators, and information and computer scientists, who focus on a variety of scientific domains, such as information retrieval, human–computer interaction, information-seeking and user-behaviour analysis, and organisational and managerial theories and practices, etc. The various interesting case studies presenting successful projects will help novice readers to conceptualise and absorb key concepts and methodologies.

Part 1 of the book refers to the people who are interested in evaluation. Librarians are an important class and the contribution by Franklin, Kyrillidou and Plum examines how assessment data are presently being used in libraries. In their chapter, they develop a set of criteria or expectations for the evaluation of digital libraries, based on the existing assessment culture in libraries and the uses to which assessment data are deployed. Khoo and Zia describe the expectations of a funding agency in terms of the results of evaluation campaigns. As a significant portion of the research in digital libraries is funded, the digital library community should acquire knowledge about the funders' requirements; the example of National Science Digital Library, a network of digital library resources and services funded by the National Science Foundation, is quite expedient.

In Part 2 of the book, the four objects of evaluation are identified, namely usability, usefulness, performance and usage. Jeng's contribution focuses on a very critical concept of digital library evaluation, that of usability. In addition to providing a panoramic view of the main usability criteria, Jeng discusses the concepts of cross-cultural usability and usability for special user groups, such as the elderly. A related concept is that of usefulness and Garoufallou, Siatri and Hartley cover significant areas of this concept, such as information behaviour and user studies. Their chapter presents the impact of information behaviour on the design of critical features and investigates the role of user studies in the evaluation of digital libraries. Ferro and Agosti's chapter discusses digital library performance evaluation methodologies and presents a new approach for the development of such systems. They argue that digital library performance evaluation creates an array of useful data ('scientific data') that must be curated properly in order to be expressive, reliable and capable of being integrated into the various development phases. Nicholas presents the value of usage data and the importance of deep log analysis, an innovative kind of log analysis. Using findings from their usage analysis of log files from the British Library Learning website, they illustrate the advantages of this method over the classic transactional log analysis, surveys and qualitative methods.

The purpose of evaluating digital libraries is investigated in Part 3 of the book. Blandford and Bainbridge discuss the definition of user needs in order to enhance digital library design. They advocate the idea that innovative digital library features may address previously unrecognised user needs. Tsakonas and Papatheodorou explore the implications of digital library evaluation on the outcome assessment of influential processes, such as education and research. Their chapter summarises the main difficulties in the generation of outcomes assessment in the digital library domain and proposes alternative, innovative approaches. Kyrillidou, Cook and Lincoln focus on the research conducted with the Science, Math, Engineering and Technology Education Digital Library (SMETE) user community, aiming to develop a protocol known as DigiQUAL®. The concept of quality is vital for user-centred digital libraries and the definition of a measuring instrument has proven laborious work.

The final part is dedicated to the methodological dimensions of evaluation. Khoo, Giersch and McArthur present a strategic list of questions that can guide evaluators to a course of activities. Their approach, which is based on the NSDL experience, takes into account the finite resources that every evaluator possesses and proposes a framework for prioritising decisions. Monopoli helps to summarise the benefits of qualitative methodologies to gain new perspectives of already known issues, or to collect in-depth data that may be difficult to convey quantitatively. Qualitative methods help evaluators to identify and to define users' perceptions, opinions and feelings about critical aspects of digital libraries, such as the degree of usefulness, usability and performance. Theng, meanwhile, uses two case studies on digital library evaluation to illustrate the power of quantitative techniques. The examples used in her chapter were conducted at appropriate stages of the software development cycle and highlight the strength of these techniques to investigate users' perceptions regarding digital library usability and usefulness.

Putting together a book with so many aspects of digital library evaluation was not an easy process. Digital libraries represent multifaceted systems and this book reflects the challenge of bringing together researchers and practitioners from the two main fields of computer science and librarianship. Moreover, the invited authors, to whom we are very grateful for the acceptance of our proposal, represent different cultural backgrounds, as is revealed in the reported case studies and examples. As any other publication, the book is amenable to further improvements. It cannot be considered exhaustive, first due to the physical constraints of every publication, and second due to the multi-prismatic substance of digital library evaluation and the liquid state of digital libraries. We believe that this book offers an insight into the most important and useful topics in digital library evaluation. Such an insight will help evaluators (both those practising and those planning evaluations) to understand the most significant aspects of this sensitive area.

Giannis Tsakonas and Christos Papatheodorou
Kerkyra, November 2008

Bibliography

Gonçalves, M. A., Fox, E. A., Watson, L. T. and Kipp, N. A. (2004) 'Streams, structures, spaces, scenarios, societies (5S): a formal model for digital libraries', *ACM Transactions of Information Systems* 22(2): 270–312.

Saracevic, T. (2004) 'Evaluation of digital libraries: an overview', paper presented at the DELOS Workshop on the Evaluation of Digital Libraries, Department of Information Engineering, University of Padua, 4–5 October, available at: *http://dlib.ionio.gr/wp7/workshop2004_program.html* (accessed 6 March 2008).

Introduction: the framework for digital library evaluation
Tefko Saracevic

This book is a compilation of a whole range of important issues, approaches and results related to the evaluation of digital libraries. It illustrates and demonstrates contemporary achievements and thinking on this important topic. The purpose of this introduction is somewhat different and much more general: it aims to offer a broader framework, context and a bit of perspective on digital library evaluation, interspersed with some musings on possible agendas for such evaluations in the future.

Digital libraries have two major orientations. On the one hand, they are deeply technical in nature – they depend totally on the digital technology of the day. On the other hand, they are social, even personal in nature – they are here for social and people purposes.

The technical part, as difficult as it may be to research, develop and operate, is relatively easier to evaluate. The social and people part is much, much harder to address in evaluation.

Broader questions

Digital libraries are often thought of as a technological fix for the traditional 'library problem', particularly given the explosion of digital knowledge records and information in the contemporary milieu. But libraries always were, and in the digital age remain, a system for resolving social problems.

Alvin Weinberg (1915–2006), the preeminent nuclear physicist who also invented the term *technological fix*, posed a number of questions that remain pertinent, even away from their original context:

In view of the simplicity of technological engineering and the complexity of social engineering, to what extent can social problems be circumvented by reducing them to technological problems? Can we identify Quick Technological Fixes for profound and almost infinitely complicated social problems, 'fixes' that are within the grasp of modern technology, and which would either eliminate the original social problem without requiring a change in the individual's social attitudes, or would so alter the problem as to make its resolution more feasible? (Weinberg, 2008: 29)

I suggest that we could and should ask these questions in the realm of digital libraries.

Since the invention of clay tablets, papyrus, and then paper, ink and printing presses, libraries have been connected with the technology of the day. They always were and always will be. Libraries have a technological imperative. They change with changes in technology. In many significant and profound ways they are changing with digital technology, and particularly with the internet and the web. But the fundamental social purpose and raison d'être remain constant. The purpose is selection, organisation, preservation and making accessible and available recorded knowledge and information. It is nothing short of remarkable that this purpose is constant across millennia, cultures, geography, technologies, societies and political systems. It is still the same purpose in the digital age with artefacts in digital formats.

From definitions to evaluation – differing perspectives

'But what is a digital library?', one might legitimately ask. Answers are sought in lexicography, philosophy and various academic pursuits, but as to practical operations, digital libraries, like many other social systems, can and do work without much concern for formal definitions. But this question is important in evaluation, for the answer sets the framework, orientation and objectives so important in any and all evaluations. One can start by asking an ancient question: 'What is a library?'

Many definitions exists, but of interest here is the one provided by Jesse H. Shera (1903–1982), the prominent library educator and author who, among other things, pioneered the introduction of information retrieval and technology in library school curricula starting in the late 1950s, orienting them toward information science. He defines the library as

> ...contributing to the total communication system in society ... Though the library is an instrumentality created to maximize the utility of graphic records for the benefits of society, it achieves that goal by working with the individual and through the individual it reaches society. (Shera, 1972: 48)

While we can clearly argue that libraries cover, particularly at present, many more types of records than the 'graphic' kind mentioned in the definition, it is important to consider a number of aspects relevant to digital libraries: communication, utility, maximisation, social and individual benefits and feedback between them. They illustrate general aspects and criteria for consideration in evaluation.

Closer to home, several definitions of digital libraries have emerged. Two are selected here to illustrate different orientations as mentioned above. From a broad and mostly technological perspective, Lesk (2005: 20) considers a digital library to be 'a collection of information which is both digitized and organized'. In a similar vein, Arms (2000: 2) provides an 'informal definition' (his words), suggesting that 'a digital library is a managed collection of information with associated services, where the information is stored in digital formats and accessible over a network. The crucial part of this definition is that information is managed.'

Hidden in these definitions are mostly technical aspects and criteria that should be considered in evaluation.

From a social perspective, a somewhat different definition is offered as derived by the Digital Libraries Federation (DLF) after a considerable amount of deliberation:

> Digital libraries are organizations that provide the resources, including the specialized staff, to select, structure, offer intellectual access to, interpret, distribute, preserve the integrity of, and ensure the persistence over time of collections of digital works so that they are readily and economically available for use by a defined community or set of communities. (DLF, 1998)

In the explanation of the definition, they emphasise that:

> It is meant here mainly to suggest that there is a set of attributes that gives coherence to the concept of digital libraries. These

attributes include functions of collection, organization, preservation, access and economy ... The proposed definition also emphasizes that 'digital libraries' need to be defined and measured in relation to the communities they serve. (DLF, 1998)

This definition is oriented not only toward a social and individual perspective, but also and strongly toward an institutional perspective, suggesting a comprehensive set of aspects and criteria for digital library evaluation. It is important to note that in a great many cases, this institutional orientation involves hybrid libraries, that is, libraries that have a major analogue component with related collections and services (print, graphic, images, sounds) along with a growing digital component with often differing collections and services. For them, evaluation also takes a differing perspective, often asking questions involving both analogue and digital aspects and relations.

Diversity in the digital library universe

The picture gets complicated when considering that the explosive growth of digital libraries over the past decade or so has increased the number of technical and social participants and stakeholders, most notably from the computer science and institutional library communities.

Digital libraries are not only based at libraries (academic, public, national etc.), but also at many other institutions and for many subjects. They take many shapes and forms. They involve a variety of context and content. Many are oriented toward a specific subject. Most importantly, they are used by a variety of users and for a variety of uses. The universe of digital libraries has become highly diversified.

Some libraries are born digital, such as the Virtual Library started by Tim Berners-Lee, the creator of the world wide web. Then there are museum-associated digital libraries, such as the one associated with the State Hermitage Museum in St. Petersburg. As to subject-oriented digital libraries, the Perseus Digital Library covers all kinds of artefacts related to antiquity and renaissance, while the ACM Digital Library covers computer science and related disciplines. There are digital libraries associated, built and maintained by historical societies, government agencies, a variety of cultural and other institutions, and even individuals. Publishers are also committed to digital libraries in a big way. And so on.

The wide and constantly increasing diversity of digital libraries and related collections and portals suggests several issues: traditional libraries are not traditional any more, but hybrid and coming in many digital library forms; many new players have entered the arena, particularly in subject areas; and many new types of use have emerged in addition to the traditional use of libraries.

This diversity has implications for evaluation as well. Diverse digital libraries require diverse evaluation objectives and criteria, among other things. It is questionable whether these are transferable among these diverse digital libraries. In and of itself, this issue is a proper agenda for evaluation research.

What does evaluation entail?

Evaluation refers to ascertaining the performance or assessment of value of some entity. There are many types of evaluation, along with many approaches, both depending on evaluation goals, questions asked and methods employed. For instance, questions and methods may be historic, ethnographic, social, economic, political, policy-related, and so on. I fully recognise the appropriateness of different approaches for different evaluation goals and audiences. However, I will concentrate here on evaluation as it relates to systems and related performance, as most, although not all, digital library evaluations take a systems approach.

To provide a context to the question asked above, first a few definitions follow, as derived from Saracevic (2000: 358–60). Then general requirements are enumerated.

A system can be considered a set of elements in interaction. A human-made system, such as a digital library, has an added aspect: it has certain objective(s) and evaluation should be related to these objectives. The elements, or the components, interact to perform certain functions or processes to achieve given objectives, thus evaluation may be limited to given elements, components or functions of a digital library and their more specific objectives. In other words, evaluation of a digital library need not involve the whole – it can concentrate on given components or functions and their specific objectives. Most digital library evaluations do just that, i.e. address some specific part or function. As a matter of fact, we do not know how to evaluate a digital library as a whole – that is, in a comprehensive manner. This is a matter for future agendas.

Furthermore, any system (digital libraries included) exists in an environment, or more precisely in a set of environments (which can also be thought of as broader systems or contexts), and interacts with its environments. It is difficult and even arbitrary to set the boundaries of a system. In the evaluation of digital libraries, as in the evaluation of any system or process, certain difficult questions arise that clearly affect the results: Where does a digital library under evaluation begin? Where does it end? What are the boundaries? What to include? What to exclude? On what environment or context should one concentrate? These questions determine the construct of digital libraries, as discussed below.

In this context, evaluation is taken to mean an appraisal of the performance or functioning of a system or part thereof, in relation to some objective(s). The performance can be evaluated with regard to:

- *Effectiveness*: How well does a system (or any of its parts) perform in terms of the purpose for which it was designed? This involves specifying or selecting particular objectives of the system, or its part or function.

- *Efficiency*: At what cost? Costs could be valued financially, or in time and effort.

- *Cost-effectiveness*: A combination of the two.

Any evaluation of a digital library must specify which of these will be evaluated. From now on, I will mostly discuss evaluation of effectiveness, with a full realisation that evaluation may involve efficiency and cost-effectiveness as well.

As in all systems, objectives occur in hierarchies, and there may be several hierarchies representing different levels – sometimes even in conflict. While the objectives may be explicitly stated or implicitly derived or assumed, they have to be reflected in an evaluation. Evaluation is not one fixed thing. For the same system, evaluation can be done on different levels, in relation to different choices of objectives, using a variety of methods, and it can be oriented toward different goals and audiences. Selection and clarification of objectives is an important starting point for all digital library evaluations. Muddled objectives result in muddled evaluations.

Any and all systems evaluations, including those of digital libraries, have to meet certain requirements. Evaluation must involve selections and decisions related to:

- *Construct* for evaluation. What to evaluate? What is actually meant by a digital library? Or any of its part or function subject to evaluation? What is encompassed? What elements (components, parts, processes etc.) should be involved in evaluation?

- *Context* of evaluation – selection of a goal, framework, viewpoint or level(s) of evaluation. What is the level of evaluation? What is critical for a selected level? Ultimately, what objective(s) will be selected for evaluation on that level?

- *Criteria* reflecting performance as related to selected objectives. What parameters of performance to concentrate on? What dimensions or characteristics to evaluate?

- *Measures* reflecting selected criteria to record the performance. What specific measure(s) should be used for a given criterion?

- *Measuring instruments*. What measuring instruments should be used to record the measures that reflect the selected criteria?

- *Methodology* for doing evaluation. What samples? What procedures should be used for data collection or for data analysis?

Let's start with an example using information retrieval systems. In terms of construct, many if not most information retrieval evaluations concentrate on functions of information organisation and/or retrieval – how well does a given indexing algorithm or retrieval method perform? In terms of context, a great many information retrieval evaluations involve retrieval in science, technology, professions or education, and a laboratory, such as the Text Retrieval Conference (TREC), with well-defined, albeit restrictive, parameters (Vorhees and Harman, 2005). In terms of criteria, most information retrieval evaluations involve relevance as the single most important criterion in retrieval. In terms of measures, familiar recall and precision are used (where recall reflects the probability that a relevant item is retrieved and precision indicates that a retrieved item is relevant). People, users or their surrogates are used as instruments to pass judgment on retrieved items. A methodology, such as the one applied in TREC, uses a set of specified items in a file for searching by various algorithms or retrieval methods; a pool of answers from all methods is compiled and given to judges for relevance assessment, and then a relative performance of each method is indicated. As a further example, a construct may be a track race, where the criterion is time, the measure is minutes and seconds, the measuring instrument is a stopwatch, and the method is timing the race from start to finish.

A clear specification on each of these six requirements is mandatory for any evaluation of digital libraries. Unfortunately, for digital libraries it is not as yet entirely clear what is to be specified in each of these six elements. There is no agreement on the criteria, measures and methodologies for digital library evaluation; nor is there agreement regarding the 'big picture', the construct and context of evaluation. The evaluation of digital libraries is still at a formative stage. Even now, after years of evaluation efforts, concepts have to be clarified first. This is the fundamental and ongoing challenge for digital library evaluation. Each evaluation effort more or less specifies these on its own. As such, there is little generalisation and agreement.

A social perspective in the evaluation of digital libraries is forcefully advocated by Marchionini et al.:

> Digital libraries serve communities of people and are created and maintained by and for people. People and their information needs · are central to all libraries, digital or otherwise. *All efforts to design, implement, and evaluate digital libraries must be rooted in the information needs, characteristics, and contexts of the people who will or may use those libraries.* (Marchionini et al., 2003: 119; authors' emphasis)

They also make some remarks related to the general requirements for evaluation as discussed above:

> Evaluation of a digital library may serve many purposes ranging from understanding basic phenomena (e.g. human information-seeking behavior) to assessing the effectiveness of a specific design to insuring sufficient return on investment. Human-centered evaluation serves many stakeholders, ranging from specific users and librarians to various groups to society in general. Additionally, evaluation may target different goals ranging from increased learning and improved research to improved dissemination to bottom line profits. Each of the evaluation goals may also have a set of measures and data collection methods. Finally, the evaluation must have a temporal component that can range from very short terms to generations. (Marchionini et al., 2003: 121).

Metrics

Clarification is needed regarding what does not fall in the realm of evaluation, even though it could be related to evaluation. In and of itself, measurement, collection of statistics, or specification of metrics for digital libraries is not evaluation – it is a quantitative or qualitative characterisation. Observation by itself, such as observing user behaviour in the use of a digital library, is not evaluation; it is a study of human information behaviour. Assessing user needs by itself is not evaluation, and neither is relating those needs to design. However, these can be linked to evaluation if they are connected to some specified performance by including all the five requirements enumerated above.

Let me concentrate on metrics, for they may be directly and fruitfully used in evaluation. 'Metrics' refers to indicators that describe in a quantitative manner specified discrete and often continuous outcomes. Metrics are important components in many fields such as econometrics, biometrics, sociometrics, bibliometrics and others where they specify the statistical properties and principles of a variety of entities and relationships.

For a long time, libraries have been involved with metrics related to the collection, synthesis, analysis and management of quantitative data on library collections, services, use, and quite a few other aspects. Library metrics are fairly well defined and widely used. Examples are data that describe the collections, staffing, expenditures and service activities, including use and other aspects. For instance, the Association of Research Libraries (ARL) (comprised of 123 member libraries in North America) regularly publishes elaborate metrics in the form of standardised statistics on many aspects of member libraries (some of these go back to 1908). The ARL report published in 2008 covers a vast array of data for 2005–06, and can serve as an illustration of the multitude of library metrics. Among other things, these metrics show a remarkable growth of digital resources over the last decade – for some libraries these now comprise up to 50–70 per cent of expenditures for total library materials.

In its report, ARL carefully warns up front, 'The tables presented in this publication are not indicative of performance and outcomes and should not be used as measures of library quality'. I agree. However, library metrics in general provide a picture of a state of a library (or a group of libraries) at a given time and/or over time. These metrics do not represent evaluation, but can be used to raise evaluation questions and suggest directions.

As yet, we are not even close to having a defined set of metrics for digital libraries. Thus, as one of the recommendations for a research agenda, I suggest addressing the development and testing of a comprehensive set of metrics to reflect the state and use of digital libraries. Establishing and then testing metrics is by no means an easy proposition. If it were, we would have plenty of them by now. These may be of help in evaluation and may also standardise many aspects of the evaluation of digital libraries.

Value of digital libraries

The definition of evaluation offered above refers to ascertaining performance or assessment of value. Performance is one thing; value is quite another. But what is value? This question has been discussed in philosophy since the time of Aristotle (384–322 BC) and in economics since the time of Adam Smith (1723–1790), considered the father of modern economics. In both philosophy and economics, value has emerged as a complex proposition.

Philosophers consider 'value' as the worth of something, and the process of valuation as an estimate, appraisal or measurement of its worth. In their works, 'worth' seems to be an undefined primitive term. They consider that value is related to, but not synonymous with, 'good', 'desirable', or 'worthwhile', and that it can be positive or negative, as well as relative or absolute. They also make a distinction between several kinds of values; of particular interest here is the distinction between *intrinsic* and *extrinsic* or *instrumental value*. Intrinsic value is being good or worthy, in and of itself, such as health or good experience. Extrinsic or instrumental value refers to means or contribution to something that is intrinsically valuable. This often relates to an activity. An example might be exercise that contributes to good health. Associated with value are also studies of impact and benefits.

Following Aristotle, Adam Smith classified economic value of two distinct kinds: *value-in-exchange* and *value-in-use*. The definitions and distinctions remain valid to this day, with, of course, some modern elaboration on the theme. The strength and wide use of value-in-exchange is attributable to the presence of the measuring-rod of money. Return on investment (ROI) is an example of a widely sought and applied measure reflecting value-in-exchange. Value-in-use does not have the luxury of having such a directly observable and countable rod as money for the basic criterion. Economists use the unifying concept of utility to extend the economic treatment of value to intrinsic value dimensions such as demands, wants, usefulness, satisfaction, pleasure, pains and the like.

For a long time, librarians and information scientists were concerned with the question of how to establish and demonstrate the value of libraries and information systems, including their impact and benefits. A continuous and lively debate regarding these questions is ongoing and a number of studies are reported in the literature (e.g. as summarised in Saracevic and Kantor, 1997, or with data in a specific study concentrating on a single public library in the Carnegie Mellon University Center for Economic Development, 2006).

As yet, similar efforts have not been extended to digital libraries. The issue of the value and impact of digital libraries has been raised, but no study has emerged. This is an important territory in need of exploration.

Digital libraries would not be supported if they were not considered to have certain value, including impact and benefits. They are used now in a great many fields and by many populations globally.

But what differences do digital libraries make?

To take one example, there is ample evidence that scholarship in the digital age has changed significantly. Borgman (2007: 29) posits that 'the growth of digital libraries, data depositories, and metadata standards are predictable outcomes of the trajectory [referring to the growth of big science and eResearch] ... Digital libraries ... can promote progress of science by facilitating collaboration'.

What differences do digital libraries make in contemporary scholarship?

Here are some more questions to contemplate as possible agendas for digital library evaluation: What difference do digital libraries make in education? For children? Other populations? For libraries themselves? What is the impact of increased availability of digitised resources (journals, books etc) on use? These and a whole host of similar questions are on the table for digital library evaluation.

Digital libraries did not appear from nowhere. They are a continuation of libraries from the past. Digital library evaluation follows in the footsteps of evaluation of libraries and information systems as technical and social systems. They have continuity. On the subject of digital scholarship, Borgman (2007: 31) says that 'Rarely is anything a complete break with the past. Digital libraries are not. Old ideas and new, old cultures and new, old artifacts and new all coexist' (Borgman 2007: 31). The same can be said for digital library evaluation.

Purpose of evaluation

At the end of this introduction, let us discuss a general question that spans across all evaluation studies: why evaluate digital libraries? The answers are not that simple.

Of course, evaluation can be done for the sake of gathering knowledge itself: to gain insight, to learn about the performance or value of digital libraries. Evaluation of a great many social and technical systems is done for the sake of gaining insight and better understanding of their operations and effects. An example is the classic and widely-cited study of the social impact of the telephone (de Sola Pool, 1977). It may be premature, but the following questions should be asked: What is the social impact of digital libraries? How do digital libraries shape society and how are digital libraries shaped by social trends?

More pragmatically, evaluation could and should be done to gather a rational and factual base for improving digital libraries – to become better, more effective, more efficient, easier to use. In science and technology, a great many evaluation studies are done to affect design and operation positively – and they do so. Many digital library evaluation studies state that results should 'affect design' or 'improve usability' or something similar. However, the majority of studies where the statement was made did not go beyond that statement, so the statement became a mantra. Even where a specific list of implications may have been given, the statement is still a mantra. I believe that the sentiment beyond the mantra is warranted, but it cannot be realised by the underlying assumption (or rather hope) that somebody, somehow, somewhere, sometime will actually do it. However, the problem of translating evaluation results into system design or operations is exceedingly difficult theoretically and pragmatically, thus, the translation problem should also become a part of evaluation.

A great many of the funders of digital libraries – institutional administrators, government and governing bodies, local authorities, investors etc. – would like to know what they are getting for their money and whether they would be better off putting their money elsewhere. The same questions are asked of all social systems. Although it may be impossible and even improper to seek a direct ROI using the measuring-rod of money, the questions are legitimate and should be addressed in value studies of digital libraries. Different measuring rods or criteria need to be used, but they need to be convincing and demonstrable. Needless to say, all managers and administrators of digital libraries would dearly like to have answers that will justify the expenditures and demonstrate the value of the digital libraries they manage. Even if metric studies of digital libraries are not evaluation, data can be oriented toward the demonstration of value. For this reason, the development and gathering of metrics for digital libraries was mentioned here in the context of evaluation.

Evaluation of digital libraries is a complex and challenging proposition, theoretically and pragmatically. The chapters in this book are meeting the challenges and contributing to a reduction of complexity in the evaluation of digital libraries.

Bibliography

Arms, W. Y. (2000) *Digital Libraries*, Cambridge, MA: MIT Press.

Association of Research Libraries (2008) 'ARL statistics 2005–06', available from: *http://www.arl.org/bm~doc/arlstats06.pdf* (accessed 28 July 2008).

Borgman, C. L. (2007) *Scholarship in the Digital Age: Information, Infrastructure and the Internet*, Cambridge, MA: MIT Press.

Carnegie Mellon University Center for Economic Development (2006) 'Carnegie Library of Pittsburgh: community impact and benefits', available from: *http://www.clpgh.org/about/economicimpact/CLP CommunityImpactFinalReport.pdf* (accessed 25 November 2008).

de Sola Pool, I. (ed.) (1977) *The Social Impact of the Telephone*, Cambridge, MA: MIT Press.

Digital Libraries Federation (1998) 'A working definition of digital library', available from: *http://www.diglib.org/about/dldefinition.htm* (accessed 26 July 2008).

Lesk, M. (2005) *Understanding Digital Libraries* (2nd edn), New York: Morgan Kaufmann – Elsevier.

Marchionini, G., Plaisant, C. and Komlodi, A. (2003) 'The people in digital libraries: multifaceted approaches to assessing needs and impact', in: A. Bishop, B. Buttenfield and N. VanHouse (eds) *Digital Library Use: Social Practice in Design and Evaluation*, Cambridge, MA: MIT Press, pp. 119–60.

Saracevic, T. and Kantor, P. (1997) 'Studying the value of library and information services: Part I – establishing a theoretical framework', *Journal of the American Society for Information Science* 48(6): 527–42.

Saracevic, T. (2000) 'Digital library evaluation: toward evolution of concepts', *Library Trends* 49(2): 350–69.

Shera, J. S. (1972) *The Foundations of Education for Librarianship*, New York: Wiley.

Voorhees, E. M. and Harman, D. K. (eds) (2005) *TREC: Experiment and Evaluation in Information Retrieval*, Cambridge, MA: MIT Press.

Weinberg, A. (2008 [1966]) 'Can technology replace social engineering?', in A. H. Teich (ed.) *Technology and the Future* (11th edn), New York: Wadsworth Publishing, pp. 28–35.

Part 1
To whom it may concern

2

From usage to user: library metrics and expectations for the evaluation of digital libraries

Brinley Franklin, Martha Kyrillidou and Terry Plum

Introduction

The refinement of e-metrics by librarians to evaluate the use of library resources and services has rapidly matured into a set of standardised tools and shared understandings about the value of e-metrics for making data-driven, managerial decisions in libraries. These measures grow out of a long history of libraries desiring to assess the usage of their resources, but only a recent history of actually being able to do it. Usage assessment of library collections began with the print materials that were collected, owned, organised and made available by the library. The methods and tools for assessment have multiplied as journals became digital and were no longer owned by the library. The assessment focus has also changed and is now on service as well as collections.

In academic libraries, the frameworks and purposes for assessments of collection usage have substantially changed, driven by the accompanying changes in the content delivery mechanisms, user behaviour, assessment tools and analytics. Not only are the assessment tools and data far better for digital materials than they ever were for print, but the frameworks for collecting, analysing and using those data have changed from the print world to the digital world, and are now consistently used and accepted across academic libraries. The collections are regarded as both a resource and a service. As a resource, assessment focuses on how the collection has been used. As a service, assessment focuses on how the patron has used the digital resource. This chapter examines the changed assessment framework for digital materials to determine what guides its development and acceptance among librarians. It looks at various projects that attempt to use usage data to learn something about user outcomes.

The scope of this survey is focused on patrons' interactions with networked electronic resources and services. This chapter does not address the current state of the evaluation of digital libraries, which is ably discussed in the other chapters in this book. It does not include web usability or usability analysis, even though the usability of the library's presentation of electronic resources and services affects patron success and therefore usage.

Interestingly, in this evaluative mini-world of networked electronic resources and services, there is a disconnection between what librarians are trying to do with their collection and analysis of evaluative data and the evaluations computer scientists are doing with digital libraries. This chapter surveys current evaluation methods and techniques used for collecting traces of patron interaction with networked electronic resources (i.e. usage data). It also looks at how those data are being used to generate information about user outcomes. The chapter then speculates qualitatively on how this assessment culture in the library world frames librarians' expectations about the assessment evidence techniques and data proposed by information scientists to evaluate or assess digital libraries. The framework of librarians' evaluative expectations is important because most production digital libraries exist within the library and not the computer science context.

Assessment and evaluation in the print library environment

Scarcely a decade into the digital library environment, librarians already know considerably more about digital library use than they did about traditional library use in the print environment. In traditional print-based libraries, librarians counted outputs such as circulating library materials, reference and information questions, and interlibrary loans to and from other libraries. In retrospect, the data collected were not reliable and, most likely, inconsistent due to varying loan periods, local practices regarding how to count informational and directional versus reference questions, and variances in how libraries classified interlibrary loans as opposed to circulation transactions.

Prior to the advent of online catalogues and integrated library systems, even circulation data for specific volumes or classes of materials were difficult to compile and analyse. Books were added to libraries' collections, but detailed information about their subsequent circulation patterns was not easily available until libraries began to automate the library equivalent of electronic inventory control systems in the last quarter of the twentieth century. The data collected by the automation of cataloguing and circulation systems made it easier to count collection size and circulation, and break them out by subject. Journal review projects in the print environment were predominantly in response to budget crises, were undertaken largely to cancel titles that were perceived as less frequently used and/or that seemed overpriced, and were frequently subject to manipulation by either librarians/selectors or the users they consulted.

Before the emergence of digital libraries during the last decade, librarians evaluated collection usage data, when they were: (a) interested in measuring library performance; (b) asked to compile statistics for professional associations or governmental agencies; or (c) confronted with budget cuts and needed to determine how the collection was being used. Librarians typically relied on gross circulation counts and routinely employed unscientific and unreliable sampling plans and simple in-house data-collection methods such as asking users not to reshelve library materials so the library could count them. These usage studies purported to measure library collection use when in fact there was never any tangible proof or consistent interpretation of what a book being removed from the shelf, or even a circulating item, really represented.

Looking back, collection development in the print environment was more of an art than a science. Libraries knew how much they were spending, but were unable to ascertain how their collections were being used or how to use the data they could collect to better inform purchasing decisions.

It is telling that the authors of one of the most commonly cited articles on print collection use in an academic library, 'Use of a university library collection', observed that:

> ...the gross data available up to this point have been too global in character and too imprecise in nature to serve as an adequate basis for the reformulation of acquisitions policies. It is not particularly helpful for a bibliographer to know that 10 per cent of the titles selected will satisfy 90 per cent of client demand for materials in a given discipline, unless we can determine which 10 per cent. It is

useless to tell the acquisitions librarian that half the monographs ordered will never be used, unless we can specify which 50 per cent to avoid buying. (Galvin and Kent, 1977)

Automated library systems changed librarians' ability to review acquisition decisions, at least for monographs. In 2003, a Mellon Foundation-funded study by the Tri-College Library Consortium (Bryn Mawr, Haverford and Swarthmore Colleges) done in conjunction with the Council on Library and Information Resources (CLIR) found that approximately 75 per cent of the items in the three libraries' collections had circulated no more than once in the past ten years. In addition, about 40 per cent of the items in the collections overlapped (i.e. they were held on more than one campus). About half of these overlapping items had not circulated in the past 11 years.

Galvin and Kent referred to the book budget in the academic world as 'the most sacred of sacred cows' and pointed out:

> The hard facts are that research libraries invest very substantial funds to purchase books and journals that are rarely, or never, called for as well as equally large sums to construct and maintain buildings designed to make accessible quickly titles that are no longer either useful to or sought by their clientele. (Galvin and Kent, 1977)

The findings of Galvin and Kent and the Tri-College Library Consortium were undoubtedly distressing to librarians, who typically based their selections in print-dominant libraries on their experience and training to correlate the literature of various genres and disciplines with their users' needs and interests in those fields. Librarians were considered the 'experts' at building collections and their purchasing decisions went largely untested and unquestioned. At the same time, librarians and their sponsoring organisations prided themselves on the size of their print collections, adding shelving at the expense of user space and building additions, new libraries, and high-density storage facilities to house their print library collections.

The older print focused model looked at the collection from the point of view of the collection as a resource. Now, as shown by statistics from the Association of Research Libraries (ARL), the collection is increasingly a service and data collection is guided toward user outcomes.

Assessment and evaluation in the electronic library environment

Networked electronic resources and services for library patrons have become more pervasive, easier to use, and have increased in number and variety since the days when patrons used predominantly print resources. As libraries devote increasingly large proportions of their materials budgets to networked electronic resources, ARL recognised the changed landscape and launched its New Measures Initiative to measure and evaluate usage of networked electronic resources.

According to ARL (2008: 22–3), expenditures for electronic resources among the major research libraries in North America exceeded $400 million during 2005–06; after including hardware and software and other operational costs, the figure increases to half a billion. This total represents close to 45 per cent of the library materials budget. The need to evaluate the return on the investment made on electronic resources was pressing. Through ARL's E-Metrics initiative (ARL, 2002), efforts were made to define the variables that would be useful to track. In addition, an experimental data collection is currently underway in the form of a supplementary statistics collection of data on searches, sessions and downloads. Evaluation in general is an activity that has increased in libraries over the last decade and it has formalised itself in a number of different ways, ranging from experiments and testbed applications to training, conferences and the emergence of a thriving community of practice (see *www.libraryassessment.org*).

Documenting contemporary interest in assessment, Wright and White (2007) examined the current state of library assessment activities in ARL libraries. One of the first steps by ARL libraries in developing an assessment programme to learn about their customers was to administer a user survey. The authors found the top five assessment methods currently used by libraries to be statistics gathering, a suggestion box, web usability testing, user-interface usability, and surveys developed outside of the library. Locally-designed user satisfaction surveys used to be more frequent, but have been replaced by the internationally implemented LibQUAL+® survey.

Increasingly, libraries are creating assessment departments, units or positions primarily responsible for assessment activities. Most of these positions or units were created after 2005. Interestingly, assessment results are wide-ranging, and are often specific to the particular library, for example, library facilities, hours, changes to the website, etc. The identified need for an infrastructure of assessment and a community of practice surrounding it is gradually being realised (DeFranco et al., 2007; Moreleli-Cacouris, 2007).

Usage measurement methods and accountability expectations have also greatly increased. Libraries have new tools for collecting usage data about how users are using digital resources. Both vendor-supplied statistics and locally-generated data through portal websites or gateways document in new ways how patrons are interacting with the library, something that was impossible in the print world. The refinement of e-metrics by librarians to evaluate the use of library resources and services has matured into a set of standardised tools and shared understandings about the value of the metrics for making data-driven, managerial decisions in libraries. E-metrics are applied to a number of library resources and service domains, some as census counts and others as samples. There are four dimensions to e-metrics:

- externally supplied e-metric usage data;
- locally captured e-metric usage data;
- full census data representing all of the usage of networked electronic resources;
- randomly or non-randomly sampled data purporting to represent all usage.

These form a helpful taxonomy to organise methods of collecting e-metric data and to discuss levels of trust by librarians.

Using these four dimensions, usage data can be organised into four categories or types of data collection processes:

- census counts:
  - externally generated, vendor usage data;
  - locally or internally generated usage data;
- sample counts:
  - externally generated, web survey data;
  - internally generated, web survey, usage data.

These four categories of collecting data sum up most of the library-initiated approaches to the evaluation of digital libraries, and define the assessment culture or evaluation environment in which librarians approach the evaluation of digital resources.

Externally-generated, vendor supplied data

Protocols for census counts include the statistics of usage of networked electronic resources collected by external vendors conforming to codes of practice, such as COUNTER, and standards-based expressions of them, such as SUSHI, a standardised transfer protocol for COUNTER-compliant statistics. As documented on its website (*www.projectcounter.org*), COUNTER proposes a code of practice and protocols covering the recording and exchange of online usage data so that librarians will have a better understanding of how their subscription information is being used, and publishers have standard data on how their products are being accessed. The constantly updated codes of practice recommend that vendors produce and the library use reports containing such variables as the 'number of successful full-text article requests by month and journal', 'turnaways by month and journal', 'total searches and sessions by month and database', in addition to other reports (see *www.projectcounter.org/code_practice.html*). The SUSHI standard (NISO Z39.93-2007) has three supporting XML schemas posted to the National Information Standards Organization (NISO) website, which also hosts retrieval envelopes for the conforming XML-formatted COUNTER reports (*www.niso.org/schemas/sushi/*). These data are analysed by libraries, either by moving the data into electronic resource management systems (ERMs) or by creating spreadsheets. The purpose of the analysis is often to generate cost-per-use data. Although the calculation is simple, collecting meaningful cost data from the complex bundling offered by vendors is not trivial.

COUNTER is a tremendous step forward, but not the total solution. From 2004 to 2007, the Institute of Museum and Library Services funded a project entitled 'Maximizing library investments in digital collections through better data gathering and analysis'. As part of the study, three research teams studied different types of usage data for electronic resources in order to develop a cost-benefit model to help librarians 'determine how best to capture, analyze and interpret usage data for their electronic resources' (Baker and Read, 2008). For their part, Baker and Read surveyed librarians at academic libraries to determine the level of effort required to process the COUNTER data, how the data are used, and which data are the most meaningful. Their findings suggest that librarians still wrestle with inconsistent data from non COUNTER-compliant reports, but surprisingly also from the reports of COUNTER-compliant vendors. The process of data analysis takes time. The most common reason for analysing the data was to make subscription decisions and to meet reporting requirements.

Census data counts like COUNTER are consistent with the tradition of collecting circulation data for print resources. They focus on the collection and not the patron; they result in decisions that create higher frequency counts but not necessarily better patron-centred services; and they measure benefit usually through some sort of cost-per-use metric, not on the value to the patron.

J. C. Bertot, C. R. McClure and D. M. Davis have been pursuing a research agenda to assess outcomes in the networked electronic environment (Bertot and McClure, 2003; Bertot and Davis, 2005; Snead et al., 2005). The approach developed for the Florida Electronic Library looks at functionality, usability and accessibility, and combines a number of iterative methods to assess outcomes. Functionality is defined as a measure of whether the digital library works as intended. Usability assesses how users interact with the programme. Accessibility measures how well the systems permit equal access for patrons with disabilities (Snead et al., 2005). This project has focused on large state digital electronic resource collections, an important target for outcomes assessment. Its strength is that it considers how the digital library (or electronic resources) serves the community as a whole. Part of the evaluation includes usage data from the resources.

The MESUR project (Bollen et al., 2007) seeks to employ usage data to expand the possibilities of scholarly assessment. The purpose is to generate a model of the scholarly communication process involving usage, citation and bibliographic data. It will create a reference set and generate a wider range of usage-based metrics than we presently use, with guidelines for their application. MESUR identifies the current datasets, such as harvestable usage statistics for scholarly journals (COUNTER and SUSHI); the Interoperable Repository Statistics Project (*irs.eprints.org*), which defines usage data for OAI-PMH-compliant repositories; and CiteBase (*www.citebase.org*) which collects citation data (Bollen et al., 2007). The deliverables from this project are a survey and model of the scholarly communication process, a large-scale reference data set for the investigation of viable usage-based metrics, an examination of the clusters of practices found in this data set, and finally the definition and validation of usage-based metrics of scholarly impact.

There are a myriad of business intelligence tools to process COUNTER data. Lakos (2007) gives a useful survey of the state of business intelligence software wedded to the integrated library system and the electronic resource management system. He lists COGNOS,

Voyager Analyzer, SirsiDynix' Directors Station, SirsiDynix' Normative Data Project for Librarians, EBSCO's effort to combine WebFeat's SMART with its A-to-Z management service, Serials Solutions' Overlap Analysis and their 360 Counter, the Ontario Council of University Libraries Scholars Portal Statistics framework, ScholarlyStats from MPS Solutions, and Blackwell's Collection Management Services. The sheer volatility and variety of these statistical reporting and analysis mechanisms speaks to great interest and few standards.

In general, the census data supplied by vendors external to the library can be useful for cost-use studies, although Conyers and Dalton (2007) provide evidence that this analysis is more difficult than it appears. There are nascent efforts to relate such data to analyse user behaviour and motivation. To become user-applicable, the data must typically be combined with locally-generated censuses of web logs or other user data. COUNTER data, though useful for making decisions regarding the collection or cost, are truly revealing regarding users' needs when combined with local data.

Internal locally-developed data

White and Kamal (2006: 129) provide a useful literature survey regarding the collection of data pertaining to the usage of networked resources at the local library level. The collection of such data can be through locally-developed census counts generated from click-through scripts, rewriting proxy server logs, virtual private networks (VPNs), or OpenURL server logs, as well as other methods. White and Kamal also present some creative models of the network infrastructure necessary to collect such data locally, including ERMs (White and Kamal, 2006: 99), VPNs (White and Kamal, 2006: 108), and rewriting proxy servers (White and Kamal, 2006: 109). Unlike external vendor-supplied data, these local data can be mapped against authenticated users or internet protocol addresses to determine usage by local demographics such as client group, school or discipline. Library websites are routinely evaluated by web server logs and web traffic analysis software. ERM applications can tie cost to usage, while enhancing access to e-journals. Interlibrary loan usage can be counted by OCLC's VDX product, Atlas Systems' ILLiad system (now licensed exclusively by OCLC) and Infotrieve's Ariel system. Finally, the online public access catalogue can collect usage data including search statements and success rates. Stemper and Jaguszewski (2003) point out that 'local use data allows us to compare usage across publishers and disciplines'. They conclude that 'it may be useful to occasionally compare local statistics with vendor statistics to understand usage in more depth', as 'both local and vendor usage data have their own strengths and weaknesses ... Both have their place in the digital library's suite of quantitative evaluation measures' (Stemper and Jaguszewski, 2003).

Transaction logs capture all local usage, yet because of the simplicity of the IP and HTTP protocol elements, they are not particularly useful. If the logs can be tied to a session, that is, one person searching over a period of time, they become more informative. The interaction within the electronic resource is unavailable to the locally collected data, but commensurable counts can be generated across disparate resources. Log files are especially attractive for closed environments, like digital libraries, OhioLINK (*www.ohiolink.edu*) and OCUL Scholar's Portal (*www.ocul.on.ca*), and they have relevance to any gateway server, through which requests to e-journal vendors must pass.

In a review of transaction log file analysis and web log analysis, Jamali et al. (2005) note that there are advantages and disadvantages to the technique and that researchers have taken both sides. The advantages include: log file data are collected automatically, data are collected unobtrusively, the data are good for longitudinal analysis, and the data are based on a census not sampling. Log analysis can provide data for the evaluation of digital library performance while providing useful data about information-seeking behaviour.

The disadvantages include the difficulty of differentiating user performance from system performance. It is difficult to identify users, and IP address alone is not sufficient; sessions are hard to determine and many researchers assume that a session lasts 30 minutes; caching proxy servers may thin out the data; and activity by spiders and other crawlers should be segregated in the data. With log file analysis we do not know why the user did what he or she did. There are some problems with caching effects on estimates of volume of use. There are several levels of caching: browser cache, local cache and large regional caching. If the IP address is treated as a user, then proxy servers, firewalls with network address translation, and VPNs bias the logs, as multi-user activity comes from one IP.

Deep log analysis (DLA – see Chapter 7 and Nicholas et al., 2005) enriches web log data with user demographic data, drawing from a user database or online questionnaires. As log files provide little explanation of behaviour, deep log analysis follows up with a survey or with interviews. DLA was developed by the CIBER (*www.ucl.ac.uk/ciber/*). DLA technique is employed with OhioLINK and is part of the MaxData project, described elsewhere in this chapter. The technique attempts to provide methods for obtaining good-quality usage data through transaction logs, and in this method items used, viewed or requested are counted as use. Unlike COUNTER, countable *use* includes such outputs as a list of journals, a table of contents page, and the full-text article. COUNTER defines *use* as the download, view, print or e-mail of a full-text journal article. Sessions are terminated after ten minutes of inactivity and there is only one session counted per day.

DLA defines site penetration as the number of items viewed during a particular visit. Time online or page view time is estimated. Users are identified by IP address. Using a reverse domain name system (DNS) lookup, sub-network names are mapped to academic departments. On-campus and off-campus users are differentiated. The user outcomes are difficult to analyse, but one can attempt to track returnees by IP, as a measure of user satisfaction, among other motivations. Assigning of dynamic IPs by internet service providers makes the off-campus returnee data even more speculative (Nicholas et al., 2005). The usage to user effort is well placed, but there appear to be a number of problems, particularly when based upon IP. However, this project seems to have disaggregating user data as one of its goals.

One of the best examples of locally-developed census collection is by Zucca (2008) and the Penn Library Data Farm. In this service-oriented data-collection tool, information is pulled from the online catalogue, acquisitions, circulation, electronic resource management systems, OpenURL link resolvers, interlibrary loan data, web service logs and rewriting proxy server logs, bringing together resources, services and the data they produce when patrons use them. The basic concept is the desire to capture library-related events or interactions in a data warehouse. Digital libraries could fit into this environment very easily. Using these data, Zucca can track resources, people and locations to create a management information framework. A sample report from this system may produce, for example, a view of 'Faculty use of electronic journals by school by journal topic'. Despite its thoroughness and census aspects, this framework would be difficult to replicate elsewhere, and therefore does not produce benchmarked data, but does successfully link usage data to users. This system is particularly useful for libraries assigning library resource and service costs to specific user groups. The possibility of extending this system through an XML schema of standardised event descriptors is under consideration.

Standardised web surveys externally collected

Though usage data from national web surveys rely mostly on perceptions and are subject to limitations of recall and second-hand reporting of user behaviour, libraries have often asked usage questions in a variety of surveys. In particular, through the well-respected, internationally practised web survey protocol known as LibQUAL+®, users are asked to report their opinions of library service quality. This extensively tested and validated web-based survey helps libraries assess and improve library services. The survey instrument measures library users' minimum, perceived and desired levels of service quality across three dimensions: information control, affect of service, and library as place. Since 2000, over 1,000 libraries and 1 million users have participated in the survey. The survey is marketed locally but administered externally, and the data are collected, analysed and reported externally (*www.libqual.org*).

Supplemented by comparable data from peer institutions, libraries can focus on the usage related to certain resources. For example, users are being asked how often they use library resources on premises, how often they use resources through library electronic gateways, and how often they use internet gateways such as Google, Yahoo, etc. Clearly the proportion of usage reported that is library-related (both gateways and physical premises) is much less than usage reported for internet gateways such as Google, Yahoo, etc. Using LibQUAL+® data provided by 295,355 of the participants who completed the LibQUAL+® survey in 2003, 2004 and 2005, Thompson et al. (2007) sought to address three research questions. First, in terms of usage of onsite library information resources versus non-library information gateways such as Google, what differences, if any, have occurred over time in the use by (a) undergraduates, (b) graduate students/postgraduates, and (c) faculty? Second, in terms of usage of onsite library information resources versus non-library information gateways such as Google, what differences, if any, have occurred across international regions in the use by (a) undergraduates, (b) graduate students/postgraduates, and (c) faculty? Third, in terms of frequency of onsite and internet gateway usage, what differences, if any, are there in perceptions of library service quality across four user types ('nonusers', 'traditionalists', 'web techies' and 'voracious users')? The results shed light on information use trends and patterns around the world (Thompson et al., 2007).

Internally collected sample counts

Most sample counts are user studies, but are not linked to systematically collected usage counts, nor are the results comparable with peer institutions. Tenopir (2003), updated by Rowlands (2007), has surveyed user studies. One web survey technique that attempts to address sampling and comparability issues is MINES for Libraries®

(*minesforlibraries.org*). The primary difference between the MINES for Libraries® approach and many of the other web-based user surveys recounted in the work of Tenopir and Rowlands is the emphasis on usage. Although user demographic information is collected, this web survey is really a usage survey rather than a user survey. The respondent must choose the web-based networked electronic resource in order to be presented with the survey, thus preventing memory or impression management errors. Once the survey is completed, the respondent's browser is forwarded to the desired networked electronic resource. This approach is based on the random moments sampling technique. Each survey period is at least two hours per month, so each survey period in itself is only a snapshot or picture of usage. Because the survey periods are randomly chosen over the course of a year and result in at least 24 hours of surveying, the total of the survey periods represents a random sample, and inferences about the population are statistically valid with a 95 per cent confidence level and a low standard error (e.g. less than 2 per cent) (Franklin and Plum, 2006).

The MINES for Libraries® survey is most accurate when the library information architecture makes it possible to survey all usage of networked electronic resources during the sample period (an assessment infrastructure), and when response is mandatory. Because the survey is a usage and a user survey, there is a real possibility of repeated surveying of the same patron. One means of reducing the inconvenience to patrons of repeated surveying is to record the values chosen in the initial survey of the patron's usage of electronic resources, and invisibly resubmit those values to the patron for subsequent use with a different networked electronic resource during the sample period. Users' demographics do not change during a session and an examination of the MINES for Libraries® data collected to date shows that repeat users rarely change their purpose of use within a session.

Although MINES for Libraries® has been used at about 50 college and university libraries, (Franklin and Plum, 2006, 2008) it has not achieved wide acceptance, possibly for two reasons: (a) it is implemented locally, and therefore requires local IT support; (b) it is a sample, albeit a well-tested representative random sample, hence it does not have the same level of trust as census counts. To address the IT issues, the MINES for Libraries® protocol is being applied to commonly accepted gateway technologies, such as EZproxy. MINES for Libraries® user data have been successfully linked to EZproxy usage log files to give a fuller picture of the usage of the user, and why resources are being used. Once this linkage is made available to all libraries running EZproxy, then the IT support issue will become much less constraining. ARL is providing analysis reports to institutions implementing the MINES for Libraries® survey. It is exploring options for scaling the application by automating the collection of data and minimising the reliance on local IT support. To date, the most scalable implementation of MINES for Libraries® is the study implemented at the OCUL Scholar's Portal where, through a central gateway, 16 different institutions participated in the study (Kyrillidou et al., 2006).

How are the data being used?

Cost-benefit analyses

One use of these assessment data is to look at the benefits, as measured in usage volume and the decreased costs of digital materials. Three ground-breaking cost-benefit analysis studies occurred between 2002 and 2004. The first, conducted at Drexel University and reported by Montgomery and King (2002), determined that, while not directly comparable, the total costs (subscription and operational) of electronic journals calculated on a cost-per-use basis were $1.85 per use, compared with $17.50 per use for print journals. These calculations were based on article views and downloads for electronic journals and four years of reshelving counts for print journals. Electronic journal use was also much higher than the print journal use measured.

A second study, performed by Obst (2003) at the Medical Branch Library of the University Library in Muenster, Germany, only considered subscription costs. Obst's study also determined considerably lower unit costs for electronic journal use (€3.47) than print journal use (€18.68). Consistent with Montgomery and King's findings, users accessed the electronic versions of journals much more frequently than the print versions. The Muenster study also found significant differences in unit costs by publisher.

A third study, published by the CLIR (Schonfeld et al., 2004), considered the non-subscription costs of current print journals, print journal back files, and electronic journals. This study was interesting in that it attempted to project cost over the estimated total lifespan for periodicals. Again, the authors concluded that, 'other things being equal, an electronic collection should achieve lower non-subscription costs than a print collection'.

Cost and use data are relatively easy to compile for digital resources. With most vendor-supplied and transaction-based usage counts, digital content usage data are based on total usage for a given year, not a sample. The data collected to date indicate that the cost per use of an article in an electronic journal is fairly inexpensive. The more often that digital content is used, the lower the unit cost, and the resulting increase in perceived value to the user population reflected by increased use does not incur additional cost. Therefore, offering digital content encourages the development of library services such as marketing, instruction and liaison outreach. Moving to digital content also nurtures the development of new technology systems to leverage already committed expenses, such as OpenURL, web usability studies, and electronic resource management systems.

Consortia like OhioLINK and OCUL mount commercially licensed digital content locally and calculate cost per use data by title, by publisher, and by member library to determine which electronic resources merit continuation of their licensing and operational costs. Individual libraries measure total use of individual electronic resources and packages and calculate unit costs, usually based on vendor-supplied usage data, to decide which titles and packages have a sufficiently low unit cost to warrant continued investment.

Many libraries now calculate the annual unit costs for electronic books, electronic journals and databases and use that information to inform collection development decisions. Unit cost analysis can help to determine whether publishers' cost increases are justified by measuring whether usage is increasing faster than the costs are inflating. While unit cost data should not be the sole determinant in buying decisions, such data can be used to explain to faculty and students why a title or package may not be a good investment at their university. Unit cost data also help to standardise different publishers, vendors and products so that titles and packages can be evaluated effectively.

As librarians at the University of Montana reported in 2004:

> For the first time, the Collection Development Team was able to review the networked resources collection from an overview of quantitative data and relate it to the collection development policy … At the same time, national-level initiatives to work with vendors to standardize vendor-supplied data provide the future opportunity to further expand the analysis to include how users actually use these resources once they are accessed. (Samson et al., 2004)

Less than a decade into its development, measuring the value and impact of digital content already provides librarians with more useful and accurate data related to collections use than was possible in the print library environment.

Yet these cost-use data are just the start. Cost-use data can be related to the size of the potential population, for example, the biology department of a university. High usage relative to the user population is also factored into cost-usage analysis. Similarly, the more data that can be brought into the analysis about the user, the more informative it is about user behaviour and user outcomes.

Linking usage data to users

One of the more exciting presentations at NISO's 2007 conference 'Understanding the data around us: gathering and analyzing usage data' was the presentation by McDonald (2007), entitled 'Usage statistics and information behaviors: understanding user behavior with quantitative indicators'. In it he made a case for using usage data to understand the impact of networked electronic resources on patrons. He proposed a series of information behaviours, for which he developed a logical outcome that could be measured with usage data. Although the focus was on testing information behaviours, libraries can use a similar methodology to test hypotheses about their users.

The future of information usage collection is linking to user outcomes. Recent refinement of web-based survey techniques promises to provide librarians with even more representative and reliable samples of digital content use. Web-based surveys can be used to measure user satisfaction and digital collection usage that is not vendor-supplied, such as locally-mounted digital collections and services and locally-hosted open access journals. Surveying at the campus router level or at the proxy rewriter provides a comprehensive sampling plan that is able to survey all electronic services users, regardless of their point of entry.

These assessment efforts allow librarians to better understand digital content usage, make more informed collection development decisions and to better justify collections management choices. However, librarians are now able to more accurately determine who is using specific digital content. Knowing the locations where networked services are being used (e.g. the majority of faculty prefer to work on campus, but not in the library) enables librarians to plan user support services accordingly. Determining purpose of use permits academic librarians to identify which electronic resources contribute most to their institutions' primary missions of instruction/education/unfunded research, funded research, patient care, public service, and other institutional activities.

The response of practising librarians to these advances in digital library evaluation has not been universally enthusiastic. Some librarians have responded positively to management information related to collection development decisions, and to the possibilities of relating usage to users, but others see usage data as threatening the values and practices that librarians cultivated in the print environment. For many years, librarians carefully reviewed published titles and selected library materials that, in their opinion, matched local users' needs and interests. Some libraries deliberately continued to build strong focused collections on particular topics that 'characterised' their library collection, sometimes on the basis of a donor's gift and often without regard for whether those collections were used sufficiently to justify their ongoing costs. Evaluation of library collections usage in the networked resource environment has, in effect, exposed some of these traditional collection development practices as failing to successfully match library collections with local users' needs and interests. The digital library environment has provided librarians with the tools to evaluate their purchasing decisions and to review usage of specific elements of the networked electronic resources, including electronic books, electronic journals and databases. Over time, usage data will become more standardised and linkages to users outcomes more routine. Service will improve and patrons will be more empowered to achieve their outcomes.

What do library metrics and librarian expectations mean for the assessment of digital libraries?

Librarians have a framework of expectations about the evaluation of digital libraries, which is part of their assessment culture. Institutional repositories are digital libraries supporting the university mission, and are the focus of much attention by librarians, particularly because of the documented non-participation by faculty (Davis and Connolly, 2007). Through interviews with faculty, Davis and Connolly sought to determine factors for faculty non-participation in Cornell University's installation of DSpace. Although a number of the reasons given by faculty for not using this particular digital library are specific to institutional repositories (such as the learning curve, redundancy with discipline repositories, copyright, intellectual property, etc.), the emphases on service and scholarly purpose were clear. Only one faculty member focused on perceived failures of the software, access, searching, retrieval or preservation. For most faculty members, the primary deterrents were the perception of problems with the service aspects of the institutional repository, and its alignment with the faculty mission of publication.

Institutional repositories are a specialised type of digital library, and the evaluation of institutional repository literature is mature, with numerous checklists, indicators for success and evaluation criteria (Center for Research Libraries, 2007; JCDL, 2006; Proudman, 2007; OARiNZ, 2007; Westell, 2006). For example, Mary Westell's 'Institutional repositories: proposed indicators of success' (2006) lists a clearly defined mandate, integration into institutional planning, ongoing funding model, relationship to digitisation centres, interoperability, measurement, promotion, and preservation strategy. Measurement includes usage data, but more importantly also includes measuring the contributions of repository content to scholarship. Demonstrating linkages between repository content and scholarship is an incentive to faculty to contribute content, but also demonstrates the alignment of the repository with the university mission.

The evaluation of institutional repositories, and the assessment culture created by the various approaches to evaluation and assessment lead to some generalisations about how libraries and librarians approach the evaluation of digital resources. The following observations about how librarians approach evaluation are not strict rules but common points taken from the evaluative efforts to date:

- *Evaluation should be based on standardised usage data collected within the local digital library, and benchmarked to national norms*: The librarian expects to see standardised data across different digital libraries and digital library platforms representing usage. The librarian understands the implications of COUNTER data, and would want to integrate digital library usage data into library data analysis systems. Evaluative systems for digital libraries producing idiosyncratic or non-standard, locally-collected data are not going to be trusted. For example, the NSDL 'Evaluating digital libraries: A user-friendly guide' (Reeves et al., 2006) lists a traditional set of evaluation tools to inform decision-making.

- *Census not samples*: The librarian is familiar with many user survey methods, but because they are based on samples, they are usually case studies in specific institutions. Ad hoc changes can be made to library facilities and websites based on user surveys, as described in Spec Kit 303, but for systematic evaluation, librarians will expect census data, or a national sampling plan such as that used by LibQUAL+®. In general, usage data are much more trusted than user survey data, unless the user surveys are very well done with a solid sampling plan, and are shown to be reliable and valid.

- *Web usability is an important, formative evaluation process rather than summative for digital libraries*: Librarians are confronted with dozens of different interfaces and systems. The best libraries regularly run web usability studies on their websites, and make changes to their web presentation based on the data. Web usability protocols are one of the methods that have had the greatest impact on libraries over the last years (Hiller et al., 2008). This is becoming an ongoing improvement process for all library systems.

- *Content is still the king*: Digital libraries represent, in some manner, a return to the ownership of collected materials, organised and made available by the library, now in digital form, but with the new digital assessment tools to collect and analyse usage data. The digital library based on usage data will live or die by its content. As Rowlands (2007) notes, researchers are not especially accomplished searchers and use various strategies including browsing to work around their own lack of familiarity with the digital collection search interface, or its limitations. Nonetheless, scholarly digital collections are perceived as increasing productivity. The content of the digital library is more important than its interface.

- *Usage data and user outcomes for service improvement*: There is an expectation that usage data will be linked to user outcomes. Librarians are protective of the privacy rights of their patrons, so if this linkage is accomplished through authentication, librarians will insist that the data are stripped of ID information after aggregation. The purpose of linking user outcomes to usage data is to inform decision-making. Assessment results in some action that improves service for patrons.

- *Service competition for users*: Digital libraries must compete with other library resources and services. The stronger the case the digital library can make for affecting user outcomes, the better it will be accepted in the library vision of service to its users. Valid usage data related to clear user outcomes tells a convincing story to the librarian, who must also assess numerous other services, often by sophisticated cost-use or cost-benefit analysis. These services all compete for funding and attention in the library world. To some extent, the bottom-line evaluation of the digital library in the library world is how it competes in the marketplace of resources and services available to users.

Bibliography

Association of Research Libraries (2002) 'Measures for electronic resources (E-Metrics)', available at: *http://www.arl.org/bm~doc/e-metrics.pdf.zip* (accessed 8 August 2008).

Association of Research Libraries (2008) 'ARL Statistics 2005–06', available at: *http://www.arl.org/bm~doc/arlstats06.pdf* (accessed 28 July 2008).

Baker, G. and Read, E. J. (2008) 'Vendor-supplied usage data for electronic resources: a survey of academic libraries', *Learned Publishing* 21(1): 48–57.

Bertot, J. C. and McClure, C. M. (2003) 'Outcomes assessment in the networked environment: Research questions, issues, considerations, and moving forward', *Library Trends* 51(4): 590–613.

Bertot, J. C. and Davis, D. M. (2005) *Planning and Evaluating Library Networked Services and Resources*, Westport, CT: Libraries Unlimited.

Bollen, J., Rodriguez, M. A. and Van de Sompel, H. (2007) 'MESUR: Usage-based metrics of scholarly impact', in *Proceedings of the 7th ACM/IEEE-CS Joint Conference on Digital Libraries Vancouver, BC, 17–23 June*, New York: ACM Press, p. 474.

Conyers, A. and Dalton, P. (2007) 'Electronic resource measurement: Linking research to practice', *Library Quarterly* 77(4): 463–70.

Center for Research Libraries (2007) *Trustworthy Repositories Audit and Certification (TRAC): Criteria and Checklist*, Chicago, IL: Center for Research Libraries and OCLC.

Davis, P. M. and Connolly, M. J. L. (2007) 'Institutional repositories: evaluating the reasons for non-use of Cornell University's installation of DSpace', *D-Lib Magazine* 12(3/4), available at: *http://www.dlib.org/dlib/march07/davis/03davis.html* (accessed 8 August 2008).

DeFranco, F., Hiller, S., Janicke Hinchliffe, L., Justh, K., Kyrillidou, M. and Self, J. (eds) (2007) *Library Assessment Conference: Building*

Effective, Sustainable and Practical Assessment, Washington, DC: ARL.

Franklin, B. and Plum, T. (2006) 'Successful web survey methodologies for Measuring the Impact of Networked Electronic Services (MINES for Libraries)', *IFLA Journal* 32(1): 28–40.

Franklin, B. and Plum, T. (2008) 'Assessing the value and impact of digital content', *Journal of Library Administration* 48(1): 1–57.

Galvin, T. and Kent, A. (1977) 'Use of a university library collection', *Library Journal* 102(20): 2317–20.

Hiller, S, Kyrillidou, M. and Self, J. (2008) 'When evidence isn't enough: Organizational factors that influence effective, sustainable and practical assessment', *Performance Measurement and Metrics* 9(3): 223–30.

Jamali, H. R., Nicholas, D. and Huntington, P. (2005) 'Use and users of scholarly e-journals: a review of log analysis studies', *Aslib Proceedings* 57(6): 554–71.

JCDL (2006) 'Digital curation and trusted repositories: seeking success', available at: *http://sils.unc.edu/events/2006jcdl/digitalcuration/* (accessed 8 August 2008).

Kyrillidou, M., Olshen T., Franklin, B. and Plum, T. (2006) *MINES for Libraries™: Measuring the Impact of Networked Electronic Services and the Ontario Council of University Libraries' Scholar Portal, Final report, January 26*, Washington, DC: ARL.

Lakos, A. (2007) 'Evidence-based library management: The leadership challenge', *portal: Libraries and the Academy* 7(4): 431–50.

McDonald, J. (2007) 'Usage statistics and information behaviors: understanding user behavior with quantitative indicators', paper presented at NISO 2007: Understanding the Data Around Us: Gathering and Analyzing Usage Data, Dallas, TX, 1–2 November, available at: *http://niso.kavi.com/news/events/niso/past/usage07/usage07mcdonald.pdf* (accessed 8 August 2008).

Montgomery, C. H. and King, D. W. (2002) 'Comparing library and user related costs of print and electronic journal collections: a first step towards a comprehensive analysis', *D-Lib Magazine* 8(10), available at: *http://www.dlib.org/dlib/october02/montgomery/10montgomery.html* (accessed 8 August 2008).

Moreleli-Cacouris, M. (ed.) (2007) *Library Assessment Conference Papers, 13–15 June 2005, Thessaloniki, Greece*, Washington, DC: ARL.

Nicholas, D., Huntington, P., Jamali, H. and Tenopir, C. (2005) 'What deep log analysis tells us about the impact of big deals: case study OhioLINK', *Journal of Documentation* 62(4): 482–508.

OARiNZ (2007) 'Evaluation criteria', available at: *http://www.oarinz .ac.nz/oarinzwiki/index.php?n=OARiNZ.EvaluationCriteria* (accessed 8 August 2008).

Obst, O. (2003) 'Patterns and cost of printed and online journal usage', *Health Information and Libraries Journal* 20(1): 22–32.

Proudman, V. (2007) 'The population of repositories', in K. Weenink, L. Waaijers and K. van Godtsenhoven (eds), *A DRIVER's Guide to European Repositories*, Amsterdam: AUP, pp. 49–101.

Reeves, T., Apedoe, X. and Woo, Y. (2006) 'Evaluating digital libraries: A user-friendly guide (revised version)', available at: *http://www.dpc .ucar.edu/projects/evalbook/index.html* (accessed 28 November 2008).

Rowlands, I. (2007) 'Electronic journals and user behavior: A review of recent research', *Library and Information Science Research* 29(3): 369–96.

Samson, S., Derry, S. and Eggleston, H. (2004) 'Networked resources, assessment and collection development', *The Journal of Academic Librarianship* 30(6): 476–81.

Schonfeld, R. C., King, D. W., Okerson, A. and Gifford Fenton, E. (2004) *The Nonsubscription Side of Periodicals: Changes in Library Operations and Costs between Print and Electronic Formats*. Washington, DC: CLIR.

Snead, J. T., Bertot, J. C., Jaeger, P. T. and McClure, C. R. (2005) 'Developing multi-method, iterative, and user-centered evaluation strategies for digital libraries: functionality, usability, and accessibility', paper presented at the Annual Meeting of the American Society for Information Science and Technology, Charlotte, NC, 28 October to 2 November, available at: *http://eprints.rclis.org/archive/ 00005268/* (accessed 8 August 2008).

Stemper, J. A. and Jaguszewski, J. M. (2003) 'Usage statistics for electronic journals: an analysis of local and vendor counts', *Collection Management* 28(4): 3–22.

Tenopir, C. (2003) *Use and Users of Electronic Library Resources: An Overview and Analysis of Recent Research Studies*. Washington, DC: CLIR.

Thompson, B., Kyrillidou, M. and Cook, C. (2008) 'On-premises library use versus Google-like information gateway usage patterns: a LibQUAL+® study', *portal: Libraries and the Academy* 7(4): 463–80.

Westell, M. (2006) Institutional repositories in Canada – institutional repositories: proposed indicators of success', *Library Hi Tech* 24(2): 211–26.

White, A. and Kamal, E. D. (2006) *E-Metrics for Library and Information Professionals: How to Use Data for Managing and Evaluating Electronic Resources Collections*, New York: Neal-Shuman.

Wright, S. and White, L. S. (2007) *Library Assessment: ARL Spec Kit 303*, Washington, DC: ARL.

Zucca, J. (2008) 'Building frameworks of organizational intelligence', paper presented at the Library Assessment Forum, University of Pennsylvania, Philadelphia, PA, 11 January, available at: *http://www.libqual.org/documents/admin/zuccaarl08.ppt* (accessed 8 August 2008).

3

An agency perspective on digital library evaluation

Michael Khoo, David McArthur and Lee Zia

Introduction

Funding agencies play key roles in digital library projects. They provide financial support, guidelines for research and development, and requirements for reporting project outcomes. In the case of publicly-supported agencies, governments in turn require such bodies to account for their own activities and expenditures. A common concern of agencies is therefore to ensure that they are obtaining good value from the projects that they fund.

Different agencies have different evaluation models and strategies. Key evaluation requirements are usually published in programme solicitations, where agencies may provide specific evaluation models and advice. In answering a solicitation, a project agrees to abide by the evaluation requirements of that solicitation. This 'contractual model' – in which an agency provides funds to a project, and that project then reports on results to the agency – constitutes a simple model of evaluation requirements, as represented in Figure 3.1a.

In practice, this simple relationship is often complicated by local conditions. To illustrate this complexity, we provide a case study of a US funding agency, the National Science Foundation (NSF), and of one of the programmes that it funds, the National Science, Technology, Engineering, and Mathematics Education Digital Library (NSDL), focusing on the example of web metrics.

Figure 3.1 (a) Simple evaluation model, showing flow of resources and results; (b) actual evaluation model in the case of NSF and the NSDL

(a)

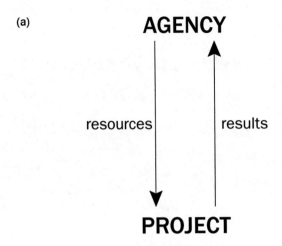

(b)

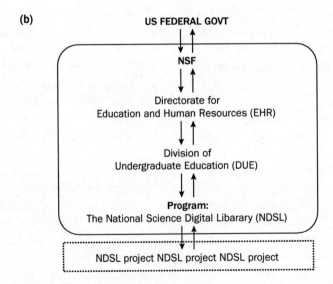

The case study is in three parts:

- the national context of digital library development in the USA;
- NSF organisation and evaluation; and
- NSDL organisation and evaluation, including a web metrics case study.

Citing a range of reports from NSF and the NSDL, we will show how NSDL evaluation is shaped by a range of national, programme and project factors, and how NSF and NSDL are linked by multiple organisational and evaluation channels, some of which arise from the position of the programme in the NSF agency structure, and others, often less clear, which stem from the collective status of the various NSDL projects as a virtual organisation that is situated within the wider NSDL programme. We argue that these multiple channels can be beneficial because they permit multiple views on the same organisation which can be triangulated with both internal project data and wider digital library research data. But we also argue that multiple channels can be challenging to manage, particularly in widely distributed organisations. Some agency evaluation requirements may be clear and compelling to projects, while others may be vague and not backed by compliance mechanisms; some requirements can be complementary, while others may be inconsistent; and balancing multiple requirements may be difficult for projects on limited resources.

We conclude with some recommendations for organisational sense-making activities in which programmes and individual projects can engage to develop successful evaluation plans. The recommendations emphasise the importance of careful planning of project-level evaluations, fully supported by the necessary resources; and also the more deliberate organisational articulation of the important connections between project and programme evaluation, taking into consideration the wider context of multiple, potentially conflicting, and changing evaluation requirements and channels.

The US context

Digital library development in the USA takes place within a range of national policy contexts, including the ongoing strategic importance of science education, and the creation of a national cyberinfrastructure to support science and engineering research and education (e.g. Atkins, 2003).

Science education in the USA

Various reports (e.g. Committee on Prospering in the Global Economy of the 21st Century, 2007) have noted the importance of science, technology, engineering and mathematics (STEM) education skills in a twenty-first century global economy, and the stagnation of these skills in the US workforce. In response, the US federal government, universities, educational foundations, and others, are applying innovations in computer and information technologies to the design of educational technologies, such as digital libraries, in order to increase STEM educational and workforce capacity. Despite the investment of billions of dollars in educational technologies, there is ongoing debate in the USA as to their effectiveness. Metastudies of the use of a range of technologies in schools (e.g. Waxman et al., 2003) have also shown improved educational outcomes in a number of areas. On the other hand, a recent report to the US Congress (Dynarski et al., 2007) on the effectiveness of reading and mathematics software found that test scores were not significantly higher in classrooms using selected reading and mathematics software products.

But this debate is not just about improvements in standardised test results. Constructivist educational theorists argue that the significance of educational technologies lies not just in their ability to promote test scores – which may in the end may just measure rote learning skills – but also in their promise to promote greater of depth of critical thinking, increase student engagement and retention, and a range of other educational outcomes (Honey, 2001; Viadero, 2007). In debates over the effectiveness of educational technologies, these more complex and qualitative learning outcomes are as significant as test scores.

Cyberinfrastructure

A second US policy context is that of the creation of a national cyberinfrastructure supporting STEM research and education. Stimulated by the blue-ribbon report on revolutionising science and engineering (Atkins, 2003), NSF has over the past several years begun to develop programmes to explore the potential of cyberinfrastructure, and this research has slowly extended from the physical sciences to the social sciences (Berman and Brady, 2005) and to education (Bernat et al., 2006). These recent reports have also suggested that cyberinfrastructure applications might transform science education as dramatically as they are now changing practice in the sciences.

The increasing emphasis on cyberinfrastructure for learning, often described by NSF as 'cyberlearning', has two broad consequences for the development and evaluation of digital learning technologies in general and digital libraries in particular. First, it places a premium on the design of innovative teaching and learning environments that extend the boundaries of what students can learn, explore the new roles teachers can play, and invigorate the processes through which learning happens.

Early work in these programmes is as much about breaking existing moulds in education, as it is about using cyberlearning to make minor enhancements in traditional pedagogies aimed at incremental improvements on standardised tests. Evaluation of cyberlearning programmes and projects, in turn, will need to reflect these priorities. Such evaluations may be very different than ones, such as those noted above, that examine the near-term effectiveness of educational technologies in helping to achieve well-defined student learning outcomes. Early cyberlearning evaluation goals are likely to emphasise the formative assessment of risky yet highly innovative educational tools and learning environments.

The second consequence of cyberlearning for digital library evaluation relates to 'virtual organisations': geographically distributed teams whose members share a common interest or goal, and work primarily or exclusively at a distance using cyberinfrastructure technologies (NSF, 2007a). Early work in virtual organisations at NSF is examining how teams come together – and split apart – to work more effectively, and how cyberinfrastructure can support such dynamic organisation synthesis and the advance work of virtual teams. In terms of evaluation, fluid virtual organisations imply that teams working together may be connected through multiple management channels, each of which may have its own evaluation priorities. Because virtual organisations may reconfigure 'on the fly', team members may not be aware of all the evaluation requirements or expectations that are imposed on them at a given time. All this is potentially far more complicated than the simple organisational connections depicted in Figure 3.1a.

The National Science Foundation

Having described the cyberinfrastructure and virtual organisation contexts within which NSF is set, we now turn to the organisational structure of NSF, and the NSDL programme within this organisation.

NSF is an independent federal agency created by Congress in 1950 'to promote the progress of science; to advance the national health, prosperity, and welfare; to secure the national defense' (NSF, 2006). NSF has an annual budget of about $6 billion, and funds basic research in many domains, including mathematics, computer science and the social sciences. The agency is composed of a hierarchy of directorates and offices, divisions, and programmes within each division responsible for funding individual projects. For instance, the NSF Directorate for Education and Human Resources (EHR) administers the Division of Undergraduate Education (DUE); DUE in turn funds the NSDL programme; and the NSDL programme funds individual NSDL projects (Figure 3.1b) (NSDL encompasses learners of all ages; the programme is in DUE for historical reasons). Each NSDL project subscribes to the research and development aims expressed in the programme-level solicitations.

Each organisational layer at NSF embraces and focuses the mission of the organisational level above it. NSF's mission as a whole is to promote US science capacity in all areas. EHR narrows that focus to formal and informal education at all levels; DUE works specifically with undergraduate education; and finally, the NSDL programme implements DUE's mission in the specific context of digital libraries. Working back up the organisational hierarchy, we can see that NSDL projects report to the NSDL programme, which reports to DUE, which reports to EHR, which reports to the NSF Director.

Programme and project-level evaluation in NSDL

Programme-level NSDL evaluation is approached as a holistic and integrative process that focuses on understanding the collective utility of the programme as a whole. Project-level evaluation focuses on the individual projects within the programme, to determine whether or not they are proceeding according to the schedules provided in the original project proposals, and whether they are meeting their stated goals (Frechtling, 2002). These two activities may appear to be mismatched, but they are actually related in complex ways: for instance, project-level evaluation data are fed back to NSF, where they may also offer the potential to be repurposed and used to answer different questions at the programme level than at the project level. In NSF's view, projects do not just succeed or fail. Rather, as many NSF projects are experimental in nature, there is an interest in data as a description of what happened, as much as an overall judgment of success or failure. In highly-experimental conditions, all data are potentially useful.

This wider perspective may not necessarily be shared by individual NSDL projects, where perceptions of success and failure may be more keenly felt, not least because the grant funding process is ultimately a competitive one, in which future success with an agency is often seen, rightly or wrongly, as being partly related to current success. To avoid this perception, programme evaluation requirements should be explained carefully to individual projects, and stress:

> the inherent relationship between evaluation and program implementation. Evaluation is not separate from, or added to, a project, but rather is part of it from the beginning. Planning, evaluation and implementation are all parts of a whole, and they work best when they work together. (Frechtling, 2002: 3)

The National Science Digital Library

The NSDL is a multi-year NSF programme that is developing a wide range of STEM educational resources, tools and services, within a distributed digital library structure. Its origins lie in discussions in the academic, pedagogical and computing science communities in the 1990s on the building of an undergraduate digital library for science, mathematics, engineering and technology education (NSF SMETE, 1998; Wattenberg, 1998). NSF subsequently developed plans for the National Science, Technology, Engineering, and Mathematics Education Digital Library Program (e.g. Zia, 2000). Officially launched in 2000, by 2006 the NSDL programme had disbursed over $150 billion to over 200 projects. The mission of the library 'to increase literacy and interest in science, mathematics, and technology; ready tomorrow's workforce for STEM-related careers; support the advance of knowledge and the solving of real-world problems; and promote continued excellence in the nation's scientific pursuits' (NSDL, 2007a), resonates both with NSF's overall mission, and also with the country's current strategic concerns with increasing STEM capacity.

Over time, the NSDL programme has moved away from funding a larger number of specific individual digital library components (tools, services, collections, etc.), and towards the support of a smaller number of integrated portals, known as 'Pathways' projects. These are:

> grouped by grade level, discipline, resource or data type ... [to] best support efficient resource discovery for broad categories of users. Pathway portals are developed and managed in partnership with organizations and institutions that have a history and expertise in

serving their portal's target audiences – in effect, they act as reference librarians for their communities. (NSDL, year unknown, a)

NSDL Pathway projects develop their own websites and catalogues. In addition, Pathway catalogues are federated at the main NSDL website (*www.nsdl.org*). NSDL users can therefore either go straight to the relevant portal or search the portals from the central site.

NSDL programme coordination

A distinctive characteristic of the NSDL programme is that individual NSDL projects are expected to collaborate among themselves in areas of programme development such as technological standards, information and library standards, programme-wide communication tools, etc. As such, NSDL projects, when taken together, constitute a virtual organisation or entity, 'NSDL', which is distinct from the NSDL programme administered by NSF (represented by the dotted line in Figure 3.1b). This virtual structure arises out of wider NSF research concerns with the management of large-scale, distributed virtual organisations. Project-level 'virtual organisation' coordination activities in NSDL are concentrated in two areas: the NSDL 'Core Integration' (NSDL-CI) project, and the NSDL community (Figure 3.2).

NSF funds a single NSDL-CI project tasked with developing programme-wide technical, logistical and managerial infrastructure.

Figure 3.2   Resource and results flows in the NSDL

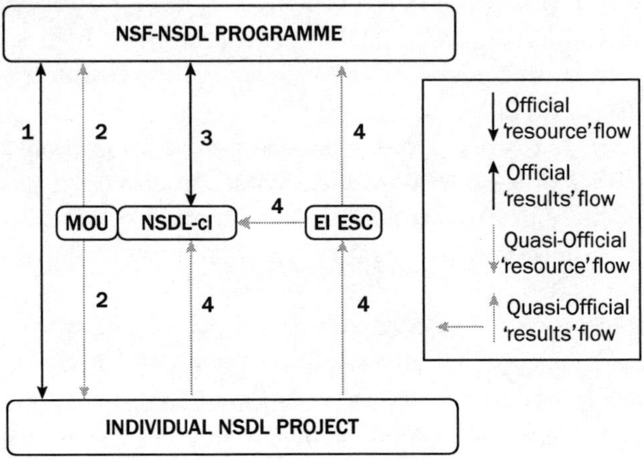

For instance, NSDL-CI maintains a portal for the NSDL at *www.nsdl.org*, and is building a federated repository, which together provides access to and search across all Pathways collections. Compared with other NSDL projects, NSDL-CI project has broader responsibilities, and deeper resources (including some full-time staff).

The NSDL-CI project has developed a quasi-official managerial relationship with Pathways projects which includes some of the oversight roles more traditionally associated with NSF programme officers. The relationship is described as 'quasi-official' because while it replicates aspects of the typical patron-client relationship between NSF programmes and individual NSF projects, it is also viewed by NSF as an experimental form of infrastructure for a large-scale virtual organisation, and is therefore open to interpretation. The relationship is described in a number of formal and informal agreements, including a memorandum of understanding (MoU) (NSDL, 2007b), which sets out the NSDL-CI requirements for Pathways projects.

Virtual management of a variety of day-to-day NSDL affairs is further coordinated by a 'community', whose members are drawn from NSDL projects, and who participate in committees, e-mail lists, conference calls, and an annual meeting. NSDL committees work to develop common NSDL policies in areas such as collection development, governance, sustainability, technical standards, and evaluation (via the Educational Impact and Evaluation Standing Committee, or EIESC, see NSDL, year unknown, b).

NSDL evaluation practices

NSDL committees and the NSDL-CI project constitute a 'middle layer' between NSF and individual NSDL projects (Figure 3.2). In this complex organisational space, evaluation involves more than the simple 'channel' model illustrated in Figure 3.1a, or even the hierarchical model of Figure 3.1b. In reality, there are a number of evaluation channels between NSF and NSDL with varying degrees of formality.

The most formal channel (arrow 1 in Figure 3.2) is between NSF and the individual Pathways projects. It is laid out in NSDL programme solicitations, which ask potential projects:

> What evidence will be sought to inform the progress towards project goals and why is this of value? As a component of NSDL, how will usage of the services offered by the project be ascertained?

What evidence of impact on users will be gathered and why? (NSF, 2007b)

Successful project applicants for NSDL programme funding have to provide a detailed account of how they would address these questions and make the data available to NSF.

A second evaluation channel is that between NSF and individual NSDL projects, mediated by NSDL-CI, and described by the MoU (see above) (arrow 2 in Figure 3.2). Pathways projects have to sign the MoU before NSF will release funds to them. In return for receiving funds, the MoU requires Pathways to participate in the larger NSDL programme evaluation effort by defining yearly benchmarks and metrics and by providing web metrics data to NSDL-CI. However, as noted above, NSDL-CI has only a quasi-official status between NSF and NSDL projects, meaning that there are no real sanctions should a Pathways project not fulfil its evaluation requirements.

The third evaluation channel depicted in Figure 3.2 is that between NSF and NSDL-CI. This channel reports the results of NSDL-CI's evaluation of its own activities. These activities include the development of evaluation capacity within the NSDL programme as a whole, and so this channel also reports Pathways evaluation data that have been collected and analysed by NSDL-CI. This relationship is a formal one – NSDL-CI's responsibilities are defined by NSDL solicitations.

Finally, there is a network of informal evaluation channels in the form of the work done by the EIESC (see above). This work includes the coordination and collection of cross-project data of interest to NSF, such as organisational structure, site usage, collection development policies, and so on (Giersch, 2005). EIESC results are presented in EIESC workshops and reports, and reported to both NSDL-CI and NSF. A significant channel here is the NSDL annual meeting, where projects can report evaluation findings. In addition, satisfaction surveys indicate that the annual meeting is very favourably rated as a venue for face-to-face interaction with colleagues in other projects. All this activity is quasi-official.

Multiple evaluation channels in NSDL

The existence of multiple official and quasi-official evaluation channels in a single programme context, as represented in Figure 3.2, is a novel experience for many NSDL projects. Usually, an NSF project has a one-on-one relationship with NSF. In the case of the NSDL, however, NSDL-CI, the MoU with the Pathways projects, and the NSDL community, constitute an additional web of organisational layers between individual projects and the NSF. While these layers do not have the authority of the traditional NSF-project relationship, they do demand attention from projects. At the same time, these multiple evaluation requirements may not necessarily be clear or useful to individual NSDL projects, for a number of reasons. The requirements may be novel; they may be in addition to the goals stated in NSDL programme solicitations; they may differ from individual project goals; and they may require a learning curve.

Individual NSDL Pathways projects therefore must identify, translate and adapt these complex NSDL evaluation channels objectives into their own strategic objectives. In cases where NSDL programme goals do not align with individual project goals, and given the limited evaluation resources sometimes available to projects, there is a danger that the programme goals will take a back seat to project goals or worse, remain unrecognised or ignored. There is the possibility that the evaluation data which NSF sees as being useful for the purpose of synthesis and programme evaluation, may not be the same data that individual projects see as being useful for their own projects. Individual projects may even see some of the data useful to NSF as being harmful to their participation in future NSF solicitations, in the sense that they could hurt a project's standing in the eyes of NSF.

Web metrics: an NSDL evaluation case study

In this section, we illustrate this multi-channel evaluation environment through a discussion of the use of web metrics in NSDL. Web metrics are methods for collecting and analysing traffic to and through a website. Apparently objective, they can yield widely different statistics. Table 3.1 presents the May 2006 figures for the NSDL portal, as measured by two different web metrics tools used by NSDL-CI, and normalised to a nominal 1,000 visits to *www.nsdl.org* as recorded by Tool B.

Table 3.1   Two versions of the web metrics for the NSDL portal

	Tool A	Tool B
Hits	37,317	n/a
Page views	14,401	4,165
Visits	1,875	1,000

The 37:1 ratio between hits recorded by Tool A and visits recorded by Tool B for the same time period underscores that data from individual NSDL projects are to be treated with caution, unless it is known how they were recorded and calculated. It follows that implementing useful NSDL programme-wide web metrics requires standardisation in tools and units of measurement.

NSDL-CI has worked for a number of years to standardise web metrics across the projects (Jones et al., 2004). However, as of 2006, NSDL projects still used a range of tools, with the attendant issues of lack of standardisation. From 2006, NSDL-CI began requiring, through a clause in the MoU, that Pathways projects implement a common javascript-based page-tagging web metrics tool on each of their sites. The implementation was supported by NSDL-CI, which paid the costs of the implementation, provided specialist technical support, and organised web metrics workshops. It was hoped that this would lead to consistency in overall programme data aggregation. However, the implementation was slower than had been expected, for several reasons.

First, there is often a lack of web metrics resources at the individual Pathway level. Pathways project managers are typically faculty who work part-time on their project, supported by part-time student assistants, and who face a learning curve with respect to implementing, configuring, and reporting web metrics. Second, implementation also requires access to individual site code (to add the javascript), and to the server (to upload the code); and some Pathways with external web developers have had trouble accessing the project servers in order to implement the code. Third, while the Pathways were required under the MoU to implement the web metrics tool, there was no formal provision for NSDL-CI to enforce either the MoU or the specific web metrics requirements that it contained. Combined with the fact that the Pathways projects often had more immediate priorities than implementing web metrics, such as getting their site up and running in the first place, it was perhaps not surprising that the web metrics implementation proceeded slowly, with the best results being obtained with Pathways that were more established or that had full-time staff with the necessary expertise.

These outcomes can be mapped onto the organisational structure in Figure 3.2, as follows:

- *Arrow 1*: There was no *official* requirement in NSDL solicitations for individual projects to report web metrics direct to NSF; consequently, little reporting took place through this channel.

- *Arrow 2*: There was a *quasi-official* requirement, described in the MoU, for projects to implement and report standardised web metrics to NSDL-CI. As described above, this implementation proceeded patchily.

- *Arrow 3*: There was an *official* requirement for NSDL-CI to report what web metrics data it did collect to NSF. This reporting occurred on a monthly basis (NSDL year unknown, c).

- *Arrow 4*: There was a *quasi-official* requirement for NSDL projects to work with the EIESC to develop and report web metrics. Once again, this work proceeded patchily.

In sum, there was no formal organisational channel that encouraged the consistent reporting of programme-wide web metrics data to NSF; however, there was a series of informal channels, which although they yielded more heterogeneous data, still provided data that were of use at the NSDL programme level.

NSF reflections on evaluation in virtual organisations

The NSDL web metrics evaluation work described above attempted to integrate a range of projects, tools and reporting channels, with varying degrees of success. The work highlights several important lessons related to project and programme evaluation, and the relationship between these two activities, especially in virtual organisations.

First, as projects need considerable expertise and resources to properly adopt an evaluation activity such as web metrics, NSF programmes must ensure at the outset that projects have adequate budget and staffing to support the appropriate implementation of the software. At an early stage in the NSDL programme, this was found not to be the case. Only with this foundation in place will it be realistic for the programme to require individual projects to implement a common set of web metrics and make the data available for shared cross-project analysis.

More broadly, agencies such as NSF must understand that the use of such tools for evaluation come with real costs as well as potential benefits. These costs not only include technical ones, but also social and strategic ones. Different projects, even within a single programme like NSDL, can have distinct goals, and the use of a common set of web metric tools and measures will not necessarily meet their evaluation requirements. A new

NSDL project, for example, may not be interested in gathering web metrics data about the volume or geographical diversity of its users; that project may be more interested in developing a website in the first place. The programme may therefore want to accommodate these diverse needs by, for example, encouraging projects to use web metric tools – or other ones – in different ways to address their specific usage and project-level evaluation questions. At the same time, however, the programme could also insist on gathering additional data using common web metrics adopted by other projects, in order to address broad programme-level evaluation questions. This, in turn, requires the programme to have a solid understanding of its key evaluation questions, and, in the case of NSDL, how innovative web metrics can be used to address them.

Supporting evaluation in virtual organisations

Ideally, a programme would establish these questions and their associated standard metrics early in the project lifecycle, thus providing clear guidelines on what to measure, when, and how. However, in dynamic programmes like NSDL that explore emerging information technologies, foster growing virtual organisations, and include multiple evaluation channels, such detailed advanced planning can be impractical. Nevertheless, there may be several ways of dealing effectively with this challenge in the future:

- *Clarity*: It would be helpful if both projects and programmes established, at least tentatively, their major evaluation goals early on, and – as such goals can change, sometimes rather radically, over time – also engaged in a continuing dialogue on evaluation goals and methods. Conversations at this level could, for example, help NSDL programme managers and the NSDL community to understand how the adoption of web metrics might address (or not) the needs of specific projects. Conversely, the discussions would also provide projects with insights about programme-level evaluation goals that web metrics might speak to, even if they do not address project-level evaluation issues.

- *Flexibility*: Many projects in programmes as diverse as NSDL will have distinct evaluation goals and will need to consider the deployment of a range of evaluation web metrics, as well as other measures of progress – as will the NSDL programme as a whole. If web metrics technologies are to be used on a broad basis to help evaluate digital library projects and programmes, they will need to be implemented in standardised ways across sites; for example, projects should adhere to common definitions of terms like 'visits', 'unique visits', and 'page views'. The tools, however, will also need to be sufficiently supple to be tailored to the evaluation needs of specific projects and programmes.

- *Research*: Finally, a significant challenge associated with the effective use of web metrics in the evaluation of NSDL projects and the programme as a whole, is that not only are the metrics new and somewhat unstable, but the science of inferring users' intentions from them is still in its infancy; we can see the results of users' interactions with a website, but we do not have access to the thought processes behind those interactions.

To make highly-effective use of the promising new ideas behind web metrics, NSDL and related programmes at NSF will therefore need to continue to support research on web metrics, not just fund their deployment. NSDL is an ideal testbed for a many interesting research studies that could, for example, track a range of metrics longitudinally, and triangulate web metrics data and other sources of information on user behaviour (Khoo et al., 2008). This sort of research could lead to a new generation of web metric tools and protocols for digital library evaluation and improvement.

Recommendations

This web metrics case study suggests several broad recommendations that agencies, their programmes, and their projects might follow to improve the success of their evaluation plans.

First, projects should have well-developed individual evaluation plans, and the programmes and agencies that support them should provide sufficient resources and requirements to ensure the project evaluations yield useful data. This seems straightforward, but project budgets are sometimes cut and evaluation plans are often compromised. In other cases, promising educational projects are still generating useful data when the project ends; absent an extension and supplementary funding, such projects may fail to deliver their most significant results.

Second, at a broader level, programmes and programme directors who understand programme-level evaluation needs should, as Frechtling (2002) notes, make clear to individual projects what the requirements of this wider context are, and how they affect the projects. Ideally, directors would articulate a logic model (Trochim et al., 2008) for the programme that encompasses all project inputs, resources, outputs and outcomes. The connections between a programme's goals, and hence its evaluation priorities, and project evaluation data may be multiple and nuanced. For example, as the web metrics case study illustrates, NSDL has a programme-level evaluation goal to track the growth of its collections. NSDL projects that manage collections would clearly provide evaluation data relevant to this programme goal; however, projects that develop specific tools and services, which rarely maintain collections, would not – although their evaluation data could inform other NSDL programme-level goals. This suggests that programmes need not only to communicate their overall evaluation goals to projects, but should also translate these into different requirements for distinct types of projects. Additional resources may be required to ensure that projects can fulfil these evaluation tasks as well as their individual project evaluation plans.

Finally, agencies and programmes will need to confront the evaluation complexities inherent in the growing trend towards programmes, like NSDL, that connect individual projects into interdependent virtual organisations. Articulating beforehand how programme-level evaluation needs translate into project-level evaluation requirements will not be possible in programmes with components that reconfigure from time to time. As new teams and committees arise, which they have done through the lifetime of NSDL, agency programme directors – as well as the virtual organisation groups that hold governing authority – will need to interpret these changes in terms of transformed programme-level goals, and translate them into new project-level evaluation needs. These same decision-makers will also have to establish the appropriate levels of compliance for new evaluation mandates, and, if they are strong requirements, programme directors will have to guarantee projects have adequate resources to comply.

Conclusion

Virtual organisations like NSDL naturally result in dynamic new relationships among teams and projects, and these connections are often less official and more informal than typical project–programme relationships. These multiple evaluation channels are useful (as the web metrics case study demonstrates), and they will become more common as virtual organisations like NSDL proliferate.

An important theme to emerge from this complexity concerns the nature and role of organisational communication in a virtual organisation. While sophisticated information and communication technologies hold the possibility of rapid and clear virtual organisational communication between funding agencies and projects, the potential of these communication tools sometimes serves as much to reveal the knowledge differences and communication difficulties between groups, as to support seamless collaboration and knowledge building. From the point of view of NSF, this suggests the importance, when planning any evaluation of a virtual organisation that goes beyond aggregating individual project results and considers broader issues, such as the value of the digital library as a whole, of ensuring that all stakeholders in the evaluation process, including agencies and projects, are on the same page with regard to aims, requirements and resources. This observation will only become more important as NSF continues to fund and evaluate large-scale virtual organisations, including digital libraries.

Bibliography

Atkins, D. (2003) 'Revolutionizing science and engineering through cyberinfrastructure', available at: *http://www.nsf.gov/od/oci/reports/toc.jsp* (accessed 6 March 2008).

Berman, F. and Brady, H. (2005) *Final Report: NSF SBE-CISE Workshop on Cyberinfrastructure and the Social Sciences*, Washington, DC: NSF.

Bernat, A., Smith, J. and Rothschild, D. (eds) (2005) *Cyberinfrastructure for Learning and Education for the Future: A Vision and Research Agenda*, Washington, DC: CRA, available at: *http://www.cra.org/reports/cyberinfrastructure.pdf* (accessed 6 March 2008).

Committee on Prospering in the Global Economy of the 21st Century (2007) *Rising above the Gathering Storm: Energizing and Employing America for a Brighter Economic Future*, Washington, DC: National Academies Press.

Dynarski, M., Agodini, R., Heaviside, S., Novak, T., Carey, N., Campuzano, L., Means, B., Murphy, R., Penuel, W., Javitz, H., Emery, D. and Sussex, W. (2007) *Effectiveness of Reading and Mathematics Software Products: Findings from the First Student Cohort*, Washington, DC: US Department of Education.

Frechtling, J. (2002) *The 2002 User-Friendly Handbook for Project Evaluation*, Washington, DC: NSF.

Giersch, S. (2005) 'EIESC activities in detail, 2001–2005', available at: *http://eval.comm.nsdl.org/docs/05_eiesc_activities.pdf* (accessed 27 March 2008).

Honey, M. (2001) 'Benefits of educational technology', Testimony and Statement for the Record before the Labor, HHS, and Education Appropriations Subcommittee of the United States Senate, available at: *http://cct.edc.org/admin/publications/speeches/testimony_lhe01 .pdf* (accessed 21 April 2008).

Jones, C., Giersch, S., Sumner, T., Wright, M., Coleman, A. and Bartolo, L. (2004) 'Developing a web analytics strategy for the National Science Digital Library', *D-Lib Magazine* 10(10), available at: *http://www .dlib.org/dlib/october04/coleman/10coleman.html* (accessed 25 November 2008).

Khoo, M., Pagano, J., Washington, A., Recker, M., Palmer, B. and Donahue, R. A. (2008) 'Using web metrics to analyze digital libraries', in *Proceedings of the 8th ACM/IEEE Joint Conference on Digital Libraries, Pittsburgh, PA, 16–20 June,* New York: ACM Press, pp. 375–84.

National Science Foundation (2006) 'Investing in America's future: strategic plan FY 2006–2011', available at: *http://www.nsf.gov/pubs/ 2006/nsf0648/NSF-06-48.pdf* (accessed 6 March 2008).

National Science Foundation (2007a) 'Cyberinfrastructure vision for the 21st Century', available at: *http://www.nsf.gov/od/oci/CI_Vision_ March07.pdf* (accessed 27 March 2008).

National Science Foundation (2007b) 'National Science Technology Engineering, Mathematics Education Digital Library (NSDL), Program Solicitation NSF 07-538', available at: *http://www.nsf .gov/pubs/2007/nsf07538/nsf07538.htm* (accessed 27 March 2008).

National Science Foundation (year unknown, a) 'NSF at a glance', available at: *http://www.nsf.gov/about/glance.jsp* (accessed 8 March 2008).

NSDL (2007a) 'NSDL collection development policy', available at: *http://onramp.nsdl.org/eserv/onramp:42/NSDL_Collection_Develop ment_Policy.pdf* (accessed 6 March 2008).

NSDL (2007b) 'Memorandum of understanding between NSDL core integration and pathways projects', available at: *http://onramp.nsdl .org/eserv/onramp:32/mou_03-14-2007.pdf* (accessed 6 March 2008).

NSDL (year unknown, a) 'What are NSDL pathways', available at: *http://nsdl.org/partners/?pager=pathways* (accessed 6 March 2008).

NSDL (year unknown, b) 'The EIESC', available at: *http://eduimpact.comm .nsdl.org* (accessed 6 March 2008).

NSDL (year unknown, c) 'The NSDL evaluation pages', available at: *http://eval.comm.nsdl.org/index.html* (accessed 6 March 2008).

NSF SMETE (1998) 'NSF SMETE-Lib Study', available at: *http://www.dlib.org/smete/public/smete-public.html* (accessed 27 February 2008).

Trochim, W., Marcus, S., Masse, L., Moser, R. and Weld, P. (2008) 'The evaluation of large initiatives', *American Journal of Evaluation* 29(1): 8–28.

Viadero, D. (2007) 'New breed of digital tutors yielding learning gains', *Education Week*, 2 April, available at: *http://www.edweek.org/ew/articles/2007/04/02/31intelligent.h26.html?qs=cognitive+tutor* (accessed 27 March 2008).

Wattenberg, F. (1998) 'A National Digital Library for Science, Mathematics, Engineering, and Technology Education', *D-Lib Magazine* 4(10), available at: *http://www.dlib.org/dlib/october98/wattenberg/10wattenberg.html* (accessed 27 February 2008).

Waxman, H., Meng-Fen, L. and Michko, G. (2003) 'A meta-analysis of the effectiveness of teaching and learning with technology on student outcomes', available at: *http://www.ncrel.org/tech/effects2/* (accessed 8 March 2008).

Zia, L. (2000) 'Growing a national learning environments and resources network for Science, Mathematics, Engineering, and Technology Education: Current issues and opportunities for the NSDL Program', *D-Lib Magazine* 7(3), available at: *http://www.dlib.org/dlib/march01/zia/03zia.html* (accessed 27 February 2008).

Part 2
What to place under the evaluation lens

4

What should we take into consideration when we talk about usability?

Judy Jeng

Introduction

Since the mid-1990s, we have seen an explosive growth of digital libraries. We have also observed an increased interest in the evaluation of digital libraries in recent years. The criteria used in the evaluations of digital libraries have included the study of impact, quality of collection, organisation of resources, metadata, cost-benefit analysis, cost-effectiveness analysis, performance evaluation, interactivity, functionality, accessibility and usability. Among these, usability has been a notion in digital library evaluation. Usability assessment is one kind of digital library evaluation and is user-centred. Usability is a multidimensional and elusive construct. Usability provides feedback on what and how to improve system performance, visual appearance, and user satisfaction. Usability is a way of learning from users.

What is usability?

Usability has a theoretical root in human–computer interaction (HCI), which attempts to bridge the gap between human goals and technology. Back when digital libraries were just beginning to emerge, Rubin (1994) suggested that system designers were slow to respond to the guidelines established from research in HCI. The problem continues today. The gap in usability knowledge between research and industry practice is an important one to bridge. It is important to keep in mind that we should shape technology to suit human needs and capabilities. Usability evaluation is a way of trying to listen to users' needs and requirements.

Because the interface is the medium through which users communicate and interact with the system, there are many usability studies focusing on interface design. Kim (2002: 26) has suggested that 'the difference between interface effectiveness and usability is not clear'. Thong et al. (2004) have reported that the quality of the system interface plays a major role in influencing the usability of a digital library. Fox et al. (1993) have stated that the interface is a key factor in user acceptance of information retrieval systems.

Among the many definitions of usability, the most concise is 'fit for use', from the *American Heritage Dictionary of the English Language* (2000: 1894). Echoing this, the Usability Professionals' Association (2005) defines usability as 'the degree to which something – software, hardware or anything else – is easy to use and a good fit for the people who use it'.

The most widely cited definition of usability is offered by Nielsen (1993). He defines usability as having five components: learnability (easy to learn), efficiency, memorability, error recovery and satisfaction. He also holds that learnability should be the most fundamental criterion. Any system needs to be easy to learn so that the user can start work with the minimum of delay.

A key definition of usability can be found in the ISO 9241-11 standard, which describes usability as 'the extent to which a product can be used by specified users to achieve specified goals with effectiveness, efficiency, and satisfaction in a specified context of use' (ISO: 1994). ISO 13407, meanwhile, provides overview guidance for designing usability (ISO, 1999). Similar to the ISO definition, Bruno and Al-Qaimari (2004) define utility as the right system for the right users and the right task.

The use of digital libraries has grown steadily and significantly since the 1990s. In their Technology Acceptance Model, Davis and colleagues have identified that perceived usefulness (the extent to which an information system will enhance a user's performance) and perceived ease of use (the extent to which a person believes a system will be free of effort) are two key factors that motivate individuals to accept specific technologies including digital libraries (Davis, 1989; Davis et al., 1989). Thomas (1998) and Jeng (2006: 33) find that usefulness is an often overlooked criterion in usability evaluation of digital libraries. Jeng has subsequently studied the usefulness of two digital libraries, including the Moving Image Collections (Jeng, 2007) and the New Jersey Digital Highway (Jeng, 2008). More research is needed to advance understanding of factors contributing to ease of use and usefulness.

Although ISO 9241-11 provides a definition of usability, the document does not specifically define each criterion. To pursue this further, the study by Jeng (2006) operationalised effectiveness, efficiency, satisfaction and learnability. In this cross-institutional study, effectiveness was measured by the number of correct answers; efficiency was measured by speed, such as the length of time to complete tasks and the number of steps (clicks, keystrokes); Likert scales were used as an economic way to measure satisfaction; and learnability was measured by observing participants' efforts to learn how to use a new system. Proposing a model of usability evaluation for digital libraries (Figure 4.1), Jeng further examined satisfaction in the areas of ease of use, organisation of information, labelling and terminology, visual appearance, content and error correction. The cross-institutional study found that the model is applicable and that there exist interlocking relationships among effectiveness, efficiency and satisfaction.

There are situations where effectiveness, in addition to counting the number of correct answers (as defined in Jeng's model), can be measured in terms of the extent to which a *goal* is achieved (Jordan and Design, 1998: 5–7). Likewise, efficiency, in Jordan and Design's definition, refers to the amount of effort required to accomplish a goal. Jordan and Design also describe satisfaction as the level of comfort that users feel when using a product and how acceptable they find the product as a means of achieving their goals. In Jordan and Design's definitions of effectiveness, efficiency, and satisfaction, the emphasis is on the relationships to *goal*. While Nielsen views learnability as the most fundamental criterion of

Figure 4.1 A model of usability evaluation for digital libraries, proposed by Jeng (2006)

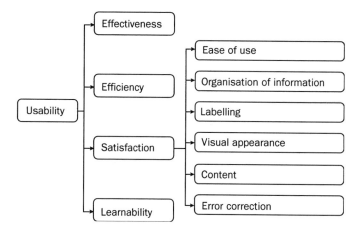

usability, Jordan and Design see satisfaction as the most important aspect of usability.

Satisfaction, according to Thomas (1998) and Jeng (2006), is the most frequently studied usability criterion. Dillon (2001) has warned that the set of metrics that falls out of the effectiveness, efficiency and satisfaction model can place undue emphasis on speed and accuracy. For many contemporary interactions, Dillon suspects that user experience will prove more complicated. He has further commented that affect covers the host of attitudinal, emotional and mood-related elements of experience. These exist in all human endeavours yet have been seriously overlooked in studies of usability. Dillon calls for more attention to user choice, preference, perception of aesthetics, frustration and sense of enhancement or accomplishment. To date, usability measures satisfaction as if it were the only affective component worthy of consideration.

Usability, as discussed earlier, is rooted in HCI and is difficult to differentiate from interface effectiveness. Usability is determined by the tasks, the users, the product and the environment. This relationship may be demonstrated as shown in Figure 4.2, which is modified from Shackel (1991: 23), Bennett (1972; 1979) and Eason (1981). This modified figure emphasises the interplaying relationships among the user, task and tool. All are in the context of the environment.

The figure demonstrates that the evaluation of usability is determined by environment, user, task and tool. A meaningful usability evaluation must take all four of these factors into account. The environment where people work influences the way in which they use artefacts. The participants in usability study must be among the specified users of the digital library. The tasks in usability testing need to be real tasks. The theory of four principal components in a human–machine system has clearly influenced the ISO 9241-11 standard on usability.

Figure 4.2 **The four principal components in a human–machine system**

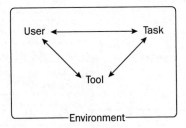

User acceptance of digital libraries may also be affected by external factors such as interface characteristics (terminology, screen design and navigation), organisational context (relevance, system accessibility, system visibility), and individual differences (computer self-efficacy, computer experience and domain knowledge) (Thong et al., 2004).

Framework of usability evaluation

Thomas (1998) recommends a framework of usability evaluation that consists of outcome, process and task. Dillon (2001) considers process (what user does), outcome (what user attains), and affect (how user feels). Saracevic (2005) recommends content, process, format and overall assessment as a framework when conducting a digital library usability evaluation.

The outcome group may include effectiveness, efficiency and satisfaction; the process group may include ease of use, interface, learnability, memorability and error recovery; the task group may include functionality and compatibility. It is important to bear in mind that all should be within the context of environment and may have interplay relationships. Jeng (2006) found that effectiveness, efficiency and satisfaction have interlocking relationships: the higher the efficiency, the higher the satisfaction; the higher the effectiveness, the higher the satisfaction; and when effectiveness is high, so is the efficiency.

When conducting a usability evaluation, we should also bear in mind the four principal components in a human–machine system (i.e. user, task, tool and environment) proposed in Figure 4.2.

Usability evaluation of a digital library is mostly user-centred. The common techniques employed in usability evaluations include formal usability testing, heuristic evaluation, usability inspection, cognitive walkthrough, claims analysis, concept-based analysis of surface and structural misfits (CASSM), card sort, paper prototyping, category membership expectation, focus groups, interviews, questionnaires, think aloud, analysis of site usage logs, and field study. Some evaluation employs one primary method. Many use more than one method.

Stefl-Mabry et al. (2003) discuss the debate regarding whether users actually know more than designers on usability needs which took place at an ASIS&T conference. Some developers have commented that usability evaluations highlight many issues that are already known to them. In a study comparing the system developers' knowledge of existing usability problems versus feedback from real users, Høegh (2006) found that the developers were aware of 38 per cent of the usability problems prior to the evaluation. The study also found that the developers were mostly able to describe the usability problems in more general terms than those identified during the usability evaluation. Nonetheless, some two-thirds of the usability problems had not been expected or acknowledged by the developers. This indicates that user-centred evaluation can provide system designers with new knowledge or awareness of new needs.

Cross-cultural usability

Culture, as we know it, is not easy to operationalise. In HCI, it is often defined as the common values, attitudes and behavioural patterns shared by a group of people. In the specific area of usability, Marcus (2006) has expressed how little we know or understand culture as it relates to user-interface usability and design.

Shneiderman (2000) has explained that 'universal usability' or 'universality' (Shneiderman and Plaisant, 2004: 12) will be met when affordable, useful and usable technology accommodates the vast majority of the global population. The development of the world wide web makes the demand of universal usability more obvious. This entails addressing challenges of technology variety (e.g. serving users with slow and fast network connections, fast and slow computers, and small and large fonts), user diversity, gaps in user knowledge, and the need to deal with multilingual international product development in ways only beginning to be acknowledged by educational, corporate and government agencies. Universal usability does not imply that a system that is well-designed for one culture will necessarily be usable in a different culture.

Barber and Badre (1998) coined the term 'culturability', indicating the merging of culture and usability. The basic premise is simple: no longer can issues of culture and usability remain separate in designing for the world wide web. What is user-friendly for one culture can be vastly different for another culture. Jeng (2006) found that although ethnic background did not have a statistically significant impact on performance such as effectiveness and efficiency, different ethnic groups seemed to rate satisfaction differently in the areas of ease of use, organisation of information, and visual attractiveness.

More and more is being learned about computer users from different cultures, but designers are still struggling to establish guidelines for designing for multiple languages and cultures. There has also been inadequate empirical evidence regarding the effects of culture in the usability engineering methods used for developing these global user interfaces, although it is clear that culture does matter for user-interface design and usability.

As discussed in the previous section, contemporary digital libraries should be designed with global users in mind. In addition to internationalisation, there are other special groups of users that usability specialists should take into consideration, such as the elderly and users with disabilities (e.g. hearing impairments, visual difficulties, mobility-impaired).

Some studies have begun to investigate how elderly users perceive usability. Browne (2000) has identified that older users represent a diverse group of multiply-disabled people who have a mix of problems with vision, manipulation, cognitive complexity, learning and general computer knowledge. Yet according to the study by Jeng (2006), age does not make statistically significant differences in performance (i.e. accuracy or speed) or in the ranking of visual attractiveness. Her study is however limited in terms of the number of subjects aged over 50. According to the study by Hawthorn (2003), older users with corrected vision do not have a preference for large fonts. However, a digital library primarily serving an elderly population may want to use large fonts and provide simple, linear and predicable search spaces.

Outlook and future research

The literature on usability is vast, including the discussions on what usability is and how to assess usability. Since the phenomenal development of digital libraries in the mid-1990s, there has been more and more evaluations of digital libraries, and usability issues have received significant attention. As we stand now, it looks like human performance and user experience with computer and information systems will remain a rapidly expanding research and development topic in the coming decades. It is up to the evaluators of digital libraries to select what criteria to use and design appropriate methodology accordingly. It is important to keep in mind that the contemporary digital libraries are on an international scale and must consider culturability or universal usability.

Usability, when well applied in digital library design, diminishes the gap between what users know and what users need to know and thus makes the site more user-friendly and intuitive. Researchers have found that current users are not dedicated to the technology and their background is more tied to their work needs (Shneiderman and Plaisant, 2004: 110–11). Around the world, usability engineering is becoming a recognised discipline with maturing practices and a growing set of standards. The Usability Professionals' Association, founded in 1991, has become a respected community with active participation from nearly 2,400 members worldwide.

Usability is a multidimensional and elusive construct. Researchers and practitioners have discussed usability from many perspectives and grouped its attributes in many ways. One way is to divide between qualitative and quantitative measures. Another way is to group into outcome, process and task. Alternatively, it can be examined from technical, cognitive and social perspectives. Yet another categorisation is interface usability, content usability, organisational usability and interorganisational usability. It is important to bring these different perspectives together to share views, experiences and insights. Usability is not an isolated quality, but a feature diffused throughout the ecology of technology. There has been a call for more benchmark data so that similar systems may compare performance data, such as effectiveness and efficiency. There has also been a call for testing mechanisms as a means to evaluate new concepts. Digital library development involves interplay among people, organisation and technology. The usability issue involves the system as a whole and must be evaluated in the context of the environment.

References

American Heritage Dictionary of the English Language (4th edn) (2000) Boston, MA: Houghton Mifflin Co.

Barber, W. and Badre, A. (1998) 'Culturability: The merging of culture and usability', paper presented at the Fourth Conference on Human Factors and the Web, Basking Ridge, NJ, 5 June, available at: *http://www.research.microsoft.com/users/marycz/hfweb98/barber/index.htm* (accessed 21 May 2008).

Bennett, J. L. (1972) 'The user interface in interactive systems', *Annual Review of Information Science and Technology* 7: 159–196.

Bennett, J. L. (1979) 'The commercial impact of usability in interactive systems', in B. Shackel (ed.) *Man-Computer Communication, Infotech State-of-the-Art* (Vol. 2), Maidenhead: Infotech International, pp. 1–17.

Browne, H. (2000) 'Accessibility and usability of information technology by the elderly', available at: *http://www.otal.umd.edu/UUGuide/hbrowne* (accessed 21 May 2008).

Bruno, V. and Al-Qaimari, G. (2004) 'Usability attributes: An initial step toward effective user-centred development', paper presented at OZCHI 2004: Supporting Community Interaction: Possibilities and Challenges, Wollongong, New South Wales, 22–24 November, available at: *http://www.brunoplace.com/~vince/Data/OZCHIU sabilityAttributesV12.pdf* (accessed 21 May 2008).

Davis, F. D. (1989) 'Perceived usefulness, perceived ease of use, and user acceptance of information technology', *MIS Quarterly* 13(3): 319–40.

Davis, F. D., Bagozzi, R. P. and Warshaw, P. R. (1989) 'User acceptance of computer technology: A comparison of two theoretical models', *Management Science* 35(8): 982–1003.

Dillon, A. (2001) 'Beyond usability: Process, outcome, and affect in human computer interactions', *The Canadian Journal of Information and Library Science* 26(4): 57–69.

Eason, K. D. (1981) 'A task-tool analysis of manager-computer interaction', in B. Shackel (ed.) *Man-Computer Interaction: Human Factors Aspects of Computers and People*, Rockville, MD: Sijthoff and Noordhoff, pp. 289–307.

Fox, E. A., Hix, D., Nowell, L. T., Brueni, D. J., Wake, W. C. and Heath, L. S. (1993) 'Users, user interfaces, and objects: Envision, a digital library', *Journal of the American Society for Information Science* 44(8): 480–91.

Hawthorn, D. (2003) 'How universal is good design for older users?', in *Proceedings of the 2003 Conference on Universal Usability, 10–11 November, Vancouver, BC*, New York: ACM Press, pp. 38–45.

Høegh, R. T. (2006) 'Usability problems: Do software developers already know?', in *Proceedings of the 18th Conference of the Computer-Human Interaction Special Interest Group (CHISIG) of Australia on Computer-Human Interaction: Design, Activities, Artifacts and Environments, Sydney, 20–24 November*, New York: ACM Press, pp. 425–28.

International Standards Organization (1994) *ISO DIS 9241 – Ergonomic Requirements for Office Work with Visual Display Terminals: Part 11 – Guidance on Usability*, London: ISO.

International Standards Organization (1999) *ISO IEC 13407 – Human-Centered Design Processes for Interactive Systems*, London: ISO.

Jeng, J. (2006) 'Usability of the digital library: An evaluation model', unpublished PhD dissertation, Rutgers University.

Jeng, J. (2007) 'Metadata usefulness evaluation of the Moving Image Collections', paper presented at the New Jersey Library Association Conference, Long Branch, NJ, 25 April, available at: *http://www.njla.org/conference/2007/presentations/Metadata.pdf* (accessed 21 May 2008).

Jeng, J. (2008) 'Evaluation of the New Jersey Digital Highway', paper presented at the New Jersey Library Association Conference, Long Branch, NJ, 1 May, available at: *http://www.njla.org/njacrl/Res_Forum_Jeng.ppt* (accessed 25 November 2008).

Jordan, P. W. and Design, P. (1998) *An Introduction to Usability*, Bristol, PA: Taylor and Francis.

Kim, K. (2002) 'A model of digital library information seeking process (DLISP model) as a frame for classifying usability problems', unpublished PhD dissertation, Rutgers University.

Marcus, A. (2006) 'Culture: Wanted? Alive or dead? '*Journal of Usability Studies* 1(2): 62–3.

Nielsen, J. (1993) *Usability Engineering*, Cambridge, MA: Academic Press.

Rubin, J. (1994) *Handbook of Usability Testing: How to Plan, Design, and Conduct Effective Tests*, New York: John Wiley and Sons.

Saracevic, T. (2005) 'How were digital libraries evaluated?', paper presented at Libraries in the Digital Age, Dubrovnik and Mljet, 30 May to 3 June, available at: *http://www.ffos.hr/lida/datoteke/DL_evaluation_LIDA.doc* (accessed 21 May 2008).

Shackel, B. (1991) 'Usability – Context, framework, definition, design and evaluation', in B. Shackel and S. J. Richardson (eds) *Human Factors for Informatics Usability*, New York: Cambridge University Press, pp. 21–37.

Shneiderman, B. (2000) 'Universal usability', *Communications of the ACM* 43(5): 85–91.

Shneiderman, B. and Plaisant, C. (2004) *Designing the User Interface* (4th edn), Boston, MA: Pearson.

Stefl-Mabry, J., Belkin, N., Dillon, A. and Marchionini, G. (2003) 'User-centered design: Science or window dressing?', in *Proceedings of the American Society for Information Science and Technology* 40(1): 441.

Thomas, R. L. (1998) 'Elements of performance and satisfaction as indicators of the usability of digital spatial interfaces for information-seeking: Implications for ISLA', unpublished PhD dissertation, University of Southern California.

Thong, J. Y. L., Hong, W. and Tam, K. Y. (2004) 'What leads to user acceptance of digital libraries?', *Communications of the ACM* 47(11): 79–83.

Usability Professionals' Association (2005) 'What is usability?', available at: *http://www.upassoc.org/usability_resources/about_usability/* (accessed 21 May 2008).

5

Users and digital libraries: an insightful story

Emmanouel Garoufallou, Rania Siatri and Richard J. Hartley

Introduction

In this chapter we seek to focus on users and digital libraries. The word *focus* is chosen deliberately as, remarkably, little has been written with regard to digital library users – a curious situation given the amount of effort that has underpinned their development. An evolution has taken place that led from a concentration on system development to a greater concern on user-centred investigations of digital libraries. However, the number of research projects that have concentrated solely on the users is strictly limited. The concept of the digital library has 'different meanings in different communities', such as to the engineering and computer science communities and to political and business communities (Marchionini, 1998). Many researchers believe that terms such as 'digital library', 'electronic library' and 'virtual library' are often used synonymously in the literature. As such, work has been undertaken to identify some common elements that characterise these definitions. To this end, the Association of Research Libraries (1995) states that a digital library is not a single entity; that technology assists in linking the resources of many; that universal access is a priority; that linkage among different digital libraries is transparent to users; and finally that digital libraries contain digital artefacts that cannot be reproduced in printed formats.

Among professionals, the most widely quoted definition of a digital library is that given by the Digital Library Federation (DLF):

> Digital libraries are organizations that provide the resources, including the specialized staff, to select, structure, offer intellectual

access to, interpret, distribute, preserve the integrity of, and ensure the persistence over time of collections of digital works so that they are readily and economically available for use by a defined community or set of communities. (DLF, 1998)

Borgman (1999) presents perspectives and definitions drawn from the research and practice communities. She presents definitions of digital libraries with regards to the content, collections and communities, research-oriented definitions, defining elements of digital libraries, digital libraries as institutions or services and digital libraries as databases.

During the 1990s and the 2000s, two main initiatives enabled digital libraries to evolve from their infancy. These were the Electronic Library Programme (eLib) in the UK and the Digital Library Initiative (DLI) in the USA. Through these two research programmes, digital libraries dominated discussion in the professional arena and imposed their presence on the information world. The major difference between these two projects was that DLI was essentially a research programme dominated by computer scientists and which concentrated on the advancement and implementation of information technology. In contrast, eLib was dominated by librarians and information scientists and was much more concerned with library service delivery, the impact on library staff and users, as well as resource-based learning and staff development and training. A similar study of the impact on academic librarians, their role and status in academic institutions was undertaken by Garoufallou (2004).

After almost 15 years of investing in research on digital libraries, it is alarming that there are so few projects concerning the impact of digital libraries on either information professionals or users.

The need for evaluation

The need for evaluation is an inherent characteristic of human beings as they are engaged in a continuous effort to make things around them better. In all these efforts there is always a question: has the purpose of a particular exercise been accomplished? 'When one examines and judges accomplishments and effectiveness, one is engaged in evaluation' (Patton, 1990: 12). An intriguingly simple definition of evaluation which nevertheless does not fail to encompass the complexity of the task, is given by Van House et al. (1990): 'Evaluation consists of comparing "what is" to "what ought to be"'.

As research in the formative years of digital libraries was oriented towards technological advancements and digitisation of material, discussion on the issue of evaluation was ignored. As Saracevic (2000) so sharply points out, 'evaluation is more conspicuous by its absence (or just minimal presence) in the vast majority of published work ... So far ... [it] has not been even specified as to what it means and how to do it'.

Digital libraries are interdisciplinary in nature, forming complex information retrieval systems with a multifaceted infrastructure. This has been acknowledged by the digital library community, which recognises that the process of evaluating digital libraries is not simple:

> As digital libraries are extensions of physical libraries, they have to be evaluated by using existing techniques and metrics. Assessing the impacts of libraries on patrons' lives and the larger social milieu are the ultimate goals of evaluation but the practical difficulties of assessing such complex and varied impacts cause us to measure the effectiveness and efficiencies of library operations and services as surrogates for these impacts. (Marchionini, 2000)

In an evaluation process, issues like usability, efficiency, effectiveness and satisfaction may be involved. Some of these measurements have relatively straightforward implementation procedures, such as measuring efficiency. Other issues, however, such as measuring satisfaction, are rather more complicated and require more complex instruments.

A shift in paradigm

In 1996, a DLI workshop on the social aspects of digital libraries raised research issues with three foci: human-centred, artefact-centred and system-centred. As an outcome, the workshop recommended that further research should be undertaken to investigate the three foci in depth. The subject of evaluation reached a critical point when it began to form an integral part of digital libraries projects; mostly, however, its role was limited to the recording of system-oriented values. However, an emerging need from the professional community began to drive calls for a shift in paradigm to incorporate and initiate the use of user-oriented qualitative measurements. This shift began slowly to take shape in the form of more comprehensive and holistic evaluation frameworks, which incorporated all the different characteristics and values while presenting the interdependent relations in digital library evaluation.

Saracevic and Covi (2000) presented an overview of digital library evaluation and laid down the main components that affect digital library evaluation. They argued that it is necessary to specify five elements in order to evaluate a digital library. They reasoned that approaches to evaluation should be implemented differently according to the evaluation goals and audiences. Thus the evaluation may concentrate on the system and its performance or take a sociological approach considering the user and the social effects of the digital library.

To answer questions like 'why', 'what' and 'how' to evaluate, and at what level to evaluate the context, Saracevic and Covi (2000) have presented a model with both a user-centred and system-centred approach. The user-centred approach includes the social, institutional and individual level, and the system-centred approach includes the engineering, processing and content level. In their opinion, these levels – in conjunction with the interface – are closely connected in real life, but not in the evaluation of digital libraries. They conclude that digital libraries 'are not evaluated on more than one level. This isolation of levels of evaluation could be considered a further and great challenge for all digital library evaluations' (Saracevic and Covi, 2000).

Führ et al. (2001) have developed a digital library evaluation scheme that includes data/collections (content, meta-content, management), technology (user technology, information access, systems structure technology and document technology), and users/uses (user = who, domain = what, info-seeking = how and purpose = why). These evaluation schemes also focus on users by setting four questions that are useful metrics for evaluating digital library users.

Nicholson (2004) has introduced a holistic conceptual framework for an overall evaluation of services. He argues for the adoption of a dual perspective in the evaluation process. The first is the internal perspective, which incorporates evaluation procedures that are generated within the library system, excluding the user. These procedures are concerned with taking measurements regarding the success of an information retrieval system, or collection development measured through use of book lists, statistics of reference desk use, etc. Although such measurements are indeed useful as quick indicators of a library service use, they are incomplete as they fail to incorporate the views and opinions of users, which is the second perspective, called the *external* in Nicholson's framework. Under this second perspective, one can include usability studies or user satisfaction surveys. Having established these two perspectives in the evaluation process, he further introduces two topics: library system and use. These need to be investigated under each perspective, thus completing the four quadrants of the evaluation matrix. This adds up to the internal view of the library system (which can be any subsystem of the library), the external view of the library system (effectiveness of the system), the external view of use (how useful it is) and finally the internal view of use (how users interact or manipulate the system in question). Although Nicholson's framework was not designed specifically for digital library evaluation, it is an evaluation process that can be utilised in the evaluation of any library including digital libraries.

Tsakonas and Papatheodorou (2006; 2008) have proposed the Interaction Triptych Framework (ITF), consisting of three main components: system, content and user. Each component interacts with the other two, defining three distinct evaluation approaches: user-centred, system-centred and content-centred, thus creating an evaluation triangle, each axis of which defines a measurement of the evaluation process as follows:

- the system-user axis defines the usability evaluation and uses efficiency, effectiveness and user satisfaction as measures;

- the system content axis defines the performance evaluation and uses precision, recall and response time as measures;

- the user-content axis defines the usefulness evaluation and uses task applicability and resource integration ability as measures.

The ITF depends on the usability of the system and the usefulness of the content provided by the digital library. In their hypothesis, the user communicates 'with both system and content in a unified and indiscriminate way and that interaction consists of the merging of physical, affective, cognitive and conceptual actions and judgments' (Tsakonas and Papatheodorou, 2006).

A newer more detailed version of the ITF incorporates new sets of attributes in the three axes (Tsakonas and Papatheodorou, 2008). Even though it is one of the most complete models of digital libraries evaluation, and certainly one that values usefulness as a main component of the digital library evaluation process, the ITF model leaves out some very important factors and evidence that affect usefulness in digital library evaluation.

By adapting the theoretical models to provide a more holistic view and address the human factor, the notion of measuring usefulness was born. Here, usefulness relates to all those issues that concern the user and their interaction with the system. In a way, this correlates to the fourth quadrant of Nicholson's matrix, the internal view of use. It is also the user-content axis in the ITF model. Can the user successfully complete a task? Does the user feel that the system has provided support in his quest for information? What criteria do users take into account in deciding whether a system can cater for their information needs? Which factors influence users' decisions in using one feature of a system rather than another? In the literature, there is little agreement regarding the precise set of criteria that constitute the notion of usefulness, in order for someone to measure and evaluate it as a whole. Various pieces of research have explored and investigated different components of usefulness including information quality, system function, helpfulness, effectiveness, value, credibility, instrumentality, practicality, serviceability. However, as Tsakonas and Papatheodorou (2008) point out, actions and information tasks are 'all combined and executed in an iterative manner'. To address these issues, there is a need to adopt a perspective that acknowledges forces like dynamic diversity, changeability and unanticipated factors which form an integral part of information-seeking in the user's daily routine.

Information-seeking and usefulness

For digital libraries, usefulness incorporates all the characteristics and attributes that relate to the user-centred approach to evaluation. As such, it would greatly benefit if it were to take into account the evolutionary process of theoretical frameworks, and application methods that have occurred in the wider field of user studies and more specifically in information-seeking. It is important to stress that while usefulness is a subcategory in the field of user studies and information-seeking, its evolution was so closely related to the formulation and development of digital libraries that it now appears somewhat alienated from its natural 'home'.

Examining the development of the conceptual frameworks in information-seeking can provide a way to understand the information needs of users and their context. A user recognising an information need articulates it as a query, which is conveyed through formal and/or informal channels of communication and information systems, in order to receive a response which will satisfy that need. A user's information-seeking behaviour consists of decisions on which communication channels and information systems to use and how to use them.

Borrowing from psychology literature, Wilson (1981) refers to the three categories of human needs: 'physiological needs, such as the need for food, etc.; affective needs (sometimes called psychological), such as the need for attainment, for domination, etc.; cognitive needs, such as the need to plan to learn skill, etc.' He continues by describing how one kind of need can trigger another kind, e.g. an affective need (recognition) may trigger a cognitive need (research).

Belkin's anomalous state of knowledge theory (Belkin et al., 1982a, 1982b) provides another dimension to the concept of information need and the origin of this need, as well as a revised view of information retrieval. According to Belkin, the information need arises from the recognition of an anomaly in the user's state of knowledge. This makes the user unable to express the information need in a precise manner. Thus, the hypothetical system should ask the user to describe this anomaly rather than express it precisely, such as by using subject keywords.

Dervin (1983) has developed the sense-making theory as a different conceptual framework and research approach to information needs. Dervin's work uses the timeline interview to assist interviewees in recalling their cognitive process during a specific information-need incident. Dervin argues that information-seeking and use should not be viewed as transmitting activities but rather as 'constructing activities – as a personal creating of sense. It is assumed that all information is simply the sense made by individuals at specific moments in time-space' (Dervin 1983).

Kuhlthau-Collier (1988) has modelled the information-seeking process into six stages:

- *initiation*: preparation for selection;
- *selection*: determination of topic;
- *prefocus exploration*: initial examination of information for narrowing down the subject;
- *focus formulation*: final decision on the main subject focus;
- *information collection*: gathering of information;
- *search closure*: completion of the information-gathering.

Kuhlthau-Collier associates the first three stages with feelings of uncertainty and confusion, while later stages are related more to feelings of confidence and optimism.

To model information-seeking behaviour, Ellis (1987) uses the grounded theory of Glaser and Strauss (1967). The Ellis model consists of:

- *starting*: actions to initiate the research;
- *chaining*: following citations or other relevant information;
- *browsing*: information-seeking without a precise knowledge of direction or structure;
- *differentiating*: comparing sources as a device to evaluate usefulness and quality;
- *monitoring*: keeping up in the subject area;
- *extracting*: the final stage, in which the researcher methodically locates information sources.

In one way or another, these conceptual frameworks moulded and changed the landscape of information-seeking, as they went beyond existing models to comprehend why users conduct their searching in a particular fashion, which forces are in place, and how the dynamic relations are shaped among them. To fully understand and gain insightful information to research questions such as the above, the use of qualitative research methods is inevitable. Quantitative methods have gained and established their place in the research world and rightfully so. They can provide, for instance, an overview of the use of any system, what is used, how often, by whom, etc., thus laying the foundation for further investigation. So, for example, if a survey demonstrates high use of a particular system, one can take this information and attempt to enrich understanding and gain more in-depth knowledge, by enquiring which features appeal to users and in what way. To achieve this, it is necessary to use qualitative research methods.

As the development of alternative theoretical frameworks in the field of user studies and information-seeking called for the use of alternative research methods (Siatri, 1999), which were used mainly in humanities and social sciences, so the conceptual frameworks of digital library evaluation are undergoing the same process with the introduction of usefulness, thus bringing qualitative research methods back into the spotlight. The following section gives some indicative examples of the use of qualitative research tools in studies of information-seeking.

Reneker (1993) adopted the naturalistic approach to investigate the information-seeking behaviour of academics. Academics were asked to collect data for a two-week period. The subjects used a tape-recorder to record questions as they arose, how the academic found an answer and whether they were satisfied with the results. The study found a very close relationship between the level of knowledge of information sources and services available and the chosen course of action of retrieving information. Furthermore, the availability of information was positively correlated with the generation of new information needs. Personal interviews followed, thus producing additional information.

The Information Access Project (Barry and Squires, 1995; Squires et al., 1995) sought to investigate the relation between IT-assisted information systems and academic research. The distinguishing feature of this project was the holistic view and the consistency with which the research methodology was formulated. The research team employed qualitative research methods, which were placed within an ethnographic conceptual framework utilising grounded theory. Data collection techniques involved the use of semi-structured interviews, diary of information activities, group discussions, information access stories and research timing. Academics indicated that although they appreciate the value of databases, they feel that delivery of information through a computer screen leads to more passive research and less creative thinking. However, academics were found to favour two particular systems to encourage creativity within academic research. The first was online discussion groups, which often trigger ideas and productive debates. The other was the world wide web, which can simulate an environment much like browsing through journals or retrieving information from a printed source. Here, it is important to note that this research was published in 1995, and although use of the web was in its infancy, it was already making a difference compared with other well-established information systems because it allowed users to feel comfortable as it did not alienate them, fulfilling an affective need as well. Such an issue could certainly be investigated in an evaluation of a digital library's usefulness.

In their conclusion, Barry and Squires hold that:

> these findings suggest the importance of a user-in-context focus not only in research but in system design and particularly in support and training ... it would seem that only if training and support can be targeted in response to meeting the perceived needs of the users, will they be useful. (Barry and Squires, 1995)

Does the user feel adequately supported by the system? Given the impossibility of providing training and support for digital libraries when they are accessed over networks, this conclusion merely serves to emphasise the importance of understanding what is useful to users and concentrating on this in system design.

Barry and Schamber (1998) have presented and compared two research investigations aiming to record users' criteria for evaluating relevance. The study used an adapted model of Dervin's timeline interviews in conjunction with inductive content analysis to investigate real-life information incidents and users' perception of information quality. For the research, a situational context was used in which users were asked to locate weather information in a multimedia environment. The primary criteria indicated by users can be summarised in ten broad categories: accuracy, currency, specificity, geographic proximity, reliability, accessibility, verifiability, clarity, dynamism and presentation quality. Barry and Schamber's study also aimed to gather data regarding real-life current information incidents. Open-ended interviews served as a data-gathering tool. Again, a situational background was drawn and users were presented with document representations as well as full-text documents. The study coded seven broad categories of relevance criteria relating to the document's information content: the document's sources, the document as a physical entity, other information or sources within the environment, the user's situation, the user's beliefs and preferences, and the user's previous experience and background. In the more detailed presentation of criteria that formed each broad category of the two studies, it becomes clear that users from both studies identified the same relevance criteria, such accuracy, depth, clarity, currency, quality of sources, etc. Differences in criteria were also recorded, but it became clear that this was informed by the different situational settings of the studies. Both studies confirmed that the 'user's relevance evaluation depends on individual perceptions of their problems ... and that their perceptions encompass many factors beyond information content' (Barry and Schamber, 2000).

Research on the evaluation of digital libraries and other electronic information resources

The majority of published research on the evaluation of digital libraries is mostly concerned with usability studies, which do not fall into the scope of this chapter. In addition, few studies have evaluated a clearly-defined digital library system. Many researchers have investigated use of internet resources and different user groups (Bilal, 2001; 2002; Cothey, 2002; Hyldegaard and Seiden, 2004; Williams and Nicholas, 2001), use of networked resources (Abels et al., 1996; Liebscher et al., 1997), and search engine use (Brophy and Bawden, 2005; Fast and Campbell, 2005; Griffiths and Brophy, 2005), but there remains little research that evaluates a digital library system as such. Many studies have observed a tendency for authors to use the term *digital library* in a flexible way, allowing the inclusion of terms such as e-journal platforms, portals, institutional repositories and web-based databases, and various forms of electronic information resources. A presentation of indicative studies on the evaluation of digital libraries and electronic information resources that have employed qualitative or mixed methodology follows.

Alexandria Digital Library (*www.alexandria.ucsb.edu*), a geolibrary, applied evaluation criteria to assess the usability and functionality of its system. The approach involved user studies focusing on the design features of the library (Hill et al., 2000). Researchers used complementary methodologies and took into account such factors as whether users would be able to perform the method and work within cost-effective time limits. Research tools including surveys, target user groups, ethnographic studies, demographic analysis of beta-tester registration data and log analysis were employed. Concerning the evaluation of the system, factors like the overall ease of use, appeal, usefulness, performance, clarity and consistency of terminology and navigation were examined and analysed (Hill et al. 1997; Frew et al., 2000).

The evaluation of the Perseus Digital Library (PDL – *www.perseus .tufts.edu*) was one of the first comprehensive longitudinal evaluation approaches. The PDL contains Greek text and English translations, maps, sites and images. The evaluation addressed four questions relating to learning, teaching, scholarly research and electronic publishing that resulted in a set of four evaluation criteria: 'learning, teaching, system (performance, interface, electronic publishing), and content (scope, accuracy)' (Marchionini et al., 2003). The evaluation involved different user communities, concentrated on different design features and applied different methodologies (observations, interviews and document analysis). The evaluation summarised in four categories: amplification and augmentation of teaching and learning, physical infrastructure, conceptual infrastructure and systemic change to the field of classics. This was a full-scale model of evaluating a digital library, a model that could be adapted and improved by other digital libraries.

PEAK was a project involving Elsevier Science and libraries and focused on observation of use and evaluation of economic factors. Access to journals to different groups, revenues and costs and pricing models were the evaluation criteria used (MacKie-Mason, 1999).

Notess (2004) employed three different research tools – a questionnaire survey, log file analysis and contextual enquiry – to investigate use of the music digital libraries of Indiana University. The questionnaire provided an 'inexpensive albeit gross measure of user satisfaction', giving an indication of frequency of use, purpose of use, satisfaction rating, positive and negative comments, and basic recommendations. Log file analysis supplied detailed quantitative data of overall use that can be employed in identifying problems with usability, although this form of data does not provide any insight into the cognitive processes and user rationale. Finally, although time-consuming, contextual enquiry provided a large volume of data (observations, note taking) that illuminated issues that put the information-seeking of users into context.

To gain a better understanding of the criteria that users employ to assess relevancy in their quest for information on the web, Tombros et al. (2005) investigated the utility of web-based resources. While various research tools were employed, data analysis was largely quantitative. The research was situationally based, as subjects were presented with specific information tasks. During the searching session, users were recorded thinking aloud and Camtasia software was used to record onscreen activity. In addition, pre-search questionnaires and a post-search satisfaction questionnaire were administered. The research identified five feature categories that users may engage to assess webpages: text, structure, quality, non-textual items and physical properties.

Using a topic-driven search, Komlodi et al. (2007) explored how users of legal information utilise search history support. Searches were conducted using the web interface of the Westlaw legal information system. Data-gathering fell into two phases; the first comprised observation notes and think-aloud protocol, followed by an interview to acquire a more detailed picture of information-seeking. The second phase consisted of a participatory design session. The newly recruited participants were presented with results of the first phase and were asked to participate in the interface design of the database by suggesting and communicating their ideas. The transcripts of these sessions were analysed using grounded theory. Results indicated that users rely heavily on search support history as well as memory aids. Researchers stress the need for 'intergrating search history information in other search systems, displays such as results lists, creating tools for planning, managing search history and results ... will result in ... higher searcher satisfaction in knowledge-intensive settings' (Komlodi et al., 2007).

Anderson (2007) evaluated The Glasgow Story project, which tells the story of the city through a sophisticated dynamic website. The evaluation of the project was designed as a two-phase process. The first phase investigated issues concerning 'site structure, navigation, functionality, and layout using questionnaires and focus groups' (Anderson, 2007). The second phase evaluated content quality also using questionnaires and specialist focus groups. Overall user satisfaction was rated as high. The impact on users included the opportunity to learn something new, trigger memories and experiences, and gaining a better understanding of certain issues; these factors indicate that users are 'not only acquiring new information but also that it is being explored and integrated with their personal experiences' (Anderson, 2007). Focus group discussion provided rich data that corroborated the findings of the questionnaires and allowed researchers to gain a better understanding of the ways that users utilised the information they extracted from the system.

Tsakonas and Papatheodorou (2008) explored usefulness and usability of open access digital libraries using the ITF. They evaluated E-LIS (*eprints.rclis.org*), an international e-print archive in the subject area of library and information science. They used an online questionnaire to collect data on the three axes of the evaluation process. The criteria that scored the highest were ease of use and learnability, both of which fell under the usability category. Although usefulness criteria scored highly, responses indicated that users expected more from the system, especially in terms of coverage. Finally in the performance category, users rated response time more highly than the recall and precision.

Xie (2008) evaluated the American Memory and the University of Wisconsin Digital Collection. Subjects were asked to locate information regarding specific topics in the two libraries, and to detail the whole search process in a diary. Users then had to prioritise listed evaluation criteria in a questionnaire, and add any other criteria that were not included. Finally, in an open-ended survey they were asked to comment on the strengths and weaknesses of the two resources, based on their previously selected criteria. The most important criteria were found to be the interface usability, performance in general, collection quality and accuracy.

Conclusion

In this chapter, we have explored users and digital libraries. We have done so by setting the exploration in context through brief considerations of definitions of digital libraries and the emergence of digital libraries as an important field of research, embracing the approaches of computer scientists as well as librarians and information scientists. We have argued that there is a strong need for the evaluation of digital libraries and demonstrated our belief that this must be undertaken from a user-centred perspective. Given that relatively little evaluation of this type has taken place, we have explored theoretical frameworks and methodological approaches from the fields of user studies and information-seeking behaviour, which appear to us to be particularly apposite to the evaluation of digital libraries. Along the way we have noted the emergence of the notion of usefulness and suggested that this concept might usefully be transferred to the digital library community.

Finally, we remain convinced that it is essential for the digital library community to adopt the appropriate frameworks and data collection methods for user-centred services evaluation. To our minds, it is inescapable that 'these are not research methods for the faint-hearted, however, they require time, effort, and skill in both development and use' (Schamber, 2000).

Bibliography

Abels, E. G., Liebscher, P. and Denman, D. W. (1996) 'Factors that influence the use of electronic networks by science and engineering faculty at small institutions: Part I – Queries', *Journal of the American Society for Information Science* 47(2): 146–58.

Anderson, I. G. (2007) 'Pure dead brilliant? Evaluating the Glasgow Story digitisation project', *Program* 41(1): 365–85.

Association of Research Libraries (1995) 'Definition and purposes of a digital library', available at: *http://www.ifla.org/documents/libraries/net/arl-dlib.txt* (accessed 30 June 2008).

Barry, C. L. and Schamber, L. (1998) 'User's criteria for relevance evaluation: a cross-situational comparison', *Information Processing and Management* 34(2/3): 219–36.

Barry, C. and Squires, D. (1995) 'Why the move from traditional information-seeking to the electronic library is not straight forward for academic users: some surprising findings', in *Proceedings of the 19th International Online Information Meeting, UK, 5–7 December*, Oxford: Learned Information, pp. 177–87.

Belkin, N., Oddy, R. N. and Brooks, H. M. (1982a) 'Ask for information retrieval: Part I – Background and theory', *Journal of Documentation* 38(2): 61–71.

Belkin, N., Oddy, R. N. and Brooks, H. M. (1982b) 'Ask for information retrieval: Part II – Results of a design study', *Journal of Documentation* 38(3): 145–64.

Bilal, D. (2001) 'Children's use of the Yahooligans web search engine: II – Cognitive, and physical behaviours on research tasks', *Journal of the American Society for Information Science* 52(2): 118–36.

Bilal, D. (2002) 'Perspectives on children's navigation of the World Wide Web: does the type of search task make a difference?', *Online Information Review* 26(2): 108–17.

Borgman, C. L. (1999) 'What are digital libraries? Competing visions', *Information Processing and Management* 35(3): 227–43.

Brophy, P. and Bawden, D. (2005) 'Is Google enough? Comparison of an international engine with academic library resources', *Aslib Proceedings* 57(6): 498–512.

Cothey, V. (2002) 'A longitudinal study of World Wide Web users' information seeking behaviour', *Journal of the American Society for Information Science and Technology* 53(2): 67–78.

Dervin, B. (1983) 'An overview of sense-making research: concepts, methods, and results to date', paper presented at the International Communication Association Annual Meeting, Dallas, TX, May. Available from the author.

Digital Library Federation (1998) 'A working definition of digital library', available at: *http://www.diglib.org/about/dldefinition.htm* (accessed 30 June 2008).

Ellis, D. (1987) 'The derivation of a behavioral model for information retrieval system design', unpublished PhD dissertation, University of Sheffield.

Fast, K. V. and Campell, D. G. (2005) 'I still like Google: university students' perceptions of searching OPACs and the web', in *Proceedings of the American Society for Information Science and Technology* 41(1): 138–46.

Frew, J., Freeston, M., Freitas, N., Hill, L., Janee, G., Lovette, K., Nideffer, R., Smith, T. and Zheng, Q. (2000) 'The Alexandria Digital Library architecture', *International Journal on Digital Libraries* 2(4): 259–68.

Führ, N., Hansen, P., Mabe, M., Micsik, A. and Sølvberg, I. (2001) 'Digital libraries: A generic classification and evaluation scheme', in *Proceedings of the 5th European Conference on Digital Libraries, Darmstadt, 4–9 September, LNCS Vol. 2163,* Berlin: Springer-Verlag, pp. 187–99.

Garoufallou, E. (2004) 'The impact of the electronic library on Greek academic libraries and librarians', unpublished PhD dissertation, Manchester Metropolitan University.

Glaser, B. and Strauss, A. (1967) *The Discovery of Grounded Theory: Strategies for Qualitative Research,* Hawthorne, NY: Aldine.

Griffiths, J. R. and Brophy, P. (2005) 'Students searching behaviour and the web', *Library Trends* 53(4): 539–54.

Hill, L. L., Dolin, R., Frew, J., Kemp, R. B., Larsgaard, M., Montello, D. R., Rae, M.-A. and Simpson, J. (1997) 'User evaluation: summary of the methodologies and results for the Alexandria Digital Library, University of California at Santa Barbara', in *Proceedings of the ASIS Annual Meeting, Washington, DC, 1–6 November*, available at: *http://www.asis.org/annual-97/alexia.htm* (accessed 25 November 2008).

Hill, L. L., Carver, L., Larsgaard, M., Dolin, R., Smith, T. R., Frew, J. and Rae, M.-A. (2000) 'Alexandria Digital Library: user evaluation studies and system design', *Journal of the American Society for Information Science* 51(3): 246–59.

Hyldegaard, J. and Seiden, P. (2004) 'My e-journal: exploring the usefulness of personalised access to scholarly articles and services', *Information Research* 9(3), available at: *http://informationr.net/ir/9-3/paper181.htm* (accessed 1 October 2008).

Komlodi, A., Marchionini, G. and Soergel, D. (2007) 'Search history for finding and using information: user interface design recommendations from a user study', *Information Processing and Management* 43(1): 10–29.

Kuhlthau-Collier, C. (1988) 'Developing a model of the library search process: cognitive and affective aspects', *RQ* 28(2): 232–42.

Liebscher, P., Abels, E. G. and Denman, D. W. (1997) 'Factors that influence the use of electronic networks by science and engineering faculty at small institutions: Part II – primary use indicators', *Journal of the American Society for Information Science* 48(6): 496–507.

MacKie-Mason, J. K. (1999) 'A report on the PEAK experiment: usage and economic behaviour', *D-Lib Magazine* 5(7/8), available at: *http://www.dlib.org/dlib/july99/mackie-mason/07mackie-mason.html* (accessed October 2008).

Marchionini, G. (1998) 'Research and development in digital libraries', in A. Kent (ed.) *Encyclopedia of Library and Information Science* (Vol. 63) New York: Marcel Dekker.

Marchionini, G. (2000) 'Evaluating digital libraries: a longitudinal and multifaceted view', *Library Trends* 49(2): 304–33.

Marchionini, G., Plaisant, C. and Komlodi, A. (2003) 'The people in digital libraries: multifaceted approaches to assessing needs and impact', in A. P. Bishop, N. A. Van House and B. P. Buttenfield (eds) *Digital Library Use: Social Practice in Design and Evaluation*, Cambridge, MA: MIT Press, pp. 119–60.

Nicholson, S. (2004) 'A conceptual framework for the holistic measurement and cumulative evaluation of library services', *Journal of Documentation* 60(2): 174–82.

Notess, M. (2004) 'Three looks at users: a comparison of methods for studying digital library use', *Information Research* 9(3), available at: *http://informationr.net/ir/9-3/paper177.html* (accessed October 2008).

Patton, M. Q. (1990) *Qualitative Evaluation and Research Methods* (2nd edn), Newbury Park, CA: Sage.

Reneker, H. M. (1993) 'A qualitative study of information seeking among members of an academic community: methodological issues and problems', *Library Quarterly* 63(4): 487–507.

Rowley, J. (2001) 'User behaviour monitoring and evaluation: Incorporating JUBILEE and JUSTEIS – Second annual report', available at: *http://www.jisc.ac.uk/pub01/m&e_rep2.html* (accessed 20 October 2008).

Saracevic, T. (2000) 'Digital library evaluation: towards an evolution of concepts', *Library Trends* 49(3): 350–69.

Saracevic, T. and Covi, L. (2000) 'Challenges for digital library evaluation', in *Proceedings of the ASIS Annual Meeting, Chicago, IL, 11–16 November,* available at: *http://www.is.informatik.uni-duisburg.de/courses/dl_ss04/folien/saracevic00.pdf* (accessed 25 November 2008).

Schamber, L. (2000) 'TimeLine interviews and inductive content analysis: their effectiveness for exploring cognitive behaviours', *Journal of the American Society for Information Science* 51(8): 734–44.

Siatri, R. (1999) 'The evolution of user studies', *Libri* 49(3): 132–41.

Squires, D., Barry, C. A. and Funston, H. T. (1995) *The Use of IT-Assisted Information Systems in Academic Research* (British Library R&D Report 6215), London: British Library Research and Development Department.

Tombros, A., Ruthven, I. and Jose, J. (2005) 'How users access web pages for information seeking', *Journal of American Society for Information Science and Technology* 56(4): 327–44.

Tsakonas, G. and Papatheodorou, C. (2006) 'Analysing and evaluating usefulness and usability in electronic information services', *Journal of Information Science* 32(5): 400–19.

Tsakonas, G. and Papatheodorou, C. (2008) 'Exploring usefulness and usability in the evaluation of open access digital libraries', *Information Processing and Management* 44(3): 1234–50.

Van House, N., Weil, B. and McClure, C. (1990) *Measuring Academic Library Performance: A Practical Approach*. Chicago, IL: ACRL.

Williams, P. and Nicholas, D. (2001) *The Internet and the Changing Information Environment*, London: Aslib.

Wilson, T. D. (1981) 'On user studies and information needs', *Journal of Documentation* 37(1): 3–15.

Xie, H. I. (2008) 'Users' evaluation of digital libraries: their uses, their criteria and their assessment', *Information Processing and Management* 44(3): 1346–73.

6

Towards an infrastructure for digital library performance evaluation

Maristella Agosti and Nicola Ferro

Introduction

A few years ago, Ioannidis et al. (2005) observed that 'Digital Library (DL) development must move from an art to a science' to give rise to digital library systems (DLS) based on reliable and extensible services and of proven quality.

Given the growth of the DLS and the need for a scientific approach in developing them, proper evaluation methodologies are needed to assess their performance along different dimensions. Such evaluation methodologies should not be perceived as something external to the design and development process of these complex systems, but rather they should be tightly integrated into it.

Moreover, the actual evaluation of a DLS is a scientific activity where the outcomes, such as performance analyses and measurements, constitute a kind of scientific data that must be properly taken into consideration and used for the design and development of DLS components and services.

Interestingly enough, this line of reasoning highlights a kind of intrinsic circularity when digital library development is viewed as a science. Indeed, achieving the necessary levels of reliability and effectiveness for such large-scale DLS calls for extensive use of evaluation methodologies which, as a result, produce a considerable amount of scientific data. These data should, in turn, be managed by a DLS that supports their enrichment, interpretation and preservation in order to yield the expected positive feedback on DLS design and development. Indeed, Ioannidis et al. (2005) argue that a DLS should support information enrichment and that provenance is 'important in judging the quality and applicability of information for a given use and for determining when changes at sources require revising derived information'. In addition, they observe that citation, intended as the possibility of explicitly mentioning and making reference to portions of a given digital object, should also be part of the information enrichment strategies supported by a DLS.

Therefore, the scientific development of the contents of a digital library would greatly benefit from the exploitation of a DLS for scientific data which provides the tools for enriching, citing, interpreting, and preserving the scientific data produced during the design and development process.

This type of DLS shall be known as a *scientific reflection DLS*, as it deals with scientific data, information, and interpretations about the design and development of another DLS. Indeed, the term *reflection* means both 'the act of reflecting or the state of being reflected' and 'careful or long consideration or thought' (Hanks, 1979). Here, the first meaning of reflection illustrates the capability of a scientific reflection DLS to show the evaluation outcomes of a target DLS, while the second meaning of reflection implies that a scientific reflection DLS provides support for designing and developing a target DLS.

The evaluation of a DLS is a non-trivial issue which should analyse different aspects, such as architecture, information access and extraction capabilities, management of multimedia content, interaction with users, and so on (Führ et al., 2001, 2007). As there are so many aspects to take into consideration, the scientific reflection DLS should be constituted by different and cooperating services, each focused on supporting the evaluation of one of the abovementioned aspects.

Attention will therefore be focused on the current evaluation methodologies for assessing the performances of the information access and extraction components of a DLS, which deal with the indexing, search and retrieval of documents in response to a user's query. In particular, these methodologies will be investigated to see whether they meet the requirements of information enrichment necessary for the scientific development of DLS.

This chapter focuses on the revision of current evaluation methodologies in order to adapt to the new way of thinking about DLS development. Furthermore, the outcomes of this revision process are applied to the design and development of a service capable of supporting the evaluation of the information access and extraction components of a DLS. This service is intended to be part of a wider scientific reflection DLS, which covers different aspects of DLS evaluation, and represents a first step towards the creation of a comprehensive evaluation infrastructure for assessing DLS performances from different viewpoints. Finally, the chapter describes a running prototype of this DLS service called DIRECT (*direct.dei.unipd.it*) which implements the proposed revision of current evaluation methodologies.

Conceptual framework for the evaluation of DLS information access components

The current approach for laboratory evaluation of information access systems relies on the Cranfield methodology, which makes use of experimental collections (Cleverdon, 1997). An experimental collection is a triple $C = (D, T, J)$, where: D is a set of documents, also called collection of documents; T is a set of topics, which expresses the user's information needs and from which the actual queries are derived; and J is a set of relevance judgments, i.e. for each topic $t \in T$ and for each document $d \in D$ it is determined whether or not d is relevant to t.

An experimental collection C allows the comparison of information access systems according to some measurements which quantify their performances. The main goal of an experimental collection is both to provide a common test-bed to be indexed and searched by information access systems and to guarantee the possibility of replicating the experiments.

When reasoning about this evaluation paradigm, a first step is to point out that the experimental evaluation is a scientific activity and, as such, its outcomes are different kinds of valuable scientific data. Therefore, the experiments themselves represent the primary scientific data and the starting point of the investigation. Using the experimental data, different performance measurements are produced, such as precision and recall, which are standard measures to evaluate the performances of an information access component for a given experiment. Starting from these performance measurements, descriptive statistics can be computed, such as mean or median, to summarise the overall performances achieved by an experiment or by a collection of experiments. Finally, hypothesis tests and other statistical analyses can be performed to conduct an in-depth analysis and comparison over a set of experiments.

The abovementioned scientific data can be framed in the context of the data, information, knowledge, wisdom (DIKW) hierarchy (Ackoff, 1989; Zeleny, 1987), represented in Figure 6.1:

Figure 6.1 The DIKW hierarchy with respect to the experimental evaluation

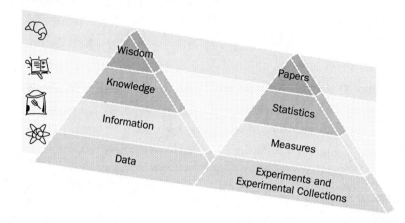

- At the *data layer* there are raw, basic elements, partial and atomised, which have little meaning by themselves and no significance beyond their immediate existence. Data are created with facts, can be measured, and can be viewed as the building blocks of the other layers. Despite the possibility of manipulation, a limited amount of actions can be performed with them. The experiments and the experimental collections correspond to the 'data level' in the hierarchy, as they represent the raw, basic elements needed for any further investigation and have little meaning by themselves. Indeed, without a relationship with the experimental collection to which the experiment pertains, an experiment and the associated results are of limited value, as these data constitute the basis for any subsequent computation.

- The *information layer* is the result of computations and processing of the data. Information comes from the form taken by the data when they are grouped and organised in different ways to create relational connections; indeed, the term 'inform' itself means etymologically to give shape, to form, thus entailing the notion of giving data a new shape by relating them together and with other entities. The performance measurements correspond to the 'information level' in the hierarchy, as they are the result of computations and processing on the data, so that a meaning is associated with the data by way of some kind of relational connection. For example, precision and recall measures are obtained by relating the results of an experiment with the relevance judgments *J*.

- The *knowledge layer* is related to the generation of appropriate actions, by using the appropriate collection of information gathered at the previous level of the hierarchy. It can be articulated into a language, more or less formal, such as words, numbers, expressions and so on, transmitted to others, or be embedded in individual experience, like beliefs or intuitions. The descriptive statistics and the hypothesis tests correspond to the 'knowledge level' in the hierarchy, as they are a further elaboration of the information carried by the performance measurements and provide some insights about the experiments.

- The *wisdom level* provides interpretation, explanation and formalisation of the content of the previous levels. Wisdom is not one thing: it is the highest level of understanding, and is a uniquely human state. The previous levels are related to the past; with wisdom people can strive to the future. Theories, models, algorithms, techniques and observations, which are usually communicated by means of papers, talks and seminars, correspond to the 'wisdom level' in the hierarchy, as they provide interpretation, explanation, and formalisation of the content of the previous levels.

As observed by Zeleny:

> while data and information (being components) can be generated per se, i.e. without direct human interpretation, knowledge and wisdom (being relations) cannot: they are human- and context-dependent and cannot be contemplated without involving human (not machine) comparison, decision-making and judgment. (Zeleny, 1987)

This observation also fits the case of the experimental evaluation. Indeed, experiments (data) and performance measurements (information) are usually generated in an automatic way by information access components, programs and tools for assessing performances. On the other hand, statistical analyses (knowledge) and models and algorithms (wisdom) require the deep involvement of researchers in order to be conducted and developed.

This view of the experimental evaluation calls into question whether the Cranfield methodology is able to support an experimental approach where the whole process from data to wisdom is taken into account (Agosti et al., 2007a; Dussin and Ferro, 2008a).

This question is made more compelling by the fact that when dealing with scientific data, 'the lineage (provenance) of the data must be tracked, as a scientist needs to know where the data came from ... and what cleaning, rescaling, or modelling was done to arrive at the data to be interpreted' (Abiteboul et al., 2005). Moreover, Ioannidis et al. (2005) point out how provenance is 'important in judging the quality and applicability of information for a given use and for determining when changes at sources require revising derived information'. Furthermore, when scientific data are maintained for further and future use, they should be enriched and, sometimes, the enrichment of a portion of scientific data can make use of a citation for explicitly mentioning and making references to useful information (Agosti et al., 2007b). Finally, the National Science Board (2005) highlights that 'digital data collections enable analysis at unprecedented levels of accuracy and sophistication and provide novel insights through innovative information integration'.

Therefore, the question turns out to be not only the degree to which the Cranfield methodology embraces the passing from data to wisdom, but also whether the proper strategies are adopted to ensure the provenance, the enrichment, the citation, and the interpretation of the scientific data.

User requirements analysis

Different types of actors are involved in an evaluation campaign (Dussin and Ferro, 2007):

- The *participant* takes part in the evaluation campaign in order to have a forum to test his new algorithms and techniques, to compare their effectiveness, and to discuss and share his proposals. He needs support for the submission of his experiments and their validation; he then expects to receive measurements about the performance of his experiments and overall indicators that allow his experiments and results to be compared with those submitted by other participants. Moreover, he should have the possibility of properly citing his experiments and other information resources and having a citation correctly resolved to the corresponding information resources.

- The *assessor* contributes to the creation of the experimental collections by both proposing the topics and assessing the relevance of the documents with respect to those topics. He needs support in both these tasks which are labour-intensive and require the inspection of great amounts of data.

- The *visitor* needs to consult, browse and access all the information resources produced during the course of an evaluation campaign in a meaningful fashion that provides insights about the conducted experiments. Moreover, he should have the possibility of properly citing the accessed information resources and having a citation correctly resolved to the corresponding information resources.

- The *organiser* manages the different aspects of an evaluation forum: he contributes to the creation of the experimental collections by preparing the documents and overseeing the creation of the topics and the relevance assessments; he provides the framework for the participants to conduct their experiments and for the assessors to create the topics and perform the relevance assessments; he computes the different measures for assessing the performances of the submitted experiments as well as descriptive statistics and statistical tests to characterise the overall features of the submitted experiments; finally, he provides the visitors with the means for accessing all the information resources they are looking for.

These actors interact together in various ways during the course of an evaluation campaign and contribute differently to the DIKW hierarchy discussed above.

Figure 6.2 shows that the early stages of an evaluation campaign are mainly devoted to the preparation of the data and require limited interaction between the different actors. As time passes and the campaign comes into full swing, there is a progressive movement from data to wisdom and also the number of actors involved and their interaction grows.

The elements shown in Figure 6.2 will now be examined in more detail:

- *Acquisition and preparation of documents*: the organisers are responsible for acquiring, formatting and preparing the set of documents that will be released to the participants. These documents are part of the data on which the experiments are built. Organisers need an interface that allows them to upload the collections of documents, which can be in diverse media, into the DLS to make them available to participants and assessors.

- *Creation of topics*: the organisers and the assessors cooperate to create the topics for the test collection. (*Topic* is the term we adopt for

Figure 6.2 Relationship between the DIKW hierarchy, the different types of actors, and the main steps of an evaluation campaign

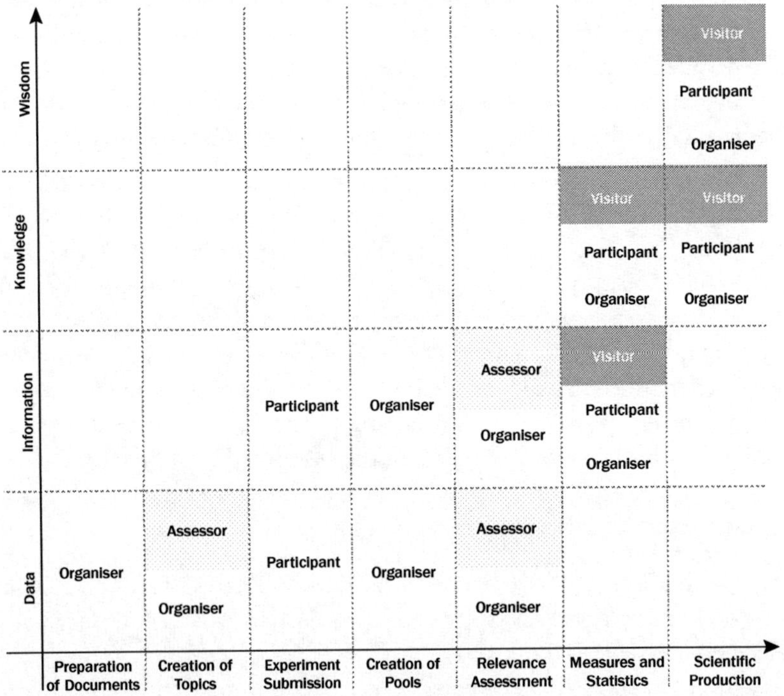

the statements of information needs which are then used by the system to derive their queries; topics can be formulated in various forms according to the particular tasks for which they will be used.) For each topic, this step usually requires preparing a first draft of the topic and searching the set of documents to verify that there are relevant documents for that topic. The topic is then refined by discussing its content and facets until a final version is reached. These topics are part of the data on which the experiments are built. Organisers need an interface that allows them to set up the topics to be created, to monitor the creation process, and to publish the topics once they are in the final form. Assessors need an interface that allows them to insert and modify the content of a topic, to search the collections of documents to verify that there are relevant documents for the topic, and to discuss the contents of the topic. Note that topics are created by inspecting the documents, which in a sense are a kind of data more basic than the topics. This fact is also reflected in the user interface, which needs to support more complex tasks that reflect the relationships between these two kinds of data.

- *Experiment submission*: the participants submit their experiments, which are built using the documents and the topics created in the previous steps. The result of each experiment is a list of retrieved documents in decreasing order of relevance for each topic and represents the output of the execution of the information retrieval system (IRS) developed by the participant. The experiments are part of the data produced during an evaluation campaign. Participants need an interface that allows them to upload their experiments into the DLS, to validate them, e.g. to check that the correct document identifiers have been used or that no topic has been skipped, and to provide all the necessary information for describing their experiments. Note that experiments are created by starting from documents and topics, and in a sense represent a kind of more complex data with respect to them. This fact is also reflected in the user interface, which provides support for checking the correctness of the experiments with respect to topics and documents.

- *Creation of pools*: the organisers collect all the experiments submitted by the participants and, using some appropriate sampling technique, select a subset of the retrieved documents to be manually assessed to determine their actual relevance. The pools are midway between data and information, as they are still quite raw elements but represent a first form of processing of the experiments. Organisers need an interface that allows them to select and sample the documents to be inserted in the pool and to see dynamically how the pools change when the selection criteria are modified to determine the best strategy for creating the pools. This hybrid nature of the pools between data and information is also reflected in the user interface, which explicitly has to show how a pool – i.e. something that relates documents, topics and experiments – changes when the selection and sampling criteria are modified.

- *Relevance assessment*: the organisers and the assessors cooperate to assess each document in the pool with respect to the topic, i.e. for determining whether or not the document is relevant for the given topic. As in the case of the pools, the relevance judgments are midway between data and information, as they are raw elements which constitute an experimental collection but represent human-added information about the relationship between the topics and documents of an experiment. Organisers need an interface that allows them to set up and monitor the relevance assessment process and to publish the relevance judgments once they are in the final form. Assessors need an interface that allows them to assess the relevance of a document with respect to a topic, to have some basic search functionalities for the documents and topics to assess, and for discussion in the event of topics that may be difficult or ambiguous to assess. This dual nature of the relevance assessment between data and information is also reflected in the user interface, which explicitly requests the assessors to enter a human judgment (relevant or not relevant) about the relationship between a document and a topic.

- *Measures and statistics*: the organisers exploit the relevance assessments to compute the performance measures and plots about each experiment submitted by a participant. These measurements are then used for computing descriptive statistics about the overall behaviour of both an experiment and all the experiments in a given task; furthermore, these measurements are also employed for conducting statistical analyses and tests on the submitted experiments. As discussed above, performance measures are information, as they are the results of data processing; descriptive statistics and hypothesis tests are knowledge, as they provide further insights into the meaning of the obtained performances. Organisers need an interface that allows them to perform all the computations and statistical analyses that are needed. Participants and visitors need an interface that gives access and presents performance measurements, plots, descriptive statistics and statistical analyses in a meaningful way in order to facilitate their comprehension and interpretation.

- *Scientific production*: both organisers and participants prepare reports where the former describe the overall trends and provide an overview for the evaluation campaign and the latter explain their experiments, the techniques that have been adopted, and the findings. This work usually continues even after the conclusion of the campaign, as the investigation and understanding of the experimental results require deep analysis and reasoning, which usually takes the form of conference papers, journal articles, talks and discussion among researchers. Furthermore, not only the organisers and the participants but also external visitors may exploit the information resources produced during the evaluation campaign to carry out their research activity. As explained above, the outcome of this process is wisdom. Organisers, participants and visitors need a user interface that provides easy access and meaningful interaction with the information resources, allows them to cite and reference the information resources relevant for their work, and supports the enrichment of the information resources available.

This discussion shows how multifaceted the needs of the users involved in a large-scale evaluation campaign are and how different and complex are the tasks that the DLS used to manage the evaluation campaign has to support. This complexity is also reflected in the user interface, which needs to offer different types of interaction with the system according to the task and user at hand.

The design of a sufficiently functional and responsive user interface must be based on the user needs, analysis of the interaction among users, and the user feedback. Furthermore, a large-scale evaluation campaign involves people from different countries, with different languages and different cultures; this factor has to be taken into account by providing a correct internationalisation and localisation of the interface in order to lower language and cultural barriers.

Key contributions

As observed in the previous section, scientific data, their curation, enrichment and interpretation are essential components of scientific research. These issues are better faced and framed in the wider context of the curation of scientific data, which plays an important role in the systematic definition of a proper methodology for managing and promoting the use of data.

The e-Science Data Curation Report gives the following definition of data curation:

> the activity of managing and promoting the use of data from its point of creation, to ensure it is fit for contemporary purpose, and available for discovery and re-use. For dynamic datasets this may mean continuous enrichment or updating to keep it fit for purpose. (Lord and MacDonald, 2003)

This definition implies the need to consider the possibility of information enrichment of scientific data, meant as archiving and preserving scientific data so that the experiments, records and observations will be available for future research, as well as provenance, curation and citation of scientific data items. The benefits of this approach include the growing involvement of scientists in international research projects and forums, and increased interest in comparative research activities. Furthermore, the definition introduced above reflects the importance of some of the many possible reasons for which keeping data is important. Such reasons include, for example, reuse of data for new research, including collection-based research to generate new science; retention of unique observational data which cannot be recreated; retention of expensively generated data which is cheaper to maintain than to regenerate; enhancing existing data available for research projects; and validating published research results.

As a concrete example in the field of information retrieval, consider the data fusion problem (Croft, 2000), where lists of results produced by different systems have to be merged into a single list. In this context, researchers do not start from scratch, but often use other researchers' results to develop their merging algorithms. In 2005, for example, the CLEF, the European initiative for the evaluation of multilingual information access components (*www.clef-campaign.org*), ran a multilingual merging track to provide results from experiments it had run in 2003 for participants to use as data for their merging algorithms (Di Nunzio et al., 2006). It is clear that such researchers would benefit from a data curation strategy which could promote the reuse of existing data and allow data fusion experiments to be traced back to the original results and, perhaps, to the analyses and interpretations of them.

However, the Cranfield methodology was developed to create comparable experiments and evaluate the performances of an IRS rather than modelling, managing and curating the scientific data produced during an evaluation campaign. The following sections present a discussion of some key points that were taken into consideration when designing the DIRECT DLS and which extend the current evaluation methodology.

Conceptual model

The definition of experimental collection does not take into consideration any kind of conceptual model (Tsichritzis and Lochovsky, 1982), neither of the experimental collection as a whole, nor its constituent parts. However, the information space implied by an evaluation campaign needs an appropriate conceptual model that takes into consideration and describes all the entities involved. An appropriate conceptual model is the necessary basis for making the scientific data produced during the evaluation an active part of any information enrichment, such as data provenance and citation. The conceptual model can also be translated into an appropriate logical model in order to manage the information of an evaluation campaign by using robust data management technology. From the conceptual model, appropriate data formats can also be derived for exchanging information among organisers and participants.

The conceptual model is built around five main modelling areas:

- *evaluation campaign*: this deals with the different aspects of an evaluation forum, such as the evaluation campaigns conducted and the different editions of each campaign, the tracks along which the campaign is organised, the subscription of the participants to the tracks, and the topics of each track;

- *collection*: this concerns the different collections made available by an evaluation forum; each collection can be organised into various files and each file may contain one or more multimedia documents; the same collection can be used by different tracks and by different editions of the evaluation campaign;

- *experiments*: this regards the experiments submitted by the participants and the evaluation metrics computed on those experiments, such as precision and recall;

- *pool/relevance assessment*: this is about the pooling method where a set of experiments is pooled and the documents retrieved in those experiments are assessed with respect to the topics of the track to which the experiments belong;

- *statistical analysis*: this models the different aspects concerning the statistical analysis of the experimental results, such as the type of statistical test employed, its parameters, the observed test statistic, and so forth.

Each entity in the conceptual model has the possibility of being enriched with various metadata objects to provide additional information about it; the different metadata objects can comply with different metadata schemes, which can be defined in an easy and extensible way, in order to describe different facets of the annotated object. Moreover, each metadata object can in turn be annotated with other metadata objects, so that is possible to have a chain of nested metadata describing a given object.

Metadata

Anderson (2004) points out that 'metadata descriptions are as important as the data values in providing meaning to the data, and thereby enabling sharing and potential future useful access'. As there is no conceptual model for an experimental collection, appropriate metadata schemes are also lacking. Consider that there are almost no metadata:

- to describe a collection of documents *D* – useful metadata would concern, at least, the creator, the creation date, a description, the context of the collection, and how the collection has been created;

- about the topics *T* – useful metadata would describe the creators and the creation date, how the creation process has taken place, if there were any issues, what documents the creators found relevant for a given topic, and so on;

- to describe the relevance judgments *J* – examples of such metadata concern creators and the creation date, the criteria leading to the creation of the relevance judgments, the problems faced by the assessors when dealing with difficult topics.

The situation is a little less problematic when it comes to experiments for which some kind of metadata may be collected, such as which topic fields have been used to create the query, and whether the query has been automatically or manually constructed from the topics. The Text Retrieval Conference (TREC) also collects more detailed information about the hardware used to run the experiments, what retrieval model has been applied, what algorithms and techniques have been adopted, what kind of stop word removal and/or stemming has been performed, and what tunings have been carried out.

A good attempt in this direction is the Reliable Information Access Workshop (Harman and Buckley, 2004), organised by the US National Institute of Standards and Technology in 2003, where an in-depth study and failure analysis of the conducted experiments was performed and valuable information about them was collected. However, the existence of a commonly agreed conceptual model and metadata schemas would have helped in defining and gathering the information to be kept.

Similar considerations also hold for the performance measurements, the descriptive statistics, and the statistical analyses that are not explicitly modelled and for which no metadata schema is defined. It would be useful to define at least the metadata that are necessary to describe which software and which version of the software were used to compute a performance measure, which relevance judgments were used to compute a performance measure, and when the performance measure was computed. Similar metadata could also be useful for descriptive statistics and statistical analyses.

All this additional information can provide useful hints about the system models as well as the context of the evaluation. The context is not simply the track or specific experiments, as more information might be needed, such as who the assessors were, how they assessed documents, what the aims of the experiment were and the circumstances in which the collection was built. Similarly, systems are more than simply a system configuration, but an overall approach for a retrieval task. Furthermore, this additional information can be used to support higher-level research activities, such as assessing the reliability of information-retrieval experiments (Zobel, 1998).

Unique identification mechanism

The lack of a conceptual model causes another relevant consequence: there is no common mechanism for uniquely identifying the different digital objects involved in an evaluation campaign, i.e. there is no way to uniquely identify and reference collections of documents, topics, relevance judgments, experiments and statistical analyses.

The absence of a mechanism to uniquely identify and reference the digital objects of an evaluation campaign prevents the direct citation of that digital object. Indeed, as recognised by Lord and MacDonald (2003), the possibility of citing scientific data and elaborating on it further is an effective way of making scientists and researchers an active part of the digital curation process. Moreover, this opportunity would strengthen the passing from data to wisdom because experimental collections and experiments would become as citable and accessible as any other item in the reference list of a paper.

Among the various identification solutions that have been proposed, the digital object identifier (DOI) is a system that provides a mechanism to interoperably identify and exchange intellectual property in the digital environment. DOI conforms to a uniform resource identifier (URI) and provides an extensible framework for managing intellectual content based on proven standards of digital object architecture and intellectual property management. Furthermore, it is an open system based on non-proprietary standards and provides facilities for resolving the identifiers (Paskin, 2006). This means that it enables direct access to each identified digital object starting from its identifier, in this way giving an interested researcher direct access to the referenced digital object together with all the information concerning it. Finally, the DOI constitutes a valuable possibility for identifying and referencing digital objects of an evaluation campaign, as there have already been successful attempts to apply it to scientific data, and it also makes possible the association of metadata with identified digital objects, as observed by Brase (2004) and Paskin (2005).

The DOI has therefore been adopted as a unique identification mechanism and DOIs are registered for different information resources of an evaluation campaign in accordance with mEDRA (*www.medra.org*).

Statistical analyses

Hull (1993) points out that, in order to evaluate retrieval performances, not only does one need an experimental collection and measures for quantifying retrieval performances, but also a statistical methodology for judging whether measured differences between retrieval methods can be considered statistically significant.

To address this issue, evaluation campaigns have traditionally supported and carried out statistical analyses which provide participants with an overview analysis of the submitted experiments. Furthermore, participants may conduct statistical analyses on their own experiments by using either ad hoc packages, such as IR-STAT-PAK, or generally available software tools with statistical analysis capabilities, like R, SPSS or MATLAB. However, the choice of whether or not to perform a statistical analysis is left up to each participant, who may even not have all the skills and resources needed to perform such analyses. Moreover, when participants perform statistical analyses using their own tools, the comparability among these analyses is not fully guaranteed. In fact, different statistical tests can be employed to analyse the data, or different choices and approximations for the various parameters of the same statistical test can be made.

Therefore, support and guidance to participants have been provided to adopt a more uniform way of performing statistical analyses on their own experiments. Indeed, not only can participants benefit from standard experimental collections which make their experiments comparable, they can also exploit standard tools for the analysis of the experimental results which make the analysis and assessment of their experiments comparable too.

As stated above, scientific data, their enrichment and interpretation are essential components of scientific research. The Cranfield methodology traces out how these scientific data have to be produced, while the statistical analysis of experiments provides the means for further elaborating and interpreting the experimental results. Nevertheless, the current methodology does not require any particular coordination or synchronisation between the basic scientific data and the analyses on them, which are treated as almost separate items. In contrast, researchers could greatly benefit from an integrated vision of them, where access to a scientific data item could also offer the possibility of retrieving all the analyses and interpretations on it. Furthermore, it should be possible to enrich the basic scientific data in an incremental way, progressively adding further analyses and interpretations of them.

Statistical analyses concerning the performances of each experiment are carried out, such as computing descriptive statistics about the experiment or providing histograms and box plots to analyse the behaviour of the experiment across different topics with respect to different metrics. Thus, through the provision of tools to ease their work, participants are encouraged to conduct in-depth analyses of their results. Moreover, statistical analyses and hypothesis tests are conducted, such as the Tukey t-test, to cross-compare all the experiments submitted for a given task and give the participants the possibility of better understanding their results with respect to the general trend and behaviour for a given task.

Architecture of the DIRECT system

As a result of an investigation of user requirements and needs, DIRECT has been designed to meet the following goals:

- to be cross-platform and easily deployable to end users;
- to be as modular as possible, clearly separating the application logic from the interface logic;
- to be intuitive and capable of providing support for the various user tasks described in the previous section, such as experiment submission, consultation of metrics and plots about experiment performances, relevance assessment, and so on;
- to support different types of users, i.e. participants, assessors, organisers and visitors, who need to have access to different kinds of features and capabilities;

- to support internationalisation and localisation – the application needs to be able to adapt to the language of the user and their country or culturally dependent data, such as dates and currencies.

Figure 6.3 shows the architecture of the proposed service. It consists of three layers – data, application and interface logic layers – in order to achieve improved modularity and to describe the behaviour of the service by isolating specific functionalities at the proper layer. In this way, the behaviour of the system is designed in a modular and extensible manner (Agosti et al., 2007a; Dussin and Ferro, 2008b).

In the following, a brief description of the architecture shown in Figure 6.3 is given from bottom to top.

Data logic

The data logic layer deals with the persistence of the different information objects coming from the upper layers. There is a set of 'storing managers' dedicated to storing the submitted experiments, the relevance assessments and so on. The data access object and the transfer object design patterns have been adopted (*java.sun.com/blueprints/ corej2eepatterns/Patterns/*). The data access object implements the access mechanism required to work with the underlying data source, acting as an adapter between the upper layers and the data source. If the underlying data source implementation changes, this pattern allows the data access object to adapt to different storage schemes without affecting the upper layers.

In addition to the other data access objects, there is the log data access object which accurately traces both system and user events. It captures information such as the user name, the IP address of the connecting host, the action that has been invoked by the user, the messages exchanged between the components of the system in order to carry out the requested action, any error condition, and so on. Thus, besides providing a log of the system and user activities, the log data access object enables the provenance of each piece of data to be accurately traced from its entrance in the system to every further processing of it.

Finally, on top of the various data access objects there is the 'DIRECT Datastore' which hides the details about the storage management to the upper layers. In this way, the addition of a new data access object is totally transparent for the upper layers.

Figure 6.3 Architecture of the DIRECT system

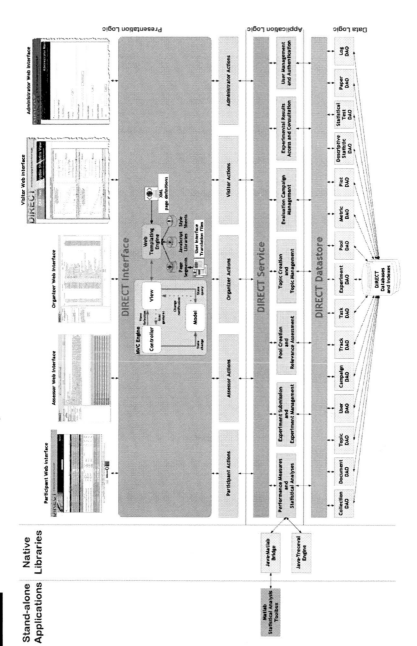

Application logic

The application logic layer deals with the flow of operations within DIRECT. It provides a set of tools capable of managing high-level tasks, such as experiment submission, pool assessment, and statistical analysis of an experiment.

For example, the 'performance measures and statistical analyses' tool offers the functionalities needed to conduct a statistical analysis on a set of experiments. In order to ensure comparability and reliability, the tool makes use of well-known and widely-used tools to implement the statistical tests, so that everyone can replicate the same test, even if they have no access to the service. In the architecture, the MATLAB Statistics Toolbox has been adopted, as MATLAB is a leader application in the field of numerical analysis which employs state-of-the-art algorithms, although other software could have been used as well. In the case of MATLAB, an additional library is needed to allow the service to access MATLAB in a programmed way; other applications might require different solutions. A further library provides an interface for the service towards the trec eval package (*trec.nist.gov/trec_eval*). Trec eval was first developed and adopted by TREC and is the standard tool for computing the basic performance figures, such as precision and recall.

Finally, the 'DIRECT Service' provides the interface logic layer with uniform and integrated access to the various tools. As with the case of the 'DIRECT Datastore', the 'DIRECT Service' makes the addition of new tools transparent for the interface logic layer too.

Interface logic

The modularity of the components has enormous benefits when building interactive applications, as it helps the designer to better understand and develop each component and modify it without affecting the others. Therefore, the model-view-controller (Krasner and Pope, 1988) approach has been used to clearly separate the following three layers:

- *model layer*: contains the underlying data structures of the application and keeps the state of the application;
- *view layer*: the way the model is presented to the user;
- *controller layer*: manages the interaction between the view and the input devices, such as the keyboard or the mouse, and updates the model accordingly.

Figure 6.3 shows the architecture of the DIRECT user interface, which is a web-based application designed to be cross-platform and easily deployable and accessible without the need to install any software on the end-user's machine.

The system also supports the internationalisation and localisation of the user interface by adapting it to the language and country of the user. The correct language and country are initially loaded according to the browser settings and, in the case of non-supported locales, it falls back to a default configuration. The user interface has been translated into Bulgarian, Czech, English, Farsi, French, German, Indonesian, Italian, Portuguese and Spanish (Dussin and Ferro, 2007).

DIRECT: the running prototype

DIRECT has been successfully adopted in the CLEF campaigns since 2005, as reported in Table 6.1. Note that the languages of the assessed documents include not only languages with a Latin alphabet, but also Bulgarian and Russian, which use the Cyrillic alphabet, and Farsi, which is written from right to left.

Table 6.1 presents the main page for the experiment management, which allows the participant to access all the relevant information about a track, related tasks, topics and experiments. The interface manages information resources which belong to different levels of the DIKW hierarchy and relates them in a meaningful way. The user can access the data produced by participants themselves, i.e. the experiments submitted; data produced by assessors, i.e. topics and relevance assessments; information produced by organisers, i.e. performance measures about the experiments submitted by a participant; and, lastly, knowledge produced by organisers, i.e. the statistics and statistical analyses about the different tasks of an evaluation campaign.

Table 6.1   Usage statistics of the DIRECT system

CLEF	Experiments	Participants/nations	Assessed documents	Assessors
2005	530	30/15 nations	160,000/7 languages	15
2006	570	75/25 nations	200,000/9 languages	40
2007	430	45/18 nations	215,000/7 languages	75
2008	490	40/20 nations	250,000/7 languages	65

The interface is based on a set of folding tables that allow participants to access their experiments, which are participant data, by structuring them in different levels based on a tree structure – tracks, tasks and experiments – well known to the user. The participant can therefore manage their own data by simply selecting and expanding the right level in the tree to facilitate the submission, editing or deletion of an experiment.

Besides experiments, further data are associated with each level of the tree in order to support the participant in accessing additional resources. By proposing only those data that are pertinent to the task currently selected by the participant, DIRECT makes available only those topics and relevance assessments which are suitable assessor data.

Moreover, the system supports the interaction of the participant with the information and knowledge produced by the organisers, i.e. performance measures and statistical analyses, by presenting the appropriate information resources at the correct level in the tree structure.

Lastly, following Zeleny (1987) who points out that knowledge is the process through which 'individual pieces of data and information (components, concepts) become connected with one another (i.e. organised) in a network of relations', the system allows users to navigate the interface and access more information resources, so that they can benefit from this 'network of relations'.

Figure 6.4 **Main page for the experiment management**

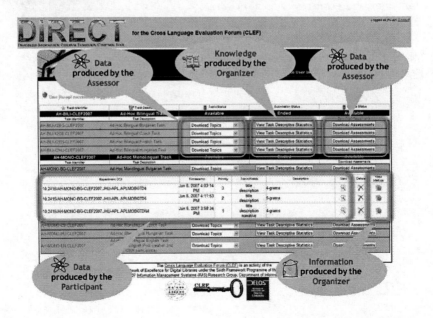

Figure 6.5 Plots about task overall performances and statistics

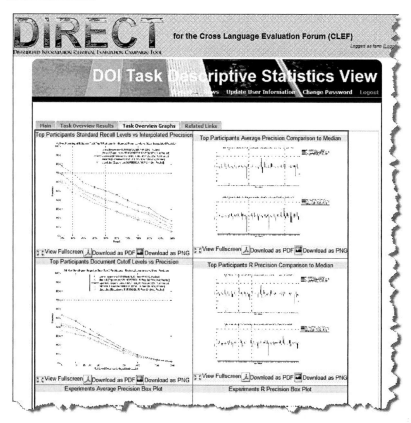

As an example, Figure 6.4 shows the information resources offered to the participant when the 'view tasks descriptive statistics' button is pressed. In particular, Figure 6.5 shows some of the plots used to summarise the overall performances achieved in the task and compare the performances of the top participants with respect to the median performances in the task. All these plots can be downloaded and used by participants and visitors, while the numerical data needed to create them can be accessed and downloaded by selecting the 'task overview results' tab.

Conclusions and future work

This chapter has described the methodology currently adopted for the experimental evaluation of the information access components of a digital library, and has shown how to extend it to include proper management, curation, archiving and enrichment of the scientific data produced while conducting an experimental evaluation in the context of large-scale evaluation campaigns.

A description has been given of the approach for maintaining the scientific output of an evaluation campaign in a DLS, in order to ensure long-term preservation, curation of data, and accessibility over time both by humans and automatic systems. The aim is to exploit the DLS for scientific data to support services for the creation, interpretation and use of multidisciplinary and multilingual digital content and to foster knowledge transfer towards relevant application communities and industry. This DLS should be constituted by several cooperating services, each focused on one aspect of digital library evaluation, where the service for managing the evaluation of the performances of the information access components represents a relevant example.

Finally, an innovative software infrastructure to support the course of an evaluation campaign, the running prototype, DIRECT, and its functionalities has been presented and discussed. DIRECT has been successfully tested and adopted as a reference tool during CLEF evaluation campaigns.

The introduction to this chapter underlined that the scientific reflection DLS being designed and developed must be constituted by different and cooperative services, each focused on supporting the evaluation of one aspect. As such, a DLS must supply coherent basic services and correspondent components that provide end users with access to information and documents. These services usually include an OPAC-like component, the information access components and a component to navigate the different collections of documents to which the digital library gives access. As this coherent set of components/ services is of great interest to end users, these can be used to start log data collection and analysis which can be considered a parallel and correspondent effort to the one conducted during the CLEF campaigns for the collection of scientific data, described previously in this work.

The relevant characteristics of a DLS suggest addressing the issue of collecting and analysing log data in a wide and comprehensive way, otherwise many aspects of the interaction between the end user and the DLS with its diversified services may be missed (Agosti, 2008). For all the different categories of DLS users, the quality of the services and documents supplied by the digital library are very important (Agosti et al., 2007c). Log data constitute a relevant aspect in evaluating the quality of a DLS and the quality of interoperability in digital library services. Work is underway to establish a framework for handling log data in the evaluation of DLS services that provide end users with access to information and documents, bearing in mind that the end users are central to any study of this sort. Indeed, the final user should be the guide of the system's designers, prompting them to conceive and invent solutions of real use for the user himself.

Acknowledgments

The authors would like to warmly thank Carol Peter, coordinator of CLEF and Project Coordinator of TrebleCLEF, for her continuous support and advice. The authors would like to thank Giorgio Maria Di Nunzio and Marco Dussin for the useful discussions on the topics addressed in this chapter.

The work reported has been partially supported by the TrebleCLEF Coordination Action, as part of the Seventh Framework Programme of the European Commission, Theme ICT-1-4-1 Digital libraries and technology-enhanced learning (Contract 215231).

Bibliography

Abiteboul, S., Agrawal, R., Bernstein, P. A., Carey, M. J., Ceri, S., Croft, W. B., DeWitt, D. J., Franklin, M. J., Garcia-Molina, H., Gawlick, D., Gray, J., Haas, L. M., Halevy, A. Y., Hellerstein, J. M., Ioannidis, Y. E., Kersten, M. L., Pazzani, M. J., Lesk, M., Maier, D., Naughton, J. F., Schek, H.-J., Sellis, T. K., Silberschatz, A., Stonebraker, M., Snodgrass, R. T., Ullman, J. D., Weikum, G., Widom, J. and Zdonik, S. B. (2005) 'The Lowell Database research self-assessment', *Communications of the ACM 48(5)*: 111–18.

Ackoff, R. L. (1989) 'From data to wisdom', *Journal of Applied Systems Analysis 16*: 3–9.

Agosti, M. (2008) 'Log data in digital libraries', in *Post-proceedings of the 4th Italian Research Conference on Digital Library Systems, Padua, 24–25 January*, Pisa: ISTI-CNR at Gruppo ALI, pp. 115–22.

Agosti, M., Di Nunzio, G. M. and Ferro, N. (2007a) 'A proposal to extend and enrich the scientific data curation of evaluation campaigns', in *Proceedings of the 1st International Workshop on*

Evaluating Information Access, Tokyo, 15 May, Tokyo: National Institute of Informatics, pp. 62–73.

Agosti, M., Di Nunzio, G. M. and Ferro, N. (2007b) 'Scientific data of an evaluation campaign: Do we properly deal with them?' In *Evaluation of Multilingual and Multi-modal Information Retrieval: 7th Workshop of the Cross-Language Evaluation Forum, Budapest, September, LNCS Vol. 4730*, Berlin, Germany: Springer-Verlag, pp. 11–20.

Agosti, M., Ferro, N., Fox, E. A. and Gonçalves, M. A. (2007c) 'Modelling DL quality – a comparison between approaches: The DELOS Reference Model and the 5S model', paper presented at the Second DELOS Conference on Digital Libraries, Tirrenia, Pisa, 5–7 December, available at: *http://www.delos.info/index.php?option= com_content&task=view&id=602&Itemid=334*.

Anderson, W. L. (2004) 'Some challenges and issues in managing, and preserving access to long-lived collections of digital scientific and technical data', *Data Science Journal* 3: 191–202.

Brase, J. (2004) 'Using digital library techniques: Registration of scientific primary data', in *Proceedings of the 8th European Conference on Digital Libraries, Bath, 12–17 September, LNCS Vol. 3232*, Berlin: Springer-Verlag, pp. 488–94.

Cleverdon, C. W. (1997) 'The Cranfield tests on index languages device', in K. Spärck Jones and P. Willet (eds) *Readings in Information Retrieval*, San Francisco, CA: Morgan Kaufmann, pp. 47–60.

Croft, W. B. (2000) 'Combining approaches to information retrieval', in W. B. Croft (ed.) *Advances in Information Retrieval: Recent Research from the Center for Intelligent Information Retrieval*, Norwell, MA: Kluwer, pp. 1–36.

Di Nunzio, G. M., Ferro, N., Jones, G. J. and Peters, C. (2006) 'CLEF 2005: Ad hoc track overview', in *Evaluation of Multilingual and Multi-modal Information Retrieval: 6th Workshop of the Cross-Language Evaluation Forum, Alicante, 17–22 September, LNCS Vol. 4022*, Berlin: Springer-Verlag, pp. 11–36.

Dussin, M. and Ferro, N. (2007) 'Design of the user interface of a scientific digital library system for large-scale evaluation campaigns', paper presented at the Second DELOS Conference on Digital Libraries, Tirrenia, Pisa, 5–7 December, available at: *http://www.delos .info/index.php?option=com_content&task=view&id=602&Itemid=334* (accessed 15 April 2009).

Dussin, M. and Ferro, N. (2008a) 'The design of the user interface of a scientific DLS in the context of the data, information, knowledge and wisdom hierarchy', in *Post-proceedings of the 4th Italian Research*

Conference on Digital Library Systems, Padua, 24–25 January, ISTI-CNR at Gruppo ALI: Pisa, pp. 105–13.

Dussin, M. and Ferro, N. (2008b) 'Design of a digital library system for large-scale evaluation campaigns', in *Proceedings of the 12th European Conference on Digital Libraries, Aarhus, 14–19 September, LNCS Vol. 5173,* Berlin: Springer-Verlag, pp. 400–1.

Führ, N., Hansen, P., Micsik, A. and Sølvberg, I. (2001) 'Digital libraries: A generic classification scheme', in *Proceedings of the 5th European Conference on Digital Libraries, Darmstadt, 4–9 September, LNCS Vol. 2163,* Berlin: Springer-Verlag, pp. 187–99.

Führ, N., Tsakonas, G., Aalberg, T., Agosti, M., Hansen, P., Kapidakis, S. Klas, C.-P., Kovács, L., Landoni, M., Micsik, A., Papatheodorou, C., Peters, C. and Sølvberg, I. (2007) 'Evaluation of digital libraries', *International Journal on Digital Libraries* 8(1): 21–38.

Hanks, P. (ed.) (1979) *Collins Dictionary of the English Language,* Glasgow: William Collins Sons and Co.

Harman, D. and Buckley, C. (2004) 'SIGIR 2004 Workshop: RIA and "Where can IR go from here?"', *ACM SIGIR Forum* 38(2): 45–9.

Hull, D. A. (1993) 'Using statistical testing in the evaluation of retrieval experiments', in *Proceedings of the 16th Annual International ACM SIGIR Conference on Research and Development in Information Retrieval, Pittsburgh, PA, 27 June to 1 July,* New York: ACM Press, pp. 329–38.

Ioannidis, Y. E., Maier, D., Abiteboul, S., Buneman, P., Davidson, S. B., Fox, E. A., Halevy, A. Y., Knoblock, C.A., Rabitti, F., Schek, H.-J. and Weikum, G. (2005) 'Digital library information-technology infrastructures', *International Journal on Digital Libraries* 5(4): 266–74.

Krasner, G. E. and Pope, S. T. (1988) 'A cookbook for using the model-view-controller user interface paradigm in Smalltalk-80', *Journal of Object-Oriented Programming* 1(3): 26–49.

Lord, P. and MacDonald, A. (2003) 'e-Science Curation Report: Data curation for e-Science in the UK – an audit to establish requirements for future curation and provision', available at: *http://www.jisc.ac.uk/uploaded_documents/e-ScienceReportFinal.pdf* (accessed 25 November 2008).

National Science Board (2005) 'Long-lived digital data collections: Enabling research and education in the 21st century', available at: *http://www.nsf.gov/pubs/2005/nsb0540/* (accessed 25 November 2008).

Paskin, N. (2005) 'Digital object identifiers for scientific data', *Data Science Journal* 4: 12–20.

Paskin, N. (ed.) (2006) 'The DOI Handbook – Edition 4.4.1', available at: *http://dx.doi.org/10.1000/186* (accessed 25 November 2008).

Tsichritzis, D. C. and Lochovsky, F. H. (1982) *Data Models*. Englewood Cliffs, NJ: Prentice Hall.

Zeleny, M. (1987) 'Management support systems: Towards integrated knowledge management', *Human Systems Management* 7(1): 59–70.

Zobel, J. (1998) 'How reliable are the results of large-scale information retrieval experiments', in *Proceedings of the 21st Annual International ACM SIGIR Conference on Research and Development in Information Retrieval, Melbourne, 24–28 August*, New York: ACM Press, pp. 307–14.

7

Employing deep log analysis to evaluate the information-seeking behaviour of users of digital libraries

David Nicholas

Introduction

This chapter describes a pioneering methodology, deep log analysis (DLA), which enables us to closely and robustly describe user activity in a virtual space such as a digital library. It also examines the strengths and weaknesses of the methodology and illustrates what the methodology can produce in regard to rich use and user data through an evaluation of the British Library's Learning website (BL Learning) for young people and their teachers (*www.bl.uk/learning/*).

What is deep log analysis?

DLA is a form of transactional log analysis, but one which goes beyond monitoring online activity of a particular information system, the territory of most log analyses, and instead turns that activity into the information-seeking behaviour of communities of users. It can also alert us to problems and failures in information-seeking and best practices. It can even tell us something about user satisfaction. It is thus a powerful methodology for evaluating the use of digital libraries.

DLA works on the raw server and search logs (the digital footprints) that are routinely recorded on the server of the service being investigated. In this way, no data are filtered out and we can squeeze them for all their worth. Data are only discarded if inspection shows that they do not contribute to the building of information-seeking portraits. Figure 7.1 shows what a typical raw log file looks like and this one comes from the academic gateway site, Intute (*www.intute.ac.uk*).

We shall now decode and demystify the log shown in Figure 7.1. The first information provided is the IP number, which is a numeric address that is given to users connected to the internet. Domain name server (DNS) registration information is available for most IP numbers via a reverse DNS lookup. DNS registration provides categories under which organisations can register, such as '.ac' for academic organisations. Reverse DNS lookup can also provide geographical location information, although more accurate data can be obtained by referring IP addresses to a database of country-allocated IP numbers. Almost all (99.4 per cent) of IP numbers are matched to a country.

The date and time comes next, and this represents the date and time stamp of when the file was sent to the user's computer as well as how this time related to GMT. The file name preceded by a GET gives an idea of the type of download. In this example, the user has viewed a page labelled 'omnilost.html' from a directory called 'healthandlifesciences'. Following the download information comes the delivery status (codes 200 and 304 are successful downloads) and number of bytes downloaded (6,336 in the above example). The referrer information follows this and gives the last page viewed by the user. In this instance, the user had entered the search expression 'funnel chest' into Google UK. The browser details of the client computer follow this.

Figure 7.1	Characteristics of the Intute server transactional log

```
82.9.66.190,62.252.64.32 - - [11/Oct/2006:00:00:17
+0100]   "GET/healthandlifesciences/omnilost.html
HTTP/1.1" 200 6336 "http://www.google.co.uk/search?
sourceid=navclient&aq=t&hl=en-GB&ie=UTF-
8&rls=GGLJ,GGLJ:2006-31,GGLJ:en-GB&q=funnel+
chest"   "Mozilla/4.0   (compatible;   MSIE   6.0;
Windows  NT  5.1;  SV1;  FunWebProducts;  .NET  CLR
1.1.4322)"
```

These logs are then processed using the Statistical Package for the Social Sciences (SPSS) to provide the detailed information-seeking patterns that are so characteristic of DLA. Where available, the usage data are related to user demographic data as contained in online questionnaires and subscriber databases. This provides particularly rich and detailed information-seeking portraits as Figure 7.2 demonstrates. On show here are the 29 characteristics that combine together to form the digital footprint of the virtual user. Not every service provides the opportunity to obtain all this information for building information-seeking portraits; the figure should thus be considered as an ideal template.

DLA provides bespoke analyses, in other words, analyses tailored to a particular system and a particular user community. This is because no log is exactly the same; nor for that matter any system or user community. Largely for this reason, as far as we know, CIBER is the only research group that employs the method. CIBER has been employing this method for more than five years now on a whole range of digital libraries and publisher platforms, including ScienceDirect, Synergy, OUP Journals, OhioLINK, Intute and BL Learning, the latter of which is featured strongly in this chapter.

Figure 7.2   The digital information footprint as portrayed by DLA

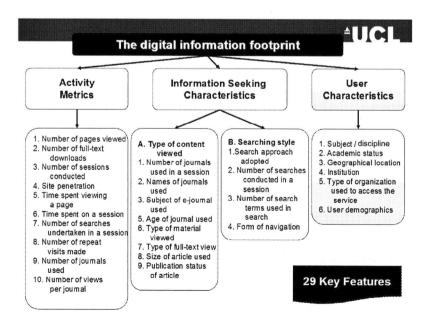

What are the benefits of deep log analysis?

We have already touched on what is, arguably, the most important benefit of the methodology and that is it focuses on users and their information-seeking rather than use, which is, surely, what is needed. However, there are numerous other unique advantages (Tenopir et al., 2007). We shall start by addressing the generic ones – those that apply to transactional log analysis, the family of methods to which DLA belongs:

- *Enormous reach*: Logs record the use by everyone who happens to engage with the digital library; this means the data yield and reach are absolutely enormous – for instance, half a million users in the case of the OhioLINK study, closer to a million in the case of Intute. There is no need to take a sample, and thus questions concerning the representativeness or validity of the findings never arise. Nothing matches logs for the size of the population studied; as such, this lends massive authority to DLA findings.

- *Direct and unfiltered*: Logs are a direct and immediately available record of what people have done: not what they say they might or would do; not what they were prompted to say; not what they thought they did. They provide an evidence base. Logs do not rely on memory; they provide 'honest' data. Studies have shown that people have poor recall of what they did even a few days ago, and this is especially true of what they did in cyberspace – they seem to leave their memory behind them (Alexander, 2008).

- *Automatic*: The data are collected routinely (24/7), automatically and quite anonymously. There is no need to contact the user or request their cooperation, as the 'users' under investigation are computers, not individuals. There are no problems with low response rates that bedevil many a survey, nor do you need a great resource to collect and analyse them – a single person working on a laptop is generally enough.

- *Detail*: Logs provide a level of detail not obtainable by any other method. They record everything that someone does online, while they are viewing, searching, browsing and navigating over the period studied – for example, 15 months in the case of the OhioLINK study. Most other methods work at a far more general level of discourse.

As mentioned earlier, DLA differs from the traditional form of log analysis as found in the COUNTER compliant log reports that libraries obtain from publishers and vendors in that it is not based on proprietary software providing processed and filtered data but on an SPSS analysis of the raw server logs, hence the word 'deep'. This brings with it the following advantages:

- Even greater detail can be furnished regarding use. Thus DLA analyses go well beyond standard 'hit' analyses (e.g. page views, full-text downloads, number of sessions), providing, for instance, data on page view and session time, number of views in a session (site penetration) and return or repeat visits. DLA also goes beyond the provision of just full-text, abstract and table of content views. It can provide usage data for added-value services, like e-mail alerts and blogs, as will be illustrated later in the chapter.

- More accurate monitoring of information-seeking can be obtained because DLA provides bespoke analyses. It can overcome the worst problems associated with log analysis which are outlined below, especially in regard to double counting, dealing with proxy servers and estimating time online more effectively.

- It is possible to cross-reference data, for instance, so demonstrating how the method of navigating towards content has an impact on what types of pages are viewed. There are tremendous opportunities for cross-referencing, as will be demonstrated.

What problems are associated with log analysis?

As with any methodology, there are problems associated with log analysis. These largely arise from: (a) the difficulty of ascribing use to individuals or groups of users, which is compounded by the sheer diversity and size of the user community; (b) the imperfect nature of the log record. Of course, DLA works to minimise these problems. The problems are as follows:

- *The basic log provides a user 'trace', but not real user identification:* Typically, all there is to work on is the IP number, which provides the name of the institution, type of organisation and country to which the user belongs. Of course, data protection laws mean that there is no possibility of obtaining individual analyses, but with this method it is impossible even to isolate classes of user, such as staff or students. With DLA, however, it is possible to identify users according to age, gender, type of organisation and subject field, for instance. This is undertaken by associating usage data with subscriber or questionnaire data, or by identifying sub-network information provided in the IP address (some networks may be closely identified with a particular user group).

- *Logs provide a partial picture of user activity*: A user may well visit a number of sites in order to meet an information need. However, logs generally only provide information about one site. In these circumstances, the more comprehensive and popular the site, the better the picture of information-seeking it will provide.

- *Robots account for a good deal of usage*: Hundreds of thousands of robots or agents harvest information on the world wide web for a wide variety of purposes, such as indexing, caching and data mining. Robots inflate usage statistics typically by as much as 50 per cent, although this can increase to 90 per cent in the case of some specialist sites that are less popular with humans. Although sites try to control robot movement, the robots mimic human behaviour to get access.

- *Use counts are not completely accurate*: This is due to a number of factors:

  - *Caching*: This affects page view calculations as some viewed pages are not recorded or attributed to a user's search session, leading to more sessions being classified as having viewed fewer pages. Caching is the storing of previously viewed pages on the client's computer for speed of retrieval; repeat in-session accesses to these pages are made from the cache and are not requested from the website's server and hence not recorded in the logs, something that underestimates use, especially that of tables of contents and other frequently consulted pages.

  - *Proxy connections*: A proxy connection is one where a number of computers are connected to the internet via a single IP number. In such cases, session details of the connected computers are muddled together and it appears that all use comes from the same 'proxy' user as they are identified by IP numbers. This leads to an underestimation of the number of users and sessions. Proxy use can be identified and excluded on the basis of the very high number of views undertaken by a particular computer.

- *The way sessions (or visits) are defined*: This can lead to variations in counting. Sessions are sometimes identified in the logs by an identification number. In such cases, logs include a session-beginning tag and a session-ending tag, which also enables us to make time calculations. Unfortunately, as far as the logs are concerned, nobody logs off on the web – they just depart anonymously. Typically, then, to estimate a log off – or a session end, and so define a session – a time lapse of inactivity has to be assumed; the industry standard for this tends to be 30 minutes. CIBER research has shown this to be a very blunt instrument indeed and it should vary according to the types of pages being viewed during and particularly towards the end of a session. Fifteen minutes should be closer to the mark.

- *Estimating time spent online*: Page view time is estimated by calculating the difference in time between one page and the next page viewed. No estimate can be generated for the last page viewed in a session because there is no logoff recorded in the logs.

- *Double counting*: If a person views a full-text document in HTML format and then goes on to view this item as a PDF, proprietary software tends to count this as two views. This particularly arises when the user comes in from a gateway or third-party site which only indexes the HTML version. Hence, when the user clicks through to the article, they are served up with the HTML version. To view the PDF version, the user has to come out of the HTML full-text version and load up the PDF version. This process results in the downloading of two items rather than one. It is possible to allow for this by only counting once when such events happen within a few seconds of each other. Even COUNTER data can now do this.

What does deep log analysis tell us about digital libraries?

We shall show what kinds of analysis can be produced by reference to a recent CIBER investigation of the BL Learning site which was conducted as part of the Google Generation project (Rowlands et al., 2007). The BL Learning website is part of the main British Library website and features on its homepage. It offers a programme of workshops, activities and resources for teachers and learners of all ages. The main topics covered are given below:

- learning;
- language and literature;
- history and citizenship;
- art and images;
- culture and knowledge;
- creative research;
- teachers' area;
- learning news.

Server transactional logs for the month of April 2007 were provided for the analysis and they were processed in the manner outlined below. Excluding robots and mechanical agents, around 2.5 million pages were viewed during this period. Of this figure, over 13 per cent were views to pages specifically located in the Learning directory. More than half a million (563,238) separate IP numbers used the service during this period, and of these, 647 related to schools, a special interest group for the study.

Types of analysis

The analysis is split into four parts: (a) a page-view analysis; (b) a session analysis; (c) search term analysis; and (d) a micro analysis. This is not the full analysis as undertaken by the project; rather it is intended to be illustrative of the kinds of analysis that can be and were conducted.

Page-view analysis

Page-view analyses provide broad, aggregated figures of use which furnish a general picture of the activity associated with the site and, in some cases, can be related to specific user communities.

Figure 7.3 shows that language and literature (langlit) attracted the most use (38 per cent of page views) and this was followed by resources (28 per cent). The latter is a directory that is used to store content files, like PDF, Flash and audio files, and its high usage is probably down to the high usage of 'Sounds Familiar', which contains Flash maps on its homepage. These subjects were followed by history and citizenship (12 per cent), and images (9 per cent). The teachers section (tarea) accounted for just 1.4 per cent of page views. However, this might be

Figure 7.3 Percentage distribution of page views by subject/topic

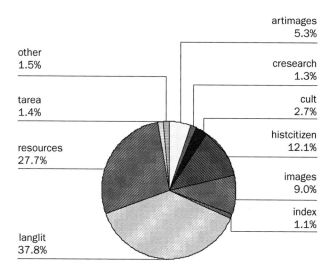

artimages
5.3%

cresearch
1.3%

cult
2.7%

histcitizen
12.1%

images
9.0%

index
1.1%

other
1.5%

tarea
1.4%

resources
27.7%

langlit
37.8%

expected as it just contains information on booking a school visit and school projects. The whole BL Learning website is for teachers (and students) and we would expect them to use the various resources for lesson ideas and in class. Culture and knowledge appeared to be a relatively unpopular area (2.7 per cent).

Logs enable us to establish on what day of the week people search the digital library. IP address identification enables us to determine what this is for particular user communities. Thus, for this particular study we were interested in identifying use emanating from universities and schools as this would indicate that the service was hitting its target audience. JANET (the UK's education and research network) provided a list of IP ranges used by schools which was used to identify school users. UK universities were identified by whether '.ac.uk' appeared in the DNS name, US universities were identified by whether '.edu' appeared in the last section of the DNS name, and EU universities were identified from a database of the top 500 EU universities assembled for the purpose. Figure 7.4 shows the results. We can see that a high proportion of EU university use was recorded on Tuesdays (31 per cent), while school usage was highest on Mondays (24 per cent), as was UK university use (27 per cent).

We can do the same for the hour of the day that people searched the system. Figure 7.5 shows that US universities mainly (57 per cent) used

Figure 7.4 Percentage distribution of page views by day of week by type of academic organisation

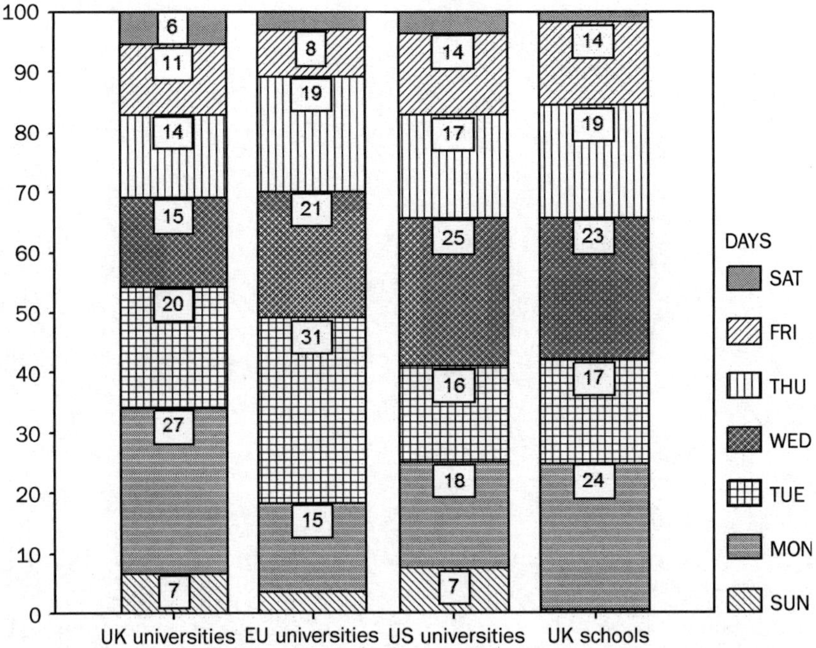

the BL Learning service in the evening (7 to 10 pm) and night (11 pm to 5 am, UK time). US users are on average about 6 hours behind and this puts their usage on a similar pattern to the UK. UK universities appeared to use the service throughout the day with a noticeable peak (29 per cent) in the morning (9 to 11 am). This was also true of school use, with over one-third (36 per cent) of usage occurring from 9 to 11 am.

The length of time a user views a page is clearly of interest as it might tell us something about the level of interest or satisfaction shown. There was quite a difference in view times between types of academic organisation, with schools generally recording a high view time of 14 seconds (Figure 7.6). EU universities recorded a low page view time of 8 seconds.

Session analysis

Session analysis gives a holistic picture of what goes on in a visit to a site, provides a context to page viewing and relates actions to an

Figure 7.5 Percentage distribution of page views by hour of day of download by type of academic organisation

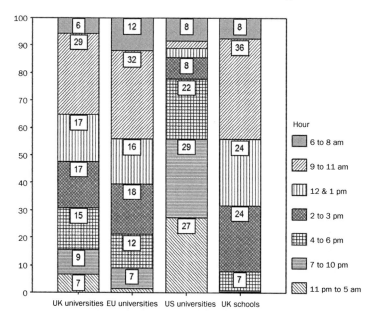

Figure 7.6 Page view time across types of academic organisation

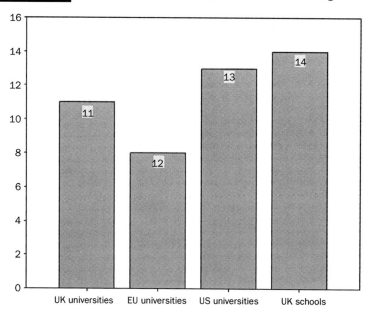

information-seeking event. Figure 7.7 examines day-of-the-week session distribution for educational organisations. There is not a great deal of difference here except that there were fewer session visits from schools at the weekend (when they were probably closed).

Figure 7.8 provides a great example of the power of DLA to produce complex cross-analyses. It shows, for UK sessions, page views by hour, according to the type of organisation through which users accessed the site. Compared with other IP providers, commercial users and internet providers showed the most use after 7 pm (between one-quarter to one-third). Compared with commercial users, UK schools and academic organisations recorded a higher use between 9 am and 11 am. About 38 per cent of schools and 24 per cent of academic institutions recorded use between these times, versus 14 per cent of commercial users.

Figures 7.9 to 7.11 look at what we call site penetration, the number of page views made in a session – an 'activity' metric. Figure 7.9 does this for hour of day for just UK academic institutions. There are marginally more active sessions conducted between 4 pm and 6 pm. The period

Figure 7.7 Percentage distribution of sessions by day of week across academic organisations

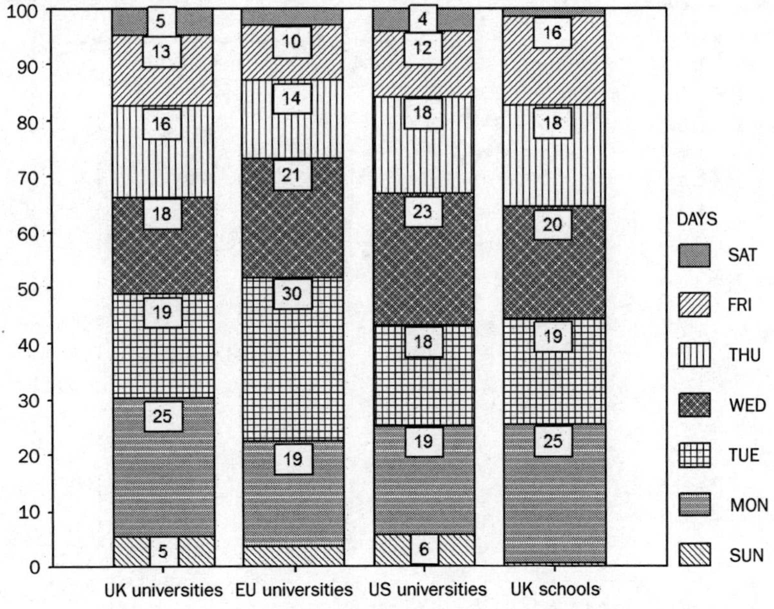

Figure 7.8 Percentage distribution of sessions by hour of day across type of organisation used to access BL Learning

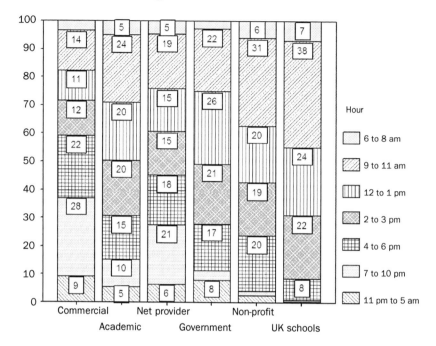

between 6 am to 8 am recorded a high percentage of sessions just viewing two or three pages – nearly half (43 per cent) of the sessions at this time saw two or three pages being viewed. Perhaps academics were checking for updates before the start of the day?

Figure 7.10 also concerns site penetration, but this time by type of organisation used to access BL Learning. Sessions conducted by academic organisations recorded the greatest number of views in a session, with 53 per cent viewing two or more pages, while net/ISP sessions viewed the least – only about 45 per cent of this group viewed two or more pages in a session. UK schools performed very similarly to academic institutions in general, and about 54 per cent of UK schools viewing BL Learning viewed two or more pages in a session.

Looking at academic sessions only, 61 per cent of UK users viewed two or more pages in a session (Figure 7.11). US universities viewed the least number of pages and just 49 per cent of these sessions viewed two or more pages. About 54 per cent of school sessions viewed only one page.

Figure 7.9 Percentage distribution of views in a session by hour of day for UK academic sessions

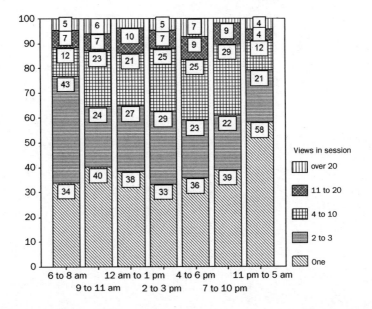

Figure 7.10 Percentage distribution of views in a session by type of organisation used to access BL Learning

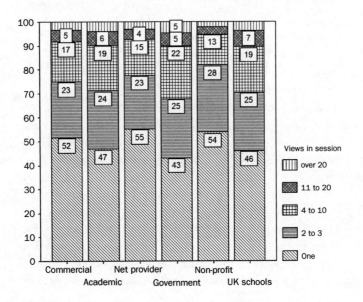

Figure 7.11 Percentage distribution of page views in a session across type of academic organisation

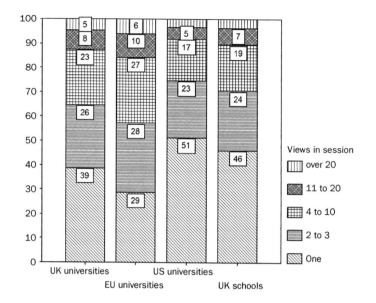

Figure 7.12 moves the analysis on to session time. In terms of session duration across academic organisations, again UK schools recorded the longest session times: 82 per cent were 30 seconds or longer, compared with 75 per cent for UK university sessions.

As mentioned at the beginning of this chapter, logs also provide information on how the virtual user searches and navigates the digital space. Thus, the search facility is prominent on the BL Learning page and it comes as a surprise perhaps that only about 10 per cent of sessions saw the facility being used. In addition, there was not much variation between organisation types (Figure 7.13). The usage distribution of the search facility within sessions was similar.

Referrer link analyses (Figures 7.14 to 7.16) yield insightful data on the behaviour of the virtual user in regard to what site (and type of site) they arrived from. Figure 7.14 shows the number of pages viewed in a session by referrer link used. People arriving via blog-type links (e.g. Wikipedia, Facebook and blogs) were most likely to view more than one page: 82 per cent did so, with 59 per cent viewing four or more pages. Previous research indicates that people using a search engine are more likely to be 'bouncers'. This was seen in the logs as those coming in via a search engine were most likely to view just one page – two-thirds (66 per cent)

Figure 7.12 Percentage distribution of session time across types of academic organisation

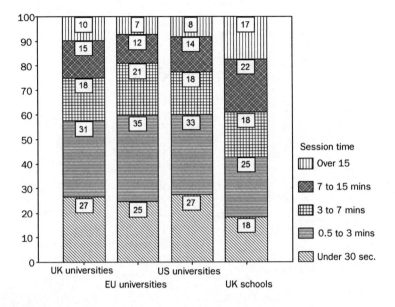

Figure 7.13 Percentage distribution of the usage of the BL Learning search facility by organisational type

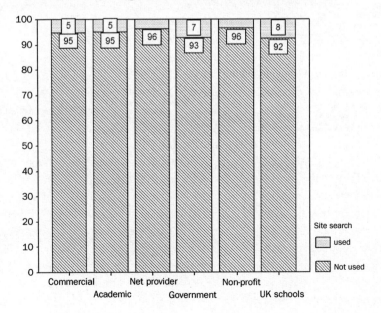

Figure 7.14 Percentage distribution of page views in a session across referrer type

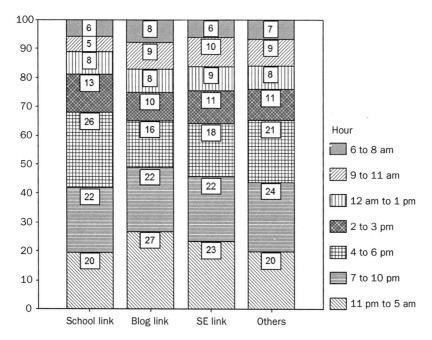

Figure 7.15 Median number of pages viewed in a session by referrer link and organisation type used to access BL Learning

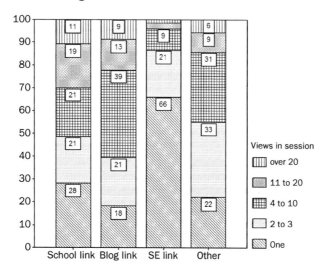

Figure 7.16 Percentage distribution of session time across referrer type

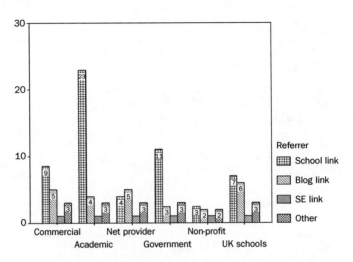

did so. With regards to BL Learning pages, those coming to the site from a blog-type link or a school link were relatively 'sticky' and went on to explore additional pages on the site.

Figure 7.15 examines the number of pages viewed in a session (median) across two groupings: referrer link and organisation used to access the service grouping. In all organisational groupings, those users that found the site using a search engine were on average likely to view just one page. It seems likely that these users were feeding off the hits returned by the search engine and cycling through them to find the information they wanted. Those sessions coming in via a school link recorded the most hits and on average viewed ten pages. In looking at UK schools, those entering the BL Learning pages either by a blog-type link or a school link recorded a relatively high usage of about 6–7 views in a session.

Sessions generated by a search engine link recorded the shortest sessions – about one-third lasted under 30 seconds. This compares with about one-quarter (23 per cent) for other referrer links (Figure 7.16). Links from schools recorded longer sessions and 19 per cent lasted over 15 minutes.

Search term used

For those people arriving at the BL Learning directory, popular search expressions used included: 'suffragists', 'medieval realms', 'sounds familiar', 'medieval food', 'beowulf', 'research ideas', 'medieval foods', 'medieval patterns', 'research ideas', 'muscle men', 'viking words', 'causes of youth crime', 'emily davison', 'shorthand alphabet', 'information on anne frank', etc.

Most search expressions were unique or rarely repeated, such as 'british nobleman hung in united kingdom for treason' (it should be pointed out, however, that this is not a typical search expression). Individual words will of course, be repeated in a number of different search strings, hence the word 'medieval' will appear in a variety of search strings.

We can compare the differing strategies used to search an internal and external search engine. Thus we might be interested in the number of words used in a search expression, first for the British Library internal search engine and then for expressions used to find the British Library site via a web search engine (for this analysis we have used Google and Yahoo only). Of course, the number of search words used does not necessarily tell us how complicated a search expression is. Wordy expressions may include a large proportion of common words such as 'the', 'of' and so on. Nonetheless, it is a metric that is relatively easy to generate and hence is provided here.

The most apparent difference was the higher levels of single word searching used for searching internally, between half to three-quarters of search expressions were composed only of a single word as compared with just 10 per cent for search engine expressions. The most probable reason for this is the number of search expressions that just had 'British Library' (19 per cent of web search expressions) or expressions that included 'British Library' in the search phrase (8 per cent). Many users (26 per cent) were using an internet-wide search facility to find the British Library site by using variations of the search expression 'British Library'; as this is a two-word search string, it will inevitably push up the percentage of two-word search string searches. A question remains as to why users are including or are just searching for the British Library site. It is possible that users are finding that search engines are not listing British Library links in response to a search query.

Figures 7.17 and 7.18 show the number of words used in a search expression by type of organisation used to access the site, first for the British Library internal search engine and then for expressions used to find the British Library site via a web search engine (for this analysis we have used Google and Yahoo only). The figures also show differences between user groups. For example, academics appear to use fewer words

Figure 7.17 Number of words used in a search expression by type of organisation used to access the site – British Library site search

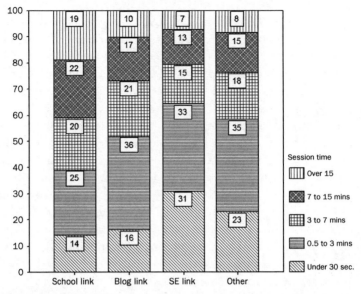

Figure 7.18 Number of words used in a search expression by type of organisation used to access the site – web search engine

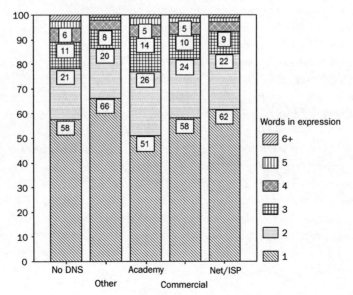

in a search engine query, but are likely to use more words when using the internal search engine. The reverse was true for net/ISP users.

Figure 7.19 and 7.20 give the same type of information broken down by type of academic organisation. The UK schools figure looks high in terms of the number of words used. However, this was influenced by one user trying out different variations of the same search query. These were: 'what does medievil means', 'medival', 'what does medival mean', 'what does medieval realms means', 'what does medieval means', 'what does medieval mean'.

Users from US universities were more likely to use a greater number of words in a search query. This was true for expressions entered into a web search engine, but not for the British Library search facility. UK-based academics were more likely to use a greater number of words on the British Library's search facility compared with other groups; 56 per cent used two or more words compared with about 40 per cent for other groups. However, UK academic users were no different from EU users and used fewer words than US users when using a search engine to access the British Library. Further research showed that US academics were

Figure 7.19 Number of words used in a search expression by type of academic organisation – British Library site search

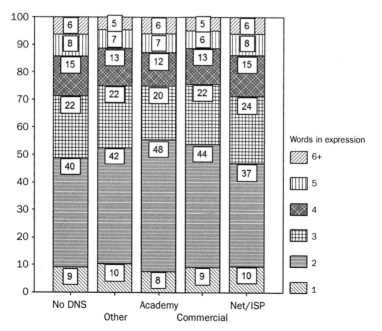

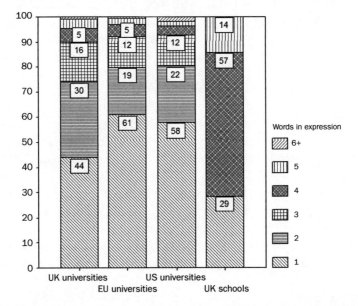

Figure 7.20 Number of words used in a search expression by type of academic organisation – web search engine

more likely than UK or EU academics to search the web using a search expression variant of 'British Library'. Clearly US academics were seeking out accredited British Library information. This is, perhaps, an indication of the standing of the British Library among US academics compared with UK or EU academics.

Micro-analysis: schools

DLA micro-analyses provide a more qualitative and personal methodology for analysing log files. They basically examine the log entries of an (anonymous) individual user's session. To illustrate the methodology, three school users of BL Learning were selected from the log file and their session information analysed. It should be pointed out that the user could be either a student or a teacher. The users' log details are as follows:

■ *User 1*: This user accessed the British Library service on 30 April at about 2 pm (Table 7.1). The (anonymised) DNS of the user was XXX.tameside.sch.uk. The user arrived at the service from a Google link. Their search expression in Google was 'britain in the 1970s' and the Google link took the user to the page 'collections/britirish/

modbrichron_70'. The user did not go on to view any additional pages. Table 7.1 summarises the data of this specific search.

- *User 2*: The DNS of the second user was XXX.pocklington.e-yorks .sch.uk. This user accessed the British Library service on 18 April at about 1:30 pm (Table 7.1). The user came into the service via a Google images link. The search expression of Google images is not recorded in the logs. The use of Google image searching is novel and previous studies by the CIBER team have not found this type of searching. However, image or picture searching may well appeal to those users who are less than 14 years old. The user viewed first one page 'Learning/histcitizen/appeasement', then returned to Google images and subsequently viewed a second page 'Onlinegallery/features/frontpage/peace'. There was approximately a ten-second gap between the first and second page. The user did not go on to view any additional pages.

- *User 3*: The DNS of the user was XXX.tameside.sch.uk. This DNS was recorded as having used the British Library service first on 24 April at around 2:45 pm and then on 30 April at about 10:45 am (Table 7.1). On the first visit, the user came into the service via a Google image link. The search expression of Google images is not recorded in the logs. The user viewed the page 'Learning/images/medeval/patterns/large4390'. On the second visit, the user employed a Google search. Their search

Table 7.1 Session information from three school users of BL Learning

User/DNS	Date/time	View	Search engine	Search expression
1 tameside.sch.uk	30-Apr-07 13:59:38	Collections/britirish/ modbrichron_70	Google	britain in the 1970s
2 pocklington.e-yorks.sch.uk	18-Apr-07 13:33:45	Learning/histcitizen/ appeasement	Google Images	n/a
	18-Apr-07 13:33:54	Onlinegallery/features/ frontpage/peace	Google Images	n/a
3 tameside.sch.uk	24-Apr-07 14:42:20	Learning/images/medeval/ patterns/large4390	GoogleI mages	n/a
	30-Apr-07 10:45:00	Learning/histcitizen/fpage/ frontpagehome	Google	front page newspaper
	30-Apr-07 10:45:34	Learning/histcitizen/21cc/ citizenship		n/a

expression was 'front page newspaper' and the Google link took them to the page 'Learning/histcitizen/fpage/ frontpagehome'. The user then navigated by a British Library site link to the page 'Learning/histcitizen/21cc/citizenship'. There was approximately a half-minute (34-second) gap between the first and second page viewed. The user did not go on to view any additional pages.

As a direct consequence of the findings of the micro-analyses it was decided to examine and compare the grouping of those sessions that had used a search engine (either Yahoo or Google) to search for images versus those that did not (Figure 7.21). About 40 per cent of UK schools found content in the learning directory by using a search engine image search (Yahoo and Google only); this compares with about 10 per cent for other directories. Further, about half of US (47 per cent) and EU universities (47 per cent) accessed the learning directory using a search engine image search (Yahoo and Google only). This was true of about 30 per cent of UK universities.

Sessions where a search engine image search was used were likely to be shorter than Yahoo and Google sessions not using an image search and were more likely to view just one page in a session. About three-quarters

Figure 7.21 Use of Yahoo and Google image search by academic status of user

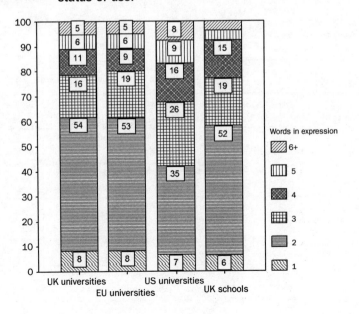

of sessions using an image search viewed one page; this was true of just 57 per cent of Google and Yahoo sessions not using an image search.

Conclusions

By reference to a recent CIBER study of the BL Learning website, we have illustrated what kinds of rich-picture analyses DLA can furnish in respect to use and users of a library service. In regards to this particular service, we can say the site succeeds in that it records the high use we are coming to expect of scholarly sites. It is particularly good to see this is the case with a site aimed at a younger group of researchers/learners. The raw figures are impressive, with 2.5 million pages used in a single month. Findings of special interest were:

- *High proportion of overseas use*: UK academics accounted for just one in ten page views, while UK users accounted for one-third of views. Nearly half of the academic use of the BL Learning site was accounted for by US universities.

- *Low levels of (direct) school use*: School use accounted for 2.5 per cent of BL Learning and 1.6 per cent of non BL Learning use. The survey period included a holiday period; allowing for this fact it might be expected that UK use in term time would make up about 5 per cent of BL Learning use. This is partly explained by the fact that most people searched the site from home.

- *Strong subject preferences*: Language and literature was, by some margin, the most popular section.

- *Busier users*: Proportionally more BL Learning sessions viewed four or more pages compared with other directories.

- *Search engine users*: Most people found the site this way and an associated questionnaire showed search engines were particularly popular with children aged between 12 and 15; however most did not go on to use the British Library's internal engine. The internal search facility is fairly prominent on the BL Learning page (and British Library homepage) and about 10 per cent of sessions saw the facility used.

- *Brand awareness*: Large US use suggests the British Library has a digital brand presence there. More generally, variations on the word string 'British Library' occurred in one-fifth of all search engine search expressions. This shows a degree of brand awareness and a keenness to find the British Library site.

- *Visual use*: There was suggestive evidence that the Google images search was attracting interest among young scholars.

In this chapter we have really only touched upon what DLA can show and more information can be found in Nicholas and Rowlands (2008). Details of individual studies conducted employing DLA can be found on the CIBER website (*www.ucl.ac.uk/slais/research/ciber/*).

Acknowledgments

Gratitude is expressed to the British Library and JISC for funding the BL Learning study.

Bibliography

Alexander, R. (2008) 'Taking the pulse of the economy', available at: *http://news.bbc.co.uk/1/hi/business/7380835.stm* (accessed 20 May 2007).

Nicholas, D. and Rowlands, I. (eds) (2008) *Digital Consumers*, London: Facet.

Rowlands, I., Nicholas, D., Huntington, P., Williams, P., Gunter, B., Tenopir, C., Fieldhouse, P., Withey, R., Jamali H. R. and Dobrowolski, T. (2007) 'The information behaviour of the researcher of the future (GoogleGeneration)', available at: *http://www.ucl.ac.uk/slais/research/ciber/downloads/ggexecutive.pdf* (accessed 14 December 2007).

Tenopir, C., Read, E., Manoff, M., Baker, G., Nicholas, D. and King, D. (2007) 'What usage data tell us about our users?' In *Proceedings of Online Information 2007*, London: Incisive Media, pp. 80–6.

Part 3
Behind the evaluation curtain

8

The pushmepullyou of design and evaluation

Ann Blandford and David Bainbridge

Introduction

In the development of digital libraries, there is a constant tension between a system-led approach of building that which is possible and a user-led approach of building that which is needed. There are many factors influencing the design and user experience of digital libraries, including traditions in librarianship and publishing, technology conventions (e.g. interoperability standards), users' expectations and their information needs. Here, we interpret the term 'need' fairly loosely to include, for example, the desire to be entertained through stories, music or multimedia.

Users' information needs, whether for particular facts, improved understanding or entertainment, do not exist in isolation, but arise in the context of their broader activities (such as writing a paper, planning a course of medical treatment, preparing a legal case or occupying leisure time). In this chapter, we consider how to establish user needs for digital libraries, recognising that those needs are situated within a broader context, both physical and activity-based.

Digital libraries have not emerged and evolved only in response to pre-existing user needs; they are also a result of technical innovation and the recognition of new possibilities. The name 'digital library' hints at an evolution that started in the library, with quality-controlled, structured collections of digital documents. Research digital libraries have expanded horizons to include novel interaction mechanisms (e.g. techniques for sorting images by similarity (Pickering and Rüger, 2003) or retrieving music by singing, as discussed below). We discuss the role of innovation in creating new possibilities that may address previously unrecognised user needs.

If they are to be taken up and used, new digital library technologies must not only address an existing or emergent user need (in the broad sense defined above); they must also be usable. We present approaches to evaluating the usability of particular digital library technologies.

These different forces (needs, possibilities and evaluations) result in a co-evolution of design and use that can result in more usable and useful digital libraries.

The user-led view: what do users need and what do they do?

To understand users' needs and identify new user-centred design possibilities, it is necessary to study the acquisition and use of information within the context of people's activities and situations. There are three common approaches to find out what people do and how they think about their needs: asking them (interviews and surveys), observing them, and gathering indirect data from them (e.g. transaction logs and participant diaries).

Because 'finding information' is rarely people's primary activity, information-seeking activities are typically interleaved with many other activities, and it can be difficult to organise observations of people finding information in their natural situations. For example, the activity of writing this chapter involved significant information-seeking activity, sometimes centring on particular concepts and sometimes on particular authors whose work was potentially relevant to the narrative, but each information-seeking episode was limited to a few minutes, while the writing took place over several days. Digital libraries have made it possible to engage in much more tightly interleaved patterns of activity, involving thinking, writing, seeking and reading, which previously would have been more demarcated as different resources were distributed through personal, institutional and public libraries.

In planning a study that involves gathering data from users, it is necessary to consider practicalities as well as the purpose of the study. Blandford et al. (2008a) propose a framework for planning studies based around the purpose of the study; resources and constraints that limit what is possible; ethical considerations; techniques for data gathering and analysis; and requirements of reporting. We talk through many of the decisions involved in designing user studies, exemplifying points using illustrative case studies.

Why? The purpose of a user study

Before designing any study, it is important to consider the purpose of the study. The focus in this section is on studies that can identify user needs and hence inform the design of future systems. Thus, the most general question is 'what does the user need of a system?' This general question can form the basis of various more detailed questions. For example, Cunningham et al. (2003) set out to identify the searching and browsing techniques employed by people looking for music so that compatible techniques could be implemented in a system, while Hertzum (2003) focused on the ways that people formulate their search requests to a film librarian (mediating between the people looking for films and the film library contents), to inform the design of future metadata for a film library. Similarly, Blandford et al. (2008b) identified the concepts (e.g. 'author', 'idea', 'domain') that people work with in a library, to highlight possible changes to metadata or interaction structures for digital libraries.

In planning a study, it is necessary not just to articulate its purpose, but also to consider practicalities, including where studies can take place, when, who can participate, and what forms of data can be gathered.

Where? The location of a user study

Many studies of information-seeking have taken place in locations where people are expected to look for information. For example, Stelmaszewska and Blandford (2004) studied people's behaviour in a physical library with a view to identifying requirements for digital libraries. Focusing on the criteria people used for assessing relevance of materials, participants were asked to think aloud while looking for the information they needed; at the same time, the authors took notes on their movements around the library, which books or journals they selected, and the criteria on which they evaluated materials. Similarly, Cunningham et al. (2003) have studied how people look for music in music stores and libraries. For this study, focus groups, semi-structured interviews and observations were conducted to build up a rich understanding of how people look for (rather than evaluate) music. Others have studied information needs and practices in the work setting, which makes it possible to relate the information-seeking to the broader work context. For example, Kuhlthau and Tama (2001) studied lawyers' information needs, while Attfield and Dowell (2003) studied the information practices of journalists. Work-based studies have typically involved interviews, with or without observation, to better understand the nature of the work and also to gather data efficiently (avoiding spending too much time observing activities that have minimal relevance to information-seeking).

When? Concurrent and retrospective data gathering

Studies of information needs and behaviours may involve concurrent or retrospective gathering of data. Retrospective data gathering is prone to bias in that people report their perceptions, rather than necessarily what they actually do. However, this may be what is required; for example Adams et al. (2005) studied users' attitudes to the introduction of digital libraries into hospitals. In this case, the focus was not on how people accessed the available resources, but on how they *perceived* the resources as changing their roles and relationships (with other clinicians and with patients). As such, interviews were an appropriate means of gathering data. Lee and Downie (2004) reported on a survey of the users of music information retrieval systems in which they probed people's music background (e.g. singing ability and instruments played), their interest in music and their usual sources of music information. By including many open-ended questions, they were able to identify practices (notably the use of reviews, ratings and recommendations from other people) that highlight requirements for future music information retrieval systems.

Concurrent data gathering may be achieved through naturalistic observation (e.g. in libraries or shops as discussed above), by recruiting participants to study and asking them to engage in information-seeking activities (as described in more detail below), or by asking people to record their own activities in a diary (e.g. Vakkari, 2001).

Who? Recruiting participants

Whatever the form of data being gathered, except for unobtrusive and anonymised data gathering such as transaction logs (for which the participant population is predetermined), it is important to consider how participants are recruited. If the interest is in systems for use by a general population then, as far as possible, a broad sample of participants will be recruited to be as representative as possible of that general population; for example, Lee and Downie (2004) recruited survey participants from their local university, randomly selecting e-mail addresses from six groups that were organised by sex and professional status to ensure coverage across the university population; they also recruited from the broader population, but in this case it was not possible to be systematic about the sampling. For studying specialist tools, it is important to recruit participants from the relevant user population; for example, Makri et al. (2008) worked with academic lawyers to study their information practices and needs when working with legal digital libraries; this study recruited a 'vertical slice' of participants, from undergraduate students to professors.

How? Instructing participants

It is also necessary to consider what instructions are given to participants. For a survey, the focus will be on the design of the questions. For a diary study, the concern is with clear instructions for participants, to ensure that they understand what kinds of data they should be recording, and when. For any study involving a concurrent protocol (e.g. observation or think-aloud), it is necessary to consider what tasks are given to participants. When gathering user requirements, these will typically be as general as possible. For example, Makri et al. (2008) asked participants to formulate their own current information need, or to recall a recent information need, and to look for documents that addressed their own need. For identifying user needs, it is rarely appropriate to specify user tasks in detail, as it is important that users' activities in the study are as natural as possible. More detailed task instructions are often useful when evaluating particular systems, as discussed below.

Data collection and analysis

What data are recorded and how they are analysed will depend on the study type and purpose. Many data-gathering approaches limit the possible forms of recording and analysing data. For example, think-aloud and observational studies yield rich, qualitative data well suited to forms of qualitative data analysis that allow new and unexpected themes to emerge from the data, whereas questionnaire data will typically be more amenable to quantitative analysis (e.g. for establishing correlations or trends). Lee and Downie (2004) focus on reporting quantitative results from their survey data; in contrast, Adams et al. (2005) develop a rich account of how digital libraries have changed clinicians' ways of working, and relate their findings to the literature on communities of practice (Wenger, 1999). This has helped to account for the roles of situated learning and evolving practices in the ways that people adopt or reject digital libraries that have been deployed in their workplaces.

Triangulating across data sources

It is also possible, and often fruitful, to combine data gathering and analysis approaches, either asynchronously or synchronously.

Asynchronous combination, or 'triangulation' (Mackay and Fayard, 1997), typically involves relating the findings from one approach to those from another, to develop a richer understanding of not only what is done but also why. For example, transaction log analysis (e.g. Jones et al., 2000; Nicholas et al., 2006) provides information about the behaviours of a large number of users of a system, filtering out the broader context within which those interactions take place; however, it provides no information about people's motivations, goals or knowledge. Interviews (e.g. Adams et al., 2005) or think-aloud studies (e.g. Blandford et al., 2001) with a representative sample of users of that system can provide a complementary view, yielding insights into how people perceive the system and what they use it for. Illustrating the approach of gathering and relating several kinds of data, Vakkari (2001) describes a study that involved triangulating across data sources including interviews, think-aloud protocols, transaction logs and search results (for particular information-seeking episodes). The study also recorded the progress of research over a three-month period, in addition to the participants' searching experiences. By gathering and relating data over an extended period of time for the same group of participants, Vakkari was able to construct a rich account of how search expertise developed over the period of his study.

Synchronous combinations of methods can also yield richer insights than the use of one method alone. Contextual inquiry (Beyer and Holtzblatt, 1998) is an example of synchronous combination. Contextual inquiry involves observing people working and recording how that work is performed, and also asking probing questions about the motivations and context for the work, to build up a richer understanding of the nature of the work and participants' perceptions of the work and the systems they use to perform that work. Makri et al. (2008) adapted the contextual inquiry approach: rather than observing people's work for an indefinite period, they scheduled focused information-seeking observation sessions. Within these sessions, they asked participants to think aloud while working and interjected with occasional probing questions to gain a deeper understanding of participants' motivations and how they understood the systems they were using. This scheduling of study sessions was necessary because, as discussed previously, it is difficult to time genuinely naturalistic observation.

From data to needs

Studies of users' needs may highlight both future possibilities and features to be avoided in the future. For example, Bainbridge et al. (2003) and Hertzum (2003) identified ways that people describe what they are looking for, with a view to supporting such searches in future systems. However, empirical techniques for identifying users' needs may not always highlight novel possibilities. For example, if we reflect on our own behaviour we might recall incidents where we have asked a friend something like 'you know that song: the one that goes...', followed by a more or less tuneful approximation of the song in question; yet Cunningham et al. (2003) did not observe people singing to find music in a shop or a public library, while Bainbridge et al. (2003) studied the queries people submitted to Google Answers (which only supports textual queries), so there were no examples of people singing in their study. Such intuitions may also lead to innovative approaches to designing interactions with digital libraries. In the next section, we describe the development of a music digital library, starting from the intuition that singing has great potential as an interaction technique, but highlighting challenges raised by the real-world practicalities of implementation that can sometimes have an impact on the quality of the user experience.

The system-led view: technology innovation

MELDEX is an innovative music digital library system, which in addition to offering commonplace digital library capabilities such as textual searching and browsing, also allows users to sing their queries. Indeed it was the first ever publicly available digital library with such capabilities. Its development spans over five years of work, encapsulated by three distinct versions of the system. In relation to its design, a theme that emerged over this time was the impact that designing for current technologies had on the user experience, particularly the issues that result from working at the limits of available technology in terms of audio capture and playback in a web browser. We expand upon this below as we describe the development of the system.

Withholding the technical complications for now, Figures 8.1 and 8.2 are representative snapshots from the original system. Figure 8.1a shows the query page to a folk song collection of nearly 10,000 songs drawn from the UK, North America, Germany, China and Ireland. The user can select to search just one of these sub-collections, or all of them together. Figure 8.1b shows the result of submitting a sung query, with the familiar ranked list of matching documents presented: in this case songs, ordered in terms of the smallest possible number of edits (add a note, delete a note, change a note pitch) that are needed to make it match an excerpt of song. From here, one can bring up the song as sheet music or play the audio file.

Putting technical complications back in the mix (and in context), the first version of the music digital library was implemented in 1998[1] and audio support on computers followed very much along the proprietary lines of the operating system used: Microsoft had the WAV format, Apple had AIFF, Sun had AU. Linux was in its infancy in terms of audio support – installing device drivers was notoriously difficult and in some instances trying to access audio recording or playback could cause a machine to lock up so badly that only a power-cycle was enough to restore the machine.

In a web browser, primary support for audio playback was through downloading the entire file and then launching the appropriate 'helper' application as designated by the file's MIME type. For audio recording, there was no off-the-shelf solution available. Even embedding a Java applet within the page would not achieve this as audio recording was not supported in Java at that time – indeed we would have to wait until Java 1.3, some years off, before the much touted Java Sound API was supported.

This situation affected the user interface. For audio capture, we decided to rely on the user using an external application, native to their computer platform, to record a query. Saved as a file, this could then be loaded in through the web page (shown in Figure 8.1a, prompted

Figure 8.1 Meldex, the music digital library: (a) query page from the original version; (b) sample result of a musical query

(a)
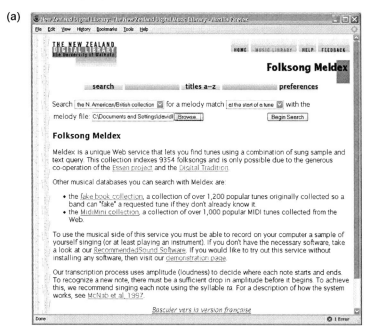

(b)
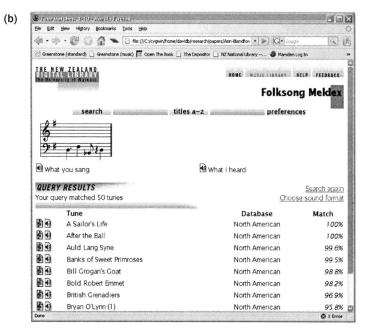

Figure 8.2 (a) Selecting an audio format for playback; (b) the preferences page

(a)

(b)

'melody file:', and accompanied by a browse button). Help file text recommended suitable audio recording software for each platform, including links to the relevant download pages. Audio playback followed similar reasoning, relying on a native application on the user's computer to perform the operation, again assisted by help text, although in practice playback has always been better set up by default than recording software on personal computers. To mitigate the effect of these proprietary file formats, we designed the music digital library server to be agnostic about file formats, converting to a canonical form for internal use. The first time the user selected some audio to listen to, an intermediate page was generated (shown in Figure 8.2a) asking them to choose a suitable output format from a given list (again, accompanying help text was provided to assist users unfamiliar with the terms displayed).

Additional features to the interfaces included a preference page (Figure 8.2b) through which the user could control search parameters, such as where the query occurred in the song. At the top of the query results page (top left of Figure 8.1b), the interface displayed an excerpt of music notation that represented how the computer had interpreted the musical query. This was produced by applying signal processing techniques to the raw audio file to establish a symbolic representation, which could then be rendered as music notation. The algorithm needed clearly accented notes to perform well, and so was not guaranteed to always capture the intent of the user. For this reason the music notation was displayed, along with two further links: 'what you sang' and 'what I heard', where the latter played a synthesised version of the symbolic representation the music digital library had derived. The intention of the 'what I heard' feature was to assist users not familiar with music notation.

Having developed this version of the interface, we released it publicly, and invited people to try it out. It generated much interest – far more than we had anticipated, even gaining coverage in the press, radio and television internationally. However, there were several aspects to the design that we were dissatisfied with, and in light of the interest shown we decided to focus on what we considered the greatest impediment to a successful user experience – the recording of audio – the rationale being that the user who does not get past the step of recording a sung query will not get to experience the primary capability of the library.

Figure 8.3 is a snapshot taken from the second version of the music digital library. The principal workflow to the digital library remains largely unchanged: submit a query to get search results, browse the collection

Figure 8.3   Recording audio natively within a web browser

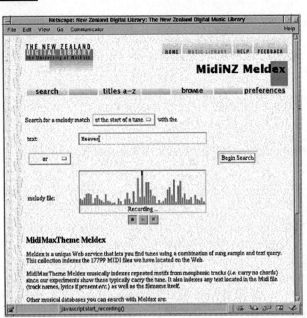

alphabetically by title, or view the preferences page. However, now when a user wants to enter a query, they click on the record button and sing directly. Orange bars, displayed in real time, provide feedback as to how the recording process is progressing: the orange bars get tipped with red should the user's singing volume get close to saturating the recording level. Upon completing the query, the user presses the stop button. The sample can be played back by pressing play. From here, pressing submit works as before. The older forms of input from the first version of the library are also available, chosen through the preferences page.

To achieve this direct audio ability we wrote our own plugin using Netscape's LiveConnect technology, customising it for each of the main platforms: Windows, Linux and Mac. At its heart is C code – specific for each platform – that accesses the user's audio hardware. For a user to take advantage of the plugin, they need to download the relevant binary file and install it in Netscape's plugin folder.

In terms of development of the user interface, there was then a hiatus. With the music digital library in this configuration, internally, we ran various musicological research projects based around it. With the advent of Java 1.3, which finally included support for audio recording, focus was once more placed on the interface and the workflow it embodied. By this time we had also performed some transaction log analysis on how people access the music digital library (McPherson and Bainbridge, 2001), the results of which also helped guide the redesign.

Figures 8.4 and 8.5 show the key areas of redevelopment, again focusing around the query page, now expanded to support queries entered by virtual piano keyboard in addition to singing directly. The former removes the possibility of transcription errors in the sung audio but requires the user to have a degree of musical (piano playing) experience (or else a panache for experimentation). Saving and loading queries in both views is also provided. For the sung query view (Figure 8.5a), transcription to symbolic form is now performed on the client side, by the applet (Figure 8.5b). This provides a faster round-trip time for the user to discover if the sung query is being decoded correctly, and the query can be re-sung again if necessary.

To achieve this in a web environment, the applet needs to request a change in security levels to permit audio recording (without such security protection, any web page could secretly embed an invisible java applet to record the user). This is accomplished through Sun's signed Java applet capability, and results in a popup window appearing to the user when they first access the page with the applet, requesting the change in security settings.

Figure 8.4 Java applet-based symbolic query interface

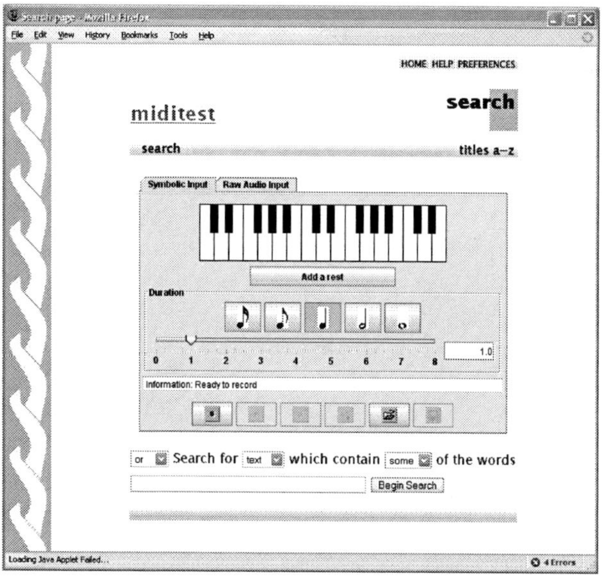

Figure 8.5 (a) Recording a sung query with the Java applet;
(b) viewing the transcribed query client side

(a)

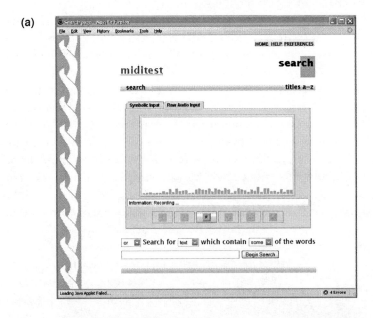

(b)

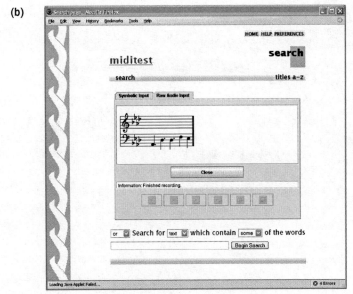

By moving to a Java applet, cross-platform and browser support was improved, but not a complete success in all cases. For instance, at the time we did this work (2003) the Java runtime available for the Mac was not even Java 1.2 compliant, let alone Java 1.3. Indeed, Apple never brought out a version of Java 1.3 for Mac OS 9, so the applet we developed simply would not work there. The situation is much improved with Mac OS X.

Using a Java applet also lowered the software entry requirement for the user. No longer did they have to know how to find an application for recording audio on their computer (and install one if nothing suitable was present); nor did they have to mess around with binary files specific to the Netscape plugin mechanism and place them in the right folder on their computer. Now, the majority of internet-capable computers have Java already installed. In terms of the user's experience, this equates to an individual (in the majority of cases) visiting the music digital library site, and – upon granting the change in security – being presented with a screen similar to Figure 8.5a. As with other websites one may have experienced, for the user who does not already have the Java plugin, the music digital library presents a page that instead activates the browser's plugin installer feature, from which installation of Java is a few clicks away.

In developing the third version of the music digital library, we were also able to take advantage of the results of some evaluation and analysis. The study by Bainbridge et al. (2003) has shown that in a broad range of music information retrieval tasks, the person posing the query can often (over 80 per cent of the time) provide some form of bibliographic information about it: a remembered fragment of title or lyrics, the year it was a written (plus or minus a year or two). This led us to add a complementary text-searching capability into the music digital library: a query could be formulated by separate text or sung query, or in combination. Browsing by textual metadata was already supported. Figure 8.5a, incidently, shows the combined text and audio search page.

In terms of workflow, this was by far the largest revision to the music digital library between versions 2 and 3. A study of the transaction logs (McPherson and Bainbridge, 2001) prompted some minor revisions to the layout and expression of information. For instance, when performing a text-only search, we noted that users sometimes also set the field 'search anywhere'. This field was in fact associated with the musical search, and so carried no meaning in a text-only query; however, while physically located with the part of the interface capturing audio, we realised it was clearly a source of confusion and something that rewording helped clarify.

On a negative front, we found that encapsulating the audio recording and playback as an applet embedded within the larger digital library framework, which was a more traditional HTML web-form based implementation, led to a disconnect that curtailed how the user interface could operate. The heart of the matter lay in where information about the state of the interface lay – in theory this could be split arbitrarily between the web form as represented by the document object model (DOM) or the Java applet – and the mechanisms available to communicate between the two. All the main browsers support Java accessing the DOM (through Javascript), but unfortunately not all browsers at the time supported communication the other way: Javascript calling methods within the Java applet. In the design, therefore, the only option was to have the Java applet call Javascript to effectively push out the data to be stored in the DOM.

Most of our interaction needs could be met this way, with one notable exception. When the users pressed the record button, sang their query and then pressed the search button (rather than pressing the stop button first), we were not able to stop the recording and have the transcribed query pushed out to the web form. Despite this being an extremely natural way for a user to formulate and then initiate a query, we were not able to support it as this would require Javascript calling Java, and we were not able to do this reliably for all browsers. However, we *were* able to detect that the Java applet was still recording (this state information is pushed out to the web form when the record button is pressed) and generate an alert window, prompting the user to press 'stop' before submitting the query.

A decade on from when we first started the music digital library project, MELDEX (now in its third incarnation) remains available online for people to try out (see *www.nzdl.org/meldex*).

Usable and useful? Evaluating digital libraries

In the previous section, we briefly sketched how evaluations of earlier versions of MELDEX were used to drive some aspects of redesign. There are many possible forms of evaluation, and many possible evaluation questions; for example, for evaluating the MELDEX system, possible evaluation questions might include:

- Information retrieval (IR) evaluation questions such as what proportion of user queries return the intended result, and how many results are returned, on average, for each query. These questions are typically best addressed by gathering quantitative data about success rates, often measured in terms of recall and precision (Tague-Sutcliffe, 1992). Analysis of recall and precision rates was used to evaluate the capabilities of the core music information retrieval algorithm used in MELDEX (McNab and Smith, 2000). This analysis proved extremely useful in choosing what features of the searching algorithm were configurable by the user through the preferences pages, and what default values to give them.

- Questions about the usability of the interface, including any difficulties or misunderstandings participants may have experienced, or inefficient navigation through the system. As noted above, transaction log analysis helped us fine-tune some aspects of the interface. We also conducted an expert review of the system (Blandford and Stelmaszewska, 2002).

- User satisfaction questions, e.g. about which interaction mechanism a user prefers and why. Such questions are typically addressed through a debriefing questionnaire or interview.

Questions about usability and use, and the methods used to address them, have much in common with the methods for establishing user needs, but focus directly on particular designs rather than the broader collection of tools that people might use to achieve their goals.

Whitefield et al. (1991) identify two dimensions on which evaluation studies vary: whether they involve the participation of users, and whether they involve access to a running (or prototype) system. Once a system exists to evaluate, it is usual to involve the system in the evaluation. A third dimension on which studies involving users may also vary is whether they take place in a controlled environment (such as a usability laboratory) or in the situation of the user (e.g. the workplace).

Studies which do not involve the user are forms of expert review. These reviews may be more or less structured. For example, Hartson et al. (2004) conducted an expert review of the Network Computer Science Technical Reference Library, which involved a team of usability experts defining a set of user tasks then 'walking through' those tasks while identifying possible user difficulties. They found two main categories of difficulties in the system: the structure of interaction was based around system functions rather than user tasks (they highlight particularly the difficulties experienced in submitting documents to the library); and the vocabulary used was typically designer rather than user-centred.

Vocabulary problems are usually more readily addressed than interaction problems, but both highlight redesign possibilities.

Expert reviews are relatively inexpensive (in time and resources) to run, and can be used to eliminate the more obvious usability problems from a system before it is released to the intended user population. However, they rely on the experts' understanding not only of usability but also of how people search for and work with information. To test systems further, it is necessary to involve users in the evaluation. If evaluation studies are run in a laboratory, participants need to be given instructions on what to do. If particular system features are the focus of the evaluation study, participants should be guided towards using those features, and given an appropriate level of detail about what is being sought or expected. The evaluator also has to design the tasks that participants are to perform. These may be quite focused; for example, Dillon and Song (1997) specified in detail what information participants were required to find. Alternatively, they may be relatively naturalistic; for example, Blandford et al. (2001) asked participants to define their own information need. As most participants in that study were research students with interests in the domain of the libraries being evaluated, it was relatively easy for them to articulate a current information need that was supported by the digital libraries being studied. There is also a question of what data are to be gathered and analysed. This will depend on the purpose of the evaluation study. It is important to devise tasks that will elicit data that address the evaluation questions of the current study, and to select appropriate data-gathering techniques.

Probably the most common approach to evaluation is to identify usability difficulties by asking participants to think aloud while interacting with the system. Thinking aloud in problem-solving (e.g. Ericsson and Simon, 1984) is a well-established process for probing cognition. More generally, think-aloud can be used to elicit people's perceptions of the system they are using. For example, participants can be asked to articulate their goals, their plans for achieving those goals (which are usually only partially formed), their expectations of the effects of actions, their understanding of the current system state, questions, uncertainties and confusions they may experience. Think-aloud data can be invaluable for identifying points in an interaction where people are uncertain or misunderstand aspects of the system design. However, two important features of think-aloud studies are that different evaluators typically draw different inferences from the same data, depending on their individual backgrounds and interests (Hertzum and Jacobsen, 2001), and that what emerges from the think-aloud data will depend on what tasks were set to participants. If the focus is on identifying user difficulties or preferences when achieving well-defined goals then the tasks should be well specified to ensure that participants make use of the system functionality that is of current interest.

If, however, the goal of the study is to discover strengths and limitations of a system more generally, it is important to gather data with real-world validity, and therefore to set tasks that are as naturalistic as possible, as discussed above.

Questions about how systems fit within people's broader lifestyles cannot easily be answered through brief studies, but require different evaluation approaches involving less intensive data gathering over an extended period of time. For example, Marshall (2007) presents a study of the Times News Reader, a specialist application for delivering news content to subscribers. Rather than creating interaction tasks and observing users, Marshall distributed the Times News Reader to participants, and asked them to keep a diary for two weeks, before completing a survey and taking part in a debriefing interview. This approach enabled her to address several questions about the use of the system within the context of people's daily lives. In particular, the study highlighted both strengths and limitations of the Times News Reader when compared with printed newspapers and web versions of newspapers that suggest design modifications, but also highlight the role for a growing set of tools that provide complementary ways of interacting with news.

Whereas general studies of user needs can often be relatively independent of particular technologies, evaluations of systems focus attention on the strengths and limitations of the systems being evaluated. Limitations represent a more localised form of user needs for revised systems. For example, in the description of the evolution of the MELDEX system, one of the important drivers was recognised problems for users in working with a separate song recorder, and then later in catering for users who could not sing but could play a keyboard: design evolution responded to both user needs (as identified through system evaluations) and new technical possibilities.

Conclusions

We have illustrated a variety of ways of identifying user needs for digital libraries, and highlighted practical considerations that need to be taken into account when designing user studies, whether early in a development process or when evaluating a prototype system. We have also described a design process that was motivated by an intuition and interest in whether singing was a usable and pleasurable way of interacting with a music digital library. This process highlighted how both technical possibilities and technical limitations influence the user experience. Many user needs are technically difficult to address, creating a tension between what is desired and what is possible. But both what is desired and what is possible change over time. There is a co-evolution between design and evaluation, whereby new designs create new opportunities which, in turn, generate new user requirements, leading to yet further new designs. A particular design and evaluation cycle may be initiated by a need or an opportunity, but both need and opportunity are necessary for a development to succeed. Every development must be technically feasible, and must also fulfil some user need, whether or not that need has already been recognised. Both technical innovation and analytical studies have a role to play in the future evolution of digital libraries.

Note

1. This was early days in terms of the web and the technology available. Users were just beginning to find their way around this exponentially expanding digitally linked environment. The World Wide Web Consortium, for instance, had only been going for four years.

Bibliography

Adams, A., Blandford, A. and Lunt, P. (2005) 'Social empowerment and exclusion: A case study on digital libraries', ACM *Transactions on CHI* 12(2): 174–200.

Attfield, S. J. and Dowell, J. (2003) 'Information seeking and use by newspaper journalists', *Journal of Documentation* 59(2): 187–204.

Bainbridge, D., Cunningham, S. J. and Downie, J. S. (2003) 'How people describe their music information needs: A grounded theory analysis of music queries', in *Proceedings of the 2003 International Symposium on Music Information Retrieval, Baltimore, MD, 26–30 October,* available at: *http://ismir2003.ismir.net/papers/Bainbridge.pdf* (accessed 26 November 2008).

Beyer, H. and Holtzblatt, K. (1998) *Contextual Design*, San Francisco, CA: Morgan Kaufmann.

Blandford, A. and Stelmaszewska, H. (2002) 'Usability of musical digital libraries: A multimodal analysis', in *Proceedings of the 2002 International Symposium on Music Information Retrieval, Paris, 13–17 October*, pp. 231–7, available at: *http://ismir2002.ismir.net/proceedings/02-FP07-5.pdf* (accessed 4 May 2009).

Blandford, A., Stelmaszewska, H. and Bryan-Kinns, N. (2001) 'Use of multiple digital libraries: a case study', in *Proceedings of the 1st ACM/IEEE-CS Joint Conference on Digital Libraries, Roanoke, VA, 24–28 June*, New York: ACM Press, pp. 179–88.

Blandford, A., Adams, A., Attfield, S., Buchanan, G., Gow, J., Makri, S., Rimmer, J. and Warwick, C. (2008a) 'PRET a rapporter: evaluating digital libraries alone and in context', *Information Processing and Management* 44(1): 4–21.

Blandford, A., Green, T. R. G., Furniss, D. and Makri, S. (2008b) 'Evaluating system utility and conceptual fit using CASSM', *International Journal of Human–Computer Studies* 66(6): 393–409.

Cunningham, S. J., Reeves, N. and Britland, M. (2003) 'An ethnographic study of music information seeking: implications for the design of a music digital library', in *Proceedings of the 3rd ACM/IEEE-CS Joint Conference on Digital Libraries, Houston, TX, 27–31 May*, New York: ACM Press, pp. 5–16.

Dillon, A. and Song, M. (1997) 'An empirical comparison of the usability for novice and expert searchers of a textual and a graphic interface to an art-resource database', *Journal of Digital Information* 1(1), available at: *http://jodi.tamu.edu/Articles/v01/i01/Dillon/* (accessed 26 November 2008).

Ericsson, K. A. and Simon, H. A. (1984) *Protocol Analysis: Verbal Reports as Data*, Cambridge, MA: MIT Press.

Hartson, H. R., Shivakumar, P. and Pérez-Quiñones, M. A. (2004) 'Usability inspection of digital libraries: A case study', *International Journal of Digital Libraries* 4(2): 108–23.

Hertzum, M. (2003) 'Requests for information from a film archive: A case study of multimedia retrieval', *Journal of Documentation* 59(2): 168–86.

Hertzum, M. and Jacobsen, N. E. (2001) 'The evaluator effect: A chilling fact about usability evaluation methods', *International Journal of Human–Computer Interaction* 13(4): 421–43.

Jones, S., Cunningham, S. J., McNab, R. and Boddie, S. (2000) 'A transaction log analysis of a digital library', *International Journal of Digital Libraries* 3(2): 152–69.

Kuhlthau, C. C. and Tama, S. L. (2001) 'Information search process of lawyers: A call for 'just for me' information services', *Journal of Documentation* 57(1): 25–43.

Lee, J. H. and Downie, J. S. (2004) 'Survey of music information needs, uses, and seeking behaviours: Preliminary findings', in *Proceedings of the 2004 International Symposium on Music Information Retrieval, Barcelona, 10–15 October*, pp. 441–6, available at: *http://ismir2004.ismir.net/proceedings/p081-page-441-paper232.pdf* (accessed 26 November 2008).

Mackay, W. E. and Fayard, A.-L. (1997) 'HCI, natural science and design: A framework for triangulation across disciplines', in *Proceedings of the 2nd Conference on Designing Interactive Systems: Processes, Practices, Methods, and Techniques, Amsterdam, 18–20 August*, New York: ACM Press, pp. 223–34.

Makri, S., Blandford, A. and Cox, A. L. (2008) 'Investigating the information-seeking behaviour of academic lawyers: From Ellis's model to design', *Information Processing and Management* 44(2): 613–34.

Marshall, C. C. (2007) 'The gray lady gets a new dress: a field study of the times news reader', in *Proceedings of the 7th ACM/IEEE-CS Joint Conference on Digital Libraries, Vancouver, BC, 17–23 June*, New York: ACM Press, pp. 259–68.

McNab, R. J. and Smith, L. A. (2000) 'Evaluation of a melody transcription system', in *Proceedings of the IEEE International Conference on Multimedia and Expo, New York City, 30 July to 2 August* (Vol 2) [s. l.], New York: IEEE, pp. 819–22.

McPherson, J. R. and Bainbridge, D. (2001) 'Usage of the MELDEX digital music library', in *Proceedings of the 2001 International Symposium on Music Information Retrieval, Bloomington, IA, 15–17 October*, available at: *http://ismir2001.ismir.net/posters/mcpherson.pdf* (accessed 28 November 2008).

Nicholas, D., Huntington, P., Jamali, H. and Watkinson, A. (2006) 'The information seeking behaviour of the users of digital scholarly journals', *Information Processing and Management* 42(5): 1345–65.

Pickering, M. J. and Rüger, S. (2003) 'Evaluation of key frame-based retrieval techniques for video', *Computer Vision and Image Understanding* 92(2–3): 217–35.

Stelmaszewska, H. and Blandford, A. (2004) 'From physical to digital: A case study of computer scientists' behaviour in physical libraries', *International Journal of Digital Libraries* 4(2): 82–92.

Tague-Sutcliffe, J. (1992) 'The pragmatics of information retrieval experimentation, revisited', *Information Processing and Management* 28(4): 467–90.

Vakkari, P. (2001) 'A theory of the task-based information retrieval process: a summary and generalisation of a longitudinal study', *Journal of Documentation* 57(1): 44–60.

Wenger, E. (1999) *Communities of Practice: Learning, Meaning and Identity*, Cambridge: Cambridge University Press.

Whitefield, A., Wilson, F. and Dowell, J. (1991) 'A framework for human factors evaluation', *Behaviour and Information Technology* 10(1): 65–79.

9

Extending borders: outcomes assessment in the era of digital libraries

Giannis Tsakonas and Christos Papatheodorou

Introduction

The present chapter discusses a critical issue of digital library evaluation, related to the wide impact of the content and services provided by digital libraries. Outcomes assessment is a multidimensional evaluation area that covers the activities of an organisation that hosts or develops a digital library, as well as its users. It is influenced by the audit community in non-financial fields of public administration and ideas such as 'performance audits', 'value for money audits', 'environmental audits', as well as by ideas from the business world such as 'strategic/operational planning' and 'performance indicators' that focus on the deliverables or results of a service or organisation. These influencing domains and ideas consider outcomes assessment as a policy tool for the reorganisation of services with the advantage of associating the well-articulated goals of an organisation with its operational effectiveness. Before any definition, it should be clarified that outcomes assessment is closely related to the institutional objectives, policies or inherent principles of an organisation.

The main targets of an outcomes assessment are thus (a) to validate the outcomes, (b) to define their extent in terms of organisational or system effectiveness – instead of inputs and processes – and correlate them with the user behaviour, and (c) if possible, to compare them with other similar outcomes. Outcomes evaluation has a number of general features of the remark by Kellaghan and Madaus (2000) that 'outcomes may be related to a target, standard of service, or achievement'. However, the range of outcomes is a considerable issue. In this regard, the outcome assessment process aims to link the outcomes of the digital library's operations with the wide aims of the institution or the community it serves. Here, digital library outcomes assessment borrows many elements and considerations from the domain of physical libraries. According to Bertot and McClure (2003) outcomes assessment 'focuses on the extent to which a library's services and/or resources made a difference in the life of the library's individual, group or institutional users'. In a wide sense, digital library services assessment aims to develop skills and competences that improve the performance of the library's users as well as its hosting institution.

Difficulties in assessing outcomes emerge from the multifaceted organisational features and operational norms which affect a variety of policies and which are reflected in different and sometimes contradictory usage behaviours. Moreover, the participation of agents outside the limits of the digital library generates significant ambiguities as regards selecting the most appropriate measurement methodologies and further complicates the outcomes assessment process.

The present chapter aims to provide an insight into the aforementioned problems as well as to analyse the crucial challenges of the outcomes assessment domain. Additionally, one of the main objectives is to present a set of recommendations on how digital libraries and related technologies, such as open access repositories, could expand their current armoury of processes and metrics for obtaining viable and reusable outcome assessment processes.

The challenge of defining outcomes assessment

One of the most significant challenges in outcomes assessment is to define outcomes in a clear and communicative form. In order to perceive outcomes and to distinguish them from outputs, Bertot and McClure (2003) have created a model of the types of evaluation in information organisations. In their model, outcomes are considered to mirror the effect of the produced and delivered library services on the sphere of community, while the service quality concept captures subjective opinions on a personal level. Both outcomes assessment and service quality evaluation are based on the outputs of an operation (resources or services), but are distinguished by the degree of objectivity in data collection and the coverage area (narrowly defined in the case of people, but more broadly defined, for example, at the community or institutional level). Outcomes assessment is a recursive process providing feedback to the earlier stages of the digital library lifecycle, such as the selection and ingestion of new resources. Kyrillidou (2002) provides in-depth analysis of this feedback process by presenting a dynamic model which encompasses characteristics of spiral development. In this chapter of substantial presentation of models and approaches, Kyrillidou suggests that complexity in understanding outcomes assessment increases as someone starts considering the involution of users, whose interaction with the library depends on various aspects of their background, such as knowledge and experience.

It is also true that some digital library services focus on users' knowledge enhancement, thus supporting the advancement of 'personal information infrastructures' (Marchionini, 1995: 61) and consequently having an impact at the community level. At the personal level, outcomes assessment is thus related to phases of information management, such as retrieval or utilisation. In other words, it effectively concentrates on whether users use information services to retrieve information or to manage and produce new knowledge. For example, outcomes assessment can explore the improvement of the design of information retrieval services, literacy programmes or bibliographic management services by monitoring any changes in users' capabilities and behaviours.

Saracevic (2000) defines seven levels (or strata) of evaluation, each corresponding to a strategic goal for performing evaluation. Each level consists of a set of processes, each of which provides significant feedback to the owners, policy makers, developers and users of the digital library. These levels are shown on the vertical axis of Figure 9.1. Figure 9.1 correlates Saracevic's evaluation strata with important evaluation areas, such as outcomes assessment and service quality, as per Bertot and McClure (2003).

According to the abovementioned definitions, outcomes assessment mainly affects the personal, institutional and community levels. However, its range is not constrained to these levels, but also provides feedback to the effectiveness and system design areas, as it offers important information for the engineering, processing and content strata. For instance, the findings in an outcomes assessment can recommend either improvements in content level (e.g. strengthening of a subject field through the acquisition of more resources), or in operation level (e.g. reconsidering improvements in systems and software).

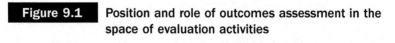

Figure 9.1 Position and role of outcomes assessment in the space of evaluation activities

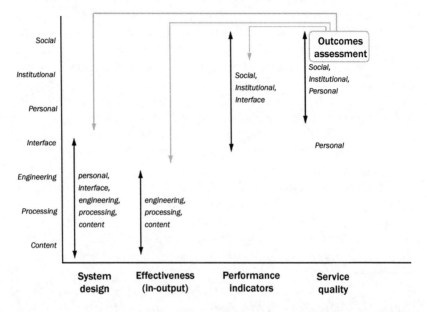

This perspective considers that this kind of assessment is part of a wider cycle of evaluation activities, the utmost target of which is to improve and adjust information services to the lives and practice of the serving communities. As such, outcomes assessment is destined to integrate other evaluation activities and to define the degree of acceptability of the offered services and their incorporation in the daily life of users. Thus, outcomes assessment is related to 'technical' or low-level evaluation activities aiming to proliferate expressions of collective information management, like reuse (Sumner and Dawe, 2001), or to enhance users' cognitive competencies (Leazer et al., 2000).

A second challenge in defining outcomes assessment is in the voluminous typology of digital libraries. As they are being developed for different purposes, such as commercial, educational or research, this evaluation area is performed under a diversity of criteria aiming at different goals. While studies in programme evaluation regard impact analysis as a subset of outcomes evaluation (Hess and Klekotla, 2005), in the library domain these terms are conceived in a different way. In general, the terms *outcomes* and *impact* are used interchangeably, with the first being related to digital libraries in the educational domain, while the latter being related to the productivity of a research community. One of the most significant problems for understanding outcomes – and possibly in establishing a common terminology – is the lack of clear distinguishing line between these concepts. Various persons hold multiple roles in different areas of outcomes assessment. The very same persons (or communities) that conduct competitive and developing research and channel their productivity through scientific publications, also perform educational activities (classes, seminars, tests and so on) in the very same institutions. As such, there is an interchange between people's multiple roles each time they are evaluated under a different lens.

Intervening factors in the generation of outcomes assessment

It is most evident that outcomes assessment is difficult to be performed. This section tries to explore the reasons causing this issue, and groups them in two broad categories, namely political and methodological factors.

Political factors

Lakos (2002) has called for the need to develop a culture of assessment in order to improve library services. However, this need is not fully comprehended and is even more difficult to realise. The lack of assessment culture is responsible for the lack of firm measures and consistent methodologies for outcomes assessment. This difficulty is more profound in the digital library area. How can someone seek digital library outcomes assessment if there is no established sense of measurement as regards traditional and long-term operating services? The lack of assessment culture is mainly caused by the inherent nature of the library mission, as witnessed by the Outcomes Project Final Report (McNichol, 2000). This project aimed to create, pilot and evaluate outcomes assessment tools for harmonising library services outcomes with the target outcomes of the parent institutions. One of the project findings was that library directors believe that their organisations 'do not need to actively demonstrate how they contribute to institutional aims or to find ways to make themselves more integral to the university' (McNichol, 2000: 76). Several other challenges arise from this lack of culture, including the tools and documents needed to promote a consensus among library administrators and evaluators.

Many digital library projects are funded by an agency that is also responsible for evaluating the overall progress of the project and the fulfilment of its aims. There is strong evidence about the role of these agents. First, evaluation activities can be misinterpreted where there is a lack of assessment culture within the authority and key concepts, such as outcomes and outputs, are misunderstood. Consequently, for digital libraries to have a positive impact on the lives of their users, project planning and target definition are necessary to align the development of digital libraries to the work tasks and needs of their users and communities. Consider, for example, the EPEAEK Project, a multi-year project jointly funded by the EU and the Greek Ministry of Education. One of the project's main activities was to focus on the development of innovative information services and infrastructures to support educational activities and to leverage the quality of the education and research in Greek universities. Through the EPEAEK programme, academic libraries in Greece received funding for the development of institutional repositories – using digital library software platforms – to fulfil the needs of their communities. The creation of the repositories represented the final deliverables of the programme, yet there was no investigation regarding the degree to which these systems made an impact on the community. In fact, some of the digital library projects were not completed properly, and were found lacking in such critical areas as content. Aside from a lack of proper control from the supervising authority, this situation highlighted the failure in policy planning, raising questions about understanding the communities' needs, the anticipated impact of these resources, and the subsequent development of the resources. The ambiguity of terms and the lack of definitions for outcomes assessment by authority agents constitute the most important inhibitory factors (Stoffle and Hitchingham, 2007). In the case of digital libraries that are detached from geographically defined communities or institutions, clear statements of the anticipated impact of their operation are essential as a means of safeguarding the evaluation activities.

Moreover, the identification and specification of the responsibility of providers and users is a significant issue. In situations in which roles may be ambiguous and not clearly separated, such as in academic repositories where researchers are concurrently the material producers and also the information seekers, it is difficult to define and apportion specific responsibilities and indicators.

One of the most important political factors is the need for collaboration. Lindauer (1998) underlines the necessity of developing synergies among librarians, faculty members and researchers. These synergies range from commonly-agreed metrics and indicators, to the identification of subtle differences that need to be taken into account, to (re)form assessment strategies and policies and to facilitate collection, analysis and interpretation of data. This remains a significant challenge, as collaboration initiatives without formal frameworks will depend on the goodwill of each agent. It should be noted that the promotion of such collaborative activities needs the appropriate time to encourage communication and understanding among the partners.

Methodological factors

Clearly stated aims are a valuable tool for outcomes assessment, as they define and discriminate the margins of the evaluation area. The multiple perspectives on outcomes assessment are logically attributed to the evaluator, his aims and the context in which he is operating. In a symbolic formulation, the evaluator is seeking findings correlated with the predefined aims of the evaluation activity, as well as any unpredicted finding that might help in sketching an integrated view of the users' demands, the system's performance, etc. Thus, the findings (F) of an evaluation can be represented as a function v, which correlates a set of criteria (c), predefined by a multitude of ways, and a number of unexpected findings (Un). In outcomes assessment, Un is often ignored due to the stress of criteria or a lack of consideration by the evaluator. Bertot and McClure (2003) undermine the oversimplified theory of a priori knowledge of the outcomes and therefore claim the existence of other types of outcomes, for example, emerging (Em) and unanticipated. According to their view, the formula can be expressed as $F = v(c, Em, Un)$.

The generation of findings is not certain and definite, but rather it might depend also on unexpected parameters. This leads to the conclusion that the evaluators should not focus on a limited range of outcomes. On the contrary, they should consider unpredicted parameters and seek emerging findings that are not included in any formal descriptions, however thorough they may be. This means that the obtained findings should be aligned with the system or organisation goals and objectives.

Unlike other areas of digital library evaluation, the methodological propositions vary and are strongly dependent on the type of digital libraries and their linkage with the community they serve. In digital libraries with a strong educational orientation, focus groups are conducted, interviews and questionnaires are performed and pre/post-test validation or other analysis techniques are utilised. For example EDNER, a formative evaluation project for the assessment of the impact of educational resources, consisted of structured telephone interviews, and paper and online questionnaire surveys covering representative classes of users, such as faculty or technical personnel (Kemp and Goodyear, 2004: 4–8). Madle et al. (2003) used pre and post-test comparison in order to trace and highlight effects in knowledge and attitude among the users of a medical digital library. Alternative methodologies include document and policy analysis in order to provide solid reference to organisational commitments or any other formal statements, library usage statistics or even semester success grades, credits and so on. However, the majority of these methods are quality-oriented and therefore issues of generalisation and possible migration are raised.

In the case of research impact, the main techniques are more distinct. For example, impact factors of publishing journals, citation analysis, single indicators of scientific excellence (e.g. the h-index), and many other metrics are available to assess the effectiveness of scientific and research literature. As well as suggesting a variety of approaches for the different types of digital libraries, this differentiation provides a classification of qualitative and quantitative methodologies. While the impact on research is depicted through numbers, ratios and other numerical indicators, the impact of educational digital libraries is hard to identify and needs to be described in other – pluralistic – ways. This challenge is related to the underlying concepts of assessment. For example, the understanding and use of digital assets by a student class cannot be traced effectively without asking students in many ways, yet the existence of citations presupposes the comprehension of the cited sources and works. Of course, this does not mean that numerical metrics are accepted without consideration and that there are no arguments about their use and their value in scientific and research assessment. A very recent review by the Joint IMU/ICIAM/IMS Committee on Quantitative Assessment of Research (2008) poses questions about the role of citation data as the sole unit qualifying the transparency of research assessment. These questions are also related to concerns about the quantitative coverage and qualitative depth of the databases and tools.

A similar issue is that usage is related to impact. Usage indicators, such as download statistics, are sometimes considered to have an effect on the reader and the community. This means that the downloaded material is actually studied, comprehended and used in an effective fashion. However, in terms of understanding how an information item has an effect on the reader, these indicators are largely peripheral. Indeed, the underlying concepts of what is actually measured represent a major issue in metrics development.

According to Kovács and Micsik (2004), an evaluation activity can be considered as a comparison of multiple evaluation atoms, in other words, multiple instances of evaluations. A comparative study concerns a strict experimental framework where particular factors may be isolated and studied. Such studies are very informative and valuable when applied in laboratory settings and mainly concern systemic evaluations. However, for outcomes assessment in a real-life context, it is difficult to fulfil the requirement for the comparison parallelism/synchronisation in time and other circumstances. Various methodologies, such as MINES for Libraries®, have been proposed to develop a reliable way of collecting statistically sound data despite the challenges of the distributed networked environment (Franklin and Plum, 2003). MINES for Libraries® has shown that it is possible to collect data from different settings and provide a homogeneous data set, despite the conditions of the different settings. Additionally, through a variety of techniques it is possible to multiply the collection methods within the evaluation atoms in order to collect data from various points in a distributed network of digital library resources, as proposed by the DLESE Evaluation Services Group (Buhr et al., 2005).

Furthermore, evaluation activities are encouraged to be iterative in order to ensure proper monitoring of operation. This is not easy in the case of outcomes assessment, however, as the whole process is regarded longitudinal, especially in the case of educational digital libraries. The use of quantitative metrics and the automation of their generation using known and reliable databases, such as ISI Web of Knowledge, seems to encourage iterative evaluation, but in the case of educational digital libraries, where more in-depth studies are required to prove proper use and understanding, the replication of evaluation activities is quite difficult. On the other hand, while it is difficult to collate the assessments for different educational digital libraries, in the field of research digital libraries this problem is pertinent at the thematic level, meaning that it is difficult to replicate evaluations for different disciplines and scientific areas.

Reforming digital libraries: alternative views on outcomes assessment

Digital libraries and repositories exploit software functionalities to record usage and provide indicators, such as number of downloads or records viewed. While download statistics are used to promote institutional repositories and provide alternative incentives, they are also used to assess the impact of research publications (Ferreira et al., 2008). In the case of institutional repositories, digital libraries not only confirm some desired outcomes, but also extend metrics and provide the ground for comparing scientific output among the various institutions.

Furthermore, download statistics and other expressions of information use, like page visits, are regarded as additional metrics for information impact, as they are generated by the visitors and readers of scientific literature. As such, the traditional author evaluation and classification methods can be enhanced by visitor-based measurements. In the case of vendors and providers this transition seems unachievable, as (a) in their current state only few of them provide such information, and (b) they hold only a part of the scientific literature. However, in the area of digital repositories and open access resources this seems more feasible. The MESUR project (Bollen et al., 2007) aimed to enrich the traditional assessment metrics with indicators based on usage statistics, citations and bibliographic data. Once again this seems reasonable and applicable in thematic areas, but this methodology might not be applicable for all kinds of impact assessment. Potential adaptations depending on the geographic consistency of a community, the method of information access and the anticipated outcomes should be also considered. Furthermore, the socio-technical dimension requires the proper exposure of repositories to retrieval mechanisms, such as Google Scholar or Scirus, or the application of interoperability protocols to increase access. Usage statistics are reliable data sources for reflecting the turnover of scientific digital libraries; in the field of education, however, digital libraries require other methodologies for the same purpose (Coleman et al., 2004).

Digital libraries and repositories, both institutional and subject-based, encourage social interaction among their users/members. The latest developments in social networking applications within the digital library domain allow data to be gathered regarding the level of impact of particular items. For example, the tagging of library catalogue records or digital library items creates a conceptual abstraction of people's understanding. Sumner and Marlino (2004) describe the role of digital libraries as knowledge networks and discuss how they could contribute to progress in learning, understanding and acceptance of resources. This approach addresses a serious problem related to the identification and measurement of the proper comprehension and integration of educational resources.

Digital libraries, research or educational, can be guided by policies, which can prescribe, among other things, a set of metrics for the assessment of their outcomes. Digital library hosting and developing authorities have full control over their design, provision and operation, and therefore it should be very easy to enforce outcome evaluation strategies. As repositories are in their infancy, but rapidly developing, the need for common ground in measurement is required. Initiatives like the Interoperable Repositories Statistics project (*http://irs.eprints.org*), address the need for a common language between the different infrastructure frameworks.

The development of new metrics is a challenge for evaluators, but important for enriching their armoury with more tools. There are two perspectives in using the new metrics and tools. The first is to focus on the creation and processing of a rich image by integrating data from different sources. The second perspective, however, is related to the need to classify the activities performed in an institution or a community, which requires new customisable and powerful metrics and measurement tools to be defined. Armbruster (2008) mentions that metric plurality may be used to provide alternative views of the activities performed by a person inside the community; such views can be essential to very specific cases. This addresses the problem of defining and classifying the activities within an institution, which may be evaluated in different fashions and for different purposes.

Conclusions

Although the current developments in digital libraries open up a number of possibilities, they should not be considered as a panacea for the largely methodological problems concerning outcomes assessment. The electronic information environment extends its influence in the outcomes assessment area and every suggestion for further development is grounded on the notion of democratisation. In a scalar perspective of the effect of digital libraries, one can see that the research field needs more evaluation resources, as well as the development of new metrics. The gradual turn to more dynamic and pluralistic metrics is gauged by the active participation of users and readers fulfilling these requirements. Instead of soliciting rankings and metrics based on networks of authors or administrators of information, modern digital libraries allow the evolution of user-based metrics. Finally, recent developments invite users to discuss information items, through tags, ratings and annotations, thus providing a more intact and apt indication of impact and comprehension.

Bibliography

Armbruster, C. (2008) 'Access, usage and citation metrics: what function for digital libraries and repositories in research evaluation?', working paper, available at: *http://ssrn.com/abstract=1088453* (accessed 26 November 2008).

Bertot, J. C. and McClure, C. R. (2003) 'Outcomes assessment in the networked environment: research questions, issues, considerations and moving forward', *Library Trends* 51(4): 590–613.

Bollen, J., Rodriquez, M. A. and Van de Sompel, H. (2007) 'MESUR: usage-based metrics of scholarly impact', in *Proceedings of the 7th ACM/IEEE-CS Joint Conference on Digital Libraries, Vancouver, BC, 18–23 June,* New York: ACM Press, p. 474.

Buhr, S., Barker, L. and Reeves, T. C. (2005) 'The DLESE Evaluation Services Group: a framework for evaluation within a digital library' in *Proceedings of the 5th ACM/IEEE-CS Joint Conference on Digital Libraries, Denver, CO, 7–11 June,* New York: ACM Press, p. 370.

Coleman, A. S., Bartolo, L. and Jones, C. (2004) 'Bricoleurs: exploring digital library evaluation as participant interactions, research and processes', in *Proceedings of the 4th ACM/IEEE-CS Joint Conference on Digital Libraries, Tucson, AZ, 7–11 June,* New York: ACM Press, p. 377.

Ferreira, M., Rodrigues, E., Baptista, A. A. and Saraiva, R. (2008) 'Carrots and sticks: some ideas on how to create a successful institutional repository', *D-Lib Magazine* 14(1/2), available at: *http://www.dlib.org/dlib/january08/ferreira/01ferreira.html* (accessed 26 November 2008).

Franklin, B. and Plum, T. (2003) 'Library usage patterns in the electronic information environment', *Information Research* 9(4), available at: *http://informationr.net/ir/9-4/paper187.html* (accessed 26 November 2008).

Hess, F. M. and Klekotla, A. L. (2005) 'Impact/outcome evaluation', in *Encyclopaedia of Social Measurement*, San Diego, CA: Elsevier, pp. 271–6.

Joint Committee on Quantitative Assessment of Research (2008) 'Citation analysis: a report from the International Mathematical

Union in cooperation with the International Council of Industrial and Applied Mathematics (ICIAM) and the Institute of Mathematical Statistics', available at: *http://www.mathunion.org/fileadmin/IMU/Report/CitationStatistics.pdf* (accessed 26 November 2008).

Kellaghan, T. and Madaus, G. F. (2000) 'Outcome evaluation', in D. L. Stufflebeam, G. F. Madaus and T. Madaus (eds) *Evaluation Models: Viewpoints on Educational and Human Services Evaluation* (2nd edn), Boston, MA: Kluwer, pp. 97–112.

Kemp, B. and Goodyear, P. (2004) *EDNER: Formative Evaluation of the Distributed National Electronic Resource: Surveys of Impact*, Lancaster: CSALT.

Kovács, L. and Micsik, A. (2004) 'The evaluation computer: a model for structuring evaluation activities', paper presented at the DELOS Workshop on the Evaluation of Digital Libraries, Padova, 4–5 October, available at: *http://dlib.ionio.gr/wp7/workshop2004_program.html* (accessed 26 November 2008).

Kyrillidou, M. (2002) 'From input and output measures to quality and outcome measures, or, from the user in the life of the library to the library in the life of the user', *The Journal of Academic Librarianship* 28(1–2): 42–6.

Lakos, A. (2002) 'Culture of assessment as a catalyst for organizational culture change in libraries', in *Proceedings of the 4th Northumbria International Conference on Performance Measurement in Libraries and Information Services, Pittsburgh, PA, 12–16 August*, Annapolis Junction, MD: ARL, pp. 311–20.

Leazer, G. H., Gilliland-Swetland, A. J. and Borgman, C. L. (2000) 'Evaluating the use of a geographic digital library in undergraduate classrooms: ADEPT', in *Proceedings of the 5th ACM Conference on Digital Libraries, Denver, CO, 7–11 June*, New York: ACM Press, pp. 248–9.

Lindauer, B. G. (1998) 'Defining and measuring the library's impact on campuswide outcomes', *College and Research Libraries* 59(6): 546–70.

Madle, G., Kostkova, P., Mani-Saada, J. and Weinberg, J. R. (2003) 'Evaluating the changes in knowledge and attitudes of digital library users', in *Proceedings of the 8th European Conference on Digital Libraries, Bath, 13–15 September, LNCS Vol. 2769*, Berlin: Springer-Verlag, pp. 29–40.

Marchionini, G. (1995) *Information Seeking in Electronic Environment*, New York: Cambridge University Press.

McNicol, S. (2000) 'Academic libraries: planning, outcomes and communication', available at: *http://www.ebase.bcu.ac.uk/docs/ Outcomes_project_report.pdf* (accessed 26 November 2008).

Saracevic, T. (2000) 'Digital library evaluation: towards an evolution of concepts', *Library Trends* 49(3): 350–69.

Stoffle, C. and Hitchingham, E. (2007) 'Learning outcomes, research outcomes, and institutional accreditation', available at: *http://www .arl.org/resources/pubs/mmproceedings/139hitchingham.shtml* (accessed 26 November 2008).

Sumner, T. and Dawe, M. (2001) 'Looking at digital library usability from a reuse perspective', in *Proceedings of the 1st ACM/IEEE-CS Joint Conference on Digital Libraries, Roanoke, VA, 24–28 June*, New York: ACM Press, pp. 416–25.

Sumner, T. and Marlino, M. (2004) 'Digital libraries and educational practice: a case for new models', in *Proceedings of the 4th ACM/IEEE-CS Joint Conference on Digital Libraries, Tucson, AZ, 7–11 June*, New York: ACM Press, pp. 170–8.

10

Digital library service quality: what does it look like?

Martha Kyrillidou, Colleen Cook and Yvonna Lincoln

Introduction

In the 500 years since the invention of the printing press, libraries have been at the centre of a remarkable flowering of the human intellect, serving as repositories of recorded human experience while promoting structured inquiry and critical thinking. Libraries are fundamental to the intellectual experience and the natural creativity of the mind; they provide core services for research, teaching and learning. What, however, defines a great library and, furthermore, a great digital library? What constitutes excellence or effectiveness in library services, especially digital library services? What constitutes quality digital library services in science, mathematics, engineering and technology education? How does the National Science Digital Library (NSDL) determine whether it is delivering the best possible service for the considerable investments made in its operations?

The problem of library service quality assessment for digital libraries is partially addressed with the establishment of the LibQUAL+® protocol at the Association of Research Libraries (ARL). LibQUAL+® identifies and measures library service quality across institutions and stands as a useful quality-assessment tool for local planning; LibQUAL+® is a full library service quality programme at ARL. LibQUAL+® was developed to assess service quality in the traditional library environment that has been historically print-based and has been thoroughly documented in a variety of studies (Cook, 2002a, 2002b; Cook and Heath, 2001; Cook and Thompson, 2001; Cook et al., 2001a, 2001b, 2002, 2003; Heath et al.,

2002, 2004; Kyrillidou, 2006; Kyrillidou and Heath, 2004; Kyrillidou and Persson, 2006; Kyrillidou et al., 2005, 2008; Thompson and Cook, 2002; Thompson, et al., 2000, 2001, 2002, 2003a, 2003b, 2005, 2006a, 2006b, 2007a, 2007b, 2008). With a grant from the National Science Foundation (NSF) NSDL, we faced the challenge of assessment in an environment where all resources were digital and the emerging community of learners, developers and teachers existed in a virtual and distributed framework of research and development activities.

ARL proposed addressing the issue of digital library service quality assessment for the NSDL by adapting the LibQUAL+® protocol for the community of faculty and students using the NSDL resources. NSDL is highly committed to advancing the effective measurement of library service quality in order to assist libraries in continually improving the service received by students, faculty and other library patrons, much like ARL. As ARL member libraries and universities support extensive digital library resources, evaluating only the service quality aspects of traditional library operations is no longer sufficient in improving library service. Digital library evaluation is a vital, yet relatively unexplored, component of research library assessment efforts.

Building, sustaining and servicing digital library resources is a major cost for an institution. Collectively, ARL member libraries spent more than $3.7 billion in 2005–06 on operating expenses, and costs are certain to rise. The escalating costs of scholarly communication – especially the prices of scholarly journals and electronic databases – are among the most volatile in postsecondary education, inflating at a rate of about 7 per cent per annum over the past three decades. The portion of the library materials budget spent on electronic resources is also growing rapidly, from an estimated 3.6 per cent in 1992–93 to more than 40 per cent in 2005–06. ARL university libraries reported spending over $431 million on electronic resources, with the majority of spending being on electronic serials and subscription services. Eighty-three ARL libraries also reported another $15 million expended on their behalf on electronic resources through centrally funded consortia (Kyrillidou and Young, 2008). Staff costs, an important component of digital library development and maintenance, account for a major portion of additional expenses.

As library expenses – including digital library expenses – continue to rise, it becomes imperative for libraries to develop more effective and efficient means of allocating scarce resources to improve the quality of services. Libraries are increasingly called upon by their institutions to demonstrate value to the research, teaching and learning enterprise in relation to the investments made in both traditional and innovative digital library services. While ARL libraries must still meet the needs of users in all formats of information, the NSDL protocol, designed to assess the digital component of research library collections and service, could be used to evaluate the electronic-based content and access services. With funding from NSF/NSDL, we proceeded in developing a process and tools to enable institutions to address the most important information needs of students and faculty, and to assess whether their research, teaching and learning needs are being met effectively within the context of the NSDL.

Concurrently driving the need for new measures of library service quality is the explosion of information in both print and electronic formats. In this information-rich era, it is vital that students acquire, through library experiences, critical information-seeking skills, and libraries must accommodate the evolving information-seeking behaviours of students and faculty in our rapidly expanding information-based economy. Enhanced service quality assessment in digital libraries will: (a) improve intelligent retrieval of relevant information, (b) promote learner preparation for working in an information-rich society, and (c) promote scholarship and lifelong learning in both individual and collaborative settings, as well as in formal and informal modes.

This ARL project was branded as DigiQUAL® and charted new territory, complementing other measurement practices now in place in digital libraries. The innovative model we proposed enhances the ability of libraries with significant digital components, such as the ARL member institution libraries, to engage a new and different assessment methodology that evaluates service quality from the point of view of library users in a consistent manner across digital library operations. The ultimate goal is to improve digital libraries by directing resources to those service quality issues identified by users as most important and in need of attention. The NSDL offered an excellent starting point for developing a digital library service quality protocol across a diverse set of digital library resources and users. Ultimately, digital library developers and maintenance agencies constantly seek new measures for outcome assessments that permit a deeper understanding of local quality issues and provide 'best practice' guides for those who wish to take corrective action in a systematic way.

The project started as adaptation of LibQUAL+® (a modification of SERVQUAL), tested in the research library environment. SERVQUAL (for SERVice QUALity) was developed for the for-profit sector in the 1980s by the marketing research group of Zeithaml et al. (1990). The

SERVQUAL instrument in its LibQUAL+® manifestation emerged as a highly reliable and valid tool in comparing service quality across libraries and across contexts, providing a consistent framework for engaging in total market surveys.

An example from Texas A&M University illustrates the power of this instrument to effect organisational change. In an iteration of the original survey on the Texas A&M campus, results from the Reliability of Library Catalog and User Records performance scores showed that services were falling outside the zone of tolerance. Armed with this information, management efforts were then concentrated on learning more about the problem and developing solutions. Through follow-up focus groups and workflow analysis, processes were re-engineered and the software for cataloguing and circulation records was replaced. Ongoing evaluation enabled refinement of the process until optimal processing was achieved.

The ARL LibQUAL+® project gained its initial impetus from the experiences derived at Texas A&M University, where, for six years, work has taken place on translating the SERVQUAL instrument for administration in the research library environment. Between October 1999 and March 2000, the SERVQUAL instrument was regrounded for libraries through a series of interviews at research libraries conducted by project managers. Building upon those interviews and adhering to the integrity of the original SERVQUAL design, a series of approximately 40 questions was developed to adapt and build a new service-directed assessment instrument to measure service outcomes as perceived by consumers of library services.

The project was endorsed as an ARL pilot project at the Association's annual meeting in October 1999. The Texas A&M design team acquired the hardware, designed a web form for collecting the data, and implemented the initial development which was carried on by ARL in more recent years (Cook and Heath, 1999; Kyrillidou et al., in press). The 12 participants in the pilot LibQUAL+® project were identified from a pool of more than 30 volunteers in late 1999. From each library, survey coordinators were appointed to work with the Texas A&M/ARL design team. In January 2000, the survey coordinators and most directors from the 12 institutions met to discuss pilot requirements and timelines. After the January 2000 meeting, most of the participating libraries were visited by the project managers with the purpose of building theory – qualitatively regrounding the SERVQUAL instrument through a series of interviews with faculty, graduate students and undergraduates. Sixty interviews were conducted on the campuses of the participating institutions to hone the questions in the SERVQUAL instrument and to assist in identifying any additional possible dimensions. The interviews of faculty and students were transcribed and then subjected to content analysis. The modified version of the SERVQUAL questionnaire was placed on the web in March 2000. Through an iterative development process, LibQUAL+® has serviced more than 1,000 libraries since 2000 across 22 countries and 15 different languages.

The qualitative work done for LibQUAL+® indicated that the concept of self-sufficiency is an important concept that needs further exploration. Self-sufficiency appears to be highly relevant to digital library development. Thus the NSDL digital library assessment, DigiQUAL®, helps us explain and understand in further detail the self-sufficiency issues and their relation to service quality issues (Lincoln, 2002). As we will see below, self-sufficiency is extended in the digital library environment as navigability and interoperability.

We studied NSDL digital environments including CITIDEL, DLESE, ENC, iLumina, MathDL, Math Forum @ Drexel, Michigan Teacher Network, MERLOT and NEEDS. We also studied a digital environment within a developing digital library within the University of Texas, Utopia. These environments were selected because of prior efforts at formative assessment and evaluation. From this initial group, DLESE and MERLOT were selected as the starting point for developing dimensions of service quality as these sites organise annual face-to-face meetings with their users. The DigiQUAL® research team conducted user focus groups that identified 250 items describing different aspects of service quality in digital libraries. Analysis of the items yielded 12 themes or dimensions of digital library service quality: accessibility/navigability; interoperability; the digital library as a community for users, developers and reviewers; collection building; role of federations; copyright; resource use; evaluating collections; and digital library sustainability.

Evaluating the NSF NSDL collections: categories and themes from MERLOT and DLESE

Reformulating and regrounding the LibQUAL+® instrument for digital libraries was accomplished with focus group interview data from both DLESE and MERLOT participants. The categories, themes and issues were identified utilising data collected at the annual meetings of the DLESE and MERLOT groups, with users, developers, reviewers and system administrators. Subjected to a formal content analysis, the data began to cluster around a dozen or more themes (Lincoln et al., 2004; 2005). Those themes, with samples of the data which prompted their identification, are presented below.

Categories and themes from the focus group data

The first several categories relate to what we have termed, broadly, 'design features': the design of the website, its initial attractiveness to users, its ease of navigation, and the critical question for its teaching potential – its interoperability.

Web attractiveness – design features

Sample items – especially those which seem the most focused, follow the category titles:

'I think the homepage is too cluttered.' (MERLOT)

'I would want a site that is truly simplistic; there's a lot of initial information on the homepage.' (MERLOT)

'I don't think about [aesthetics] much. Yeah, I like the newer version; I think it's prettier.' (DLESE)

'The graphics [in version #1] wasn't anything moving around; nowhere to go. But it's okay [now].' (DLESE)

'I really appreciate no pop-ups.' (DLESE)

'I don't like the webpage. There's so much stuff going on, but there is a problem in the way it is listed.' (MERLOT)

'And then the other way I think about it is the theory or concept behind MERLOT, which is very attractive, more so than is the actual physical site.' (MERLOT)

Accessibility – navigability

This category related not only to the ease of usage of the websites themselves, but also to the users' perceptions of their own ability to be self-sufficient by navigating successfully to the materials and objects they desired to utilise. Access is not only a feature of the libraries' websites;

it works in the opposite direction. That is, it also permits a user to feel efficacious in acquiring mobility throughout the site, successfully locating materials needed, and assigning parameters to limit an individual's search and focus more tightly on specific information needed. Accessibility and navigability enable searches to proceed more swiftly, but also enable searchers to have a greater sense of self-sufficiency in achieving their own purposes. Some of the typical comments from focus groups include the following:

'...we see some problems with the initial accessibility.' (MERLOT)

'Actually, the former version of DLESE I had a pretty easy time using.' (DLESE)

'I think it's fairly accessible once you are accustomed to the site.' (MERLOT)

'...there's a lot of links, you know, like that [unusable without a username].' (MERLOT)

'On the other hand, I do like to have an advanced search where I can specify the format and that only things with peer review [come up], so those are features that are also very important to me.' (MERLOT)

'In terms of accessibility, I think one thing that I also find good is they open the gateway to other digital libraries.' (MERLOT)

'Use and experience count for a lot.' (MERLOT)

'Actually, one of the things (and this is coming from the librarian's point of view)... In the Version I ... you could do a lot of limiting, but to do so, you had to go to "Advance Search".' (DLESE)

'Vocabulary is an issue.' (DLESE)

'...You can select a group, like age groups, and I think with finding information as with traditional libraries and graphic databases is on the vocabulary, and the vocabulary isn't clear in this library.' (DLESE)

'I think with anything, if you use it over and over again, it's easier to navigate.' (MERLOT)

'But I think another step is that the interfacing needs to be designed in such a way that the data are taken advantage of in simple, easy-to-use, and intuitive [form].' (DLESE)

'The more fields the person has to complete each time, the more awesome the task is to the user.' (MERLOT)

Other technical aspects of the sites

This is a slim category which pertains directly to the reformulation and redesign of the DLESE website, which occurred in 2002–03. This comment should likely be added to other technical aspects in the previous categories, or additional, follow-up data should be collected on the design and navigability of the new and more sophisticated website.

'Well, I reviewed a site yesterday, because I was in one of the workshops, and I actually did ask questions about the technical aspects of the site. I don't know if that referred more to whether or not you could go to the links, or it meant that the actual texts, the content material, were correct or not.' (DLESE)

Interoperability of the sites

'I've had mixed results in terms of either use [around interoperability]. I had an easy time using it, but when I let them loose to go do certain things, I had to do a lot of explaining [to the teachers with whom I was working]; I had to kind of get them into the groove, so the speak, in order to be able to use those types of things.' (DLESE)

'I think that the major complaint that I had ... we do what we call a learning log. It's a little activity we do with teachers ... and I ask specific questions about how they did some of the things, and they ... it's not so much that the content is beyond them, but just some of the ways of going about using [interoperable functions].' (DLESE)

'I think there's a large group of educators out there that are certainly capable, knowing content, but actually using the computer, using things in that domain – it's very difficult for them. Again, it's something new to them; not that they're stupid or something like that.' (DLESE)

The three foregoing comments clearly relate to the self-sufficiency issue, and, like the issues of accessibility and navigability, work not only forward, with website design and construction, but also backward, to users' ability to see themselves as self-sufficient and competent to navigate to materials which are of immediate use to them, especially in creating teaching modules and lesson plans.

'Yes and no. [Interoperability] depends on the learning object that you access.' (MERLOT)

'As part of the review process, you have to indicate whether or not the learning object is or is not inter-operable when you review the website.' (MERLOT)

Social and psychosocial aspects of digital libraries

These concepts of community and culture in the online environment may map to the 'library as place' dimension measured by the LibQUAL+® survey instrument. With minor modifications, many of the questions used to measure that dimension may resonate with the online community and provide a valid means of measuring the concept of virtual community and online space. For example, the item, 'A getaway for study, learning, or research' may be changed to 'A gateway for study, learning, or research' in order to better suit the online environment.

Library/digital library as 'community': users, developers and reviewers

We have grouped these without reference to whether the responses were from users, developers or reviewers, but we believe it is fairly easy to see who is contributing when you read the comments, as they are frequently self-identifying in terms of their usage or involvement.

'I think it [community] brings to mind two very important things: (1) the notion of community within and between MERLOT ... and (2) I was just kind of blown away by the fact that they (physicists) would completely ignore any kind of "knowledge" that we obviously have in the library community on how things should be done, and they built this thing along the lines of how they actually think.' (MERLOT)

'[In building the physics part of the digital library], it's the community base, because it's the way they think, because now you get to CINDY and you realize CINDY is not concept-based. Bingo, it's time, space and matter! It's really cool...' (MERLOT)

'I'm beginning to understand now that this whole notion of community is incredibly important – probably far more important than us coming up with any "grand schema" if you will.' (MERLOT)

'At my college, we have an undergraduate library and lots of other libraries. It is busy there. It is a place that people can [use to] study and come together.' (MERLOT)

'But notice what we're saying: That the library as a resource area where you went for stored knowledge has shifted suddenly now to a place where we look at community and social community which many librarians would say, "Sure, it's always been that way". But perhaps not to the extent that we're talking about now.' (MERLOT)

'There's a certain ... what I kind of noticed is that DLESE has its own certain language and sort of approach to all sorts of things, and I'm wondering how an "outsider" would approach it...' (DLESE)

'It's a multi-step process. I would say there's – you've got researchers producing the data; you've got the digital library developers producing tools, portals and stuff like that, maybe the metadata material; you've got educational material developers who are going ahead and building these lesson plans, along with teachers who may be building these lesson plans and the materials around it. And it may wrap all the way around...' (DLESE)

'And that's a perfect example of something that DLESE should be, a circle where it goes around. Now, students have produced data that teachers have mentored the students into producing data ... [And that addresses] also the issue of community, because you know that you are collecting data in California and someone in New York is using the same protocols and collecting data there, and you compare your points.' (DLESE)

'One of the big advantages, or the benefits, I get from MERLOT is the community and the collaborative nature of the organization as a whole.' (MERLOT)

'But we need them [feedback forms on sites], because we are a community-driven resource.' (DLESE)

'And if we are a community-driven resource, we need to hear from the community loud and often.' (DLESE)

'That's why it's called a community, because you're contributing to the community.' (DLESE)

One of the issues to be addressed at some later point is the larger issue of 'community' and what counts for a community. We already know that the term 'community' no longer means the same as it did 50, or even 25, years ago. But the meaning of community here is far different from its original meaning. It is intimately wrapped up in a project which creates a common 'product' or service (the blurring of product and service aspects is another interesting aspect of digital libraries) – a digital library and its archives – but its 'members', particularly its users, may be unknown to each other, and indeed, many of them will never meet. Nor will some of them ever even 'chat' with each other. They provide input, learning objects, materials and data, and they withdraw from common source materials, data or learning objects which they themselves might need. But some of this activity is done relatively anonymously, and with no contact other than the common resource which is being both built and drawn from. The idea of 'community' is therefore related to the process of building and using a common project (or service, perhaps?). Contributors and users alike see themselves as drawing from a project which has meaning larger than them. This entire issue may be related to more symbolic meanings and roles of the library, and its metamorphoses through the ages (Lincoln, 2002).

Collection-building: how it is done, how it will be done in the future

There is great concern about how the collections in the digital libraries are built and maintained, that is, updated, renewed, and new scientific findings (as well as teaching units) included and integrated. There is no small amount of concern about ongoing funding, as well as simple manpower to update, vet, referee and manage submissions. While thousands of users appreciate having the digital libraries as resources, it is quite clear that far fewer are willing to be involved in the time-intensive labour necessary to build and maintain them. In fact, Marianna Torgovnick (2008) suggests that archives of all sorts, particularly digital, microfilm and microfiche, are far more fragile and 'ephemeral' than we would like to believe. Torgovnick suggests that 'the idea of the archive, independent of any specific topic, has itself become an object of obsession', simply because '...they depend on living beings to animate them'. Most assuredly, the 'living beings' who animate the NSDL's digital libraries must expend enormous amounts of time, energy and data collection and object-development to prevent the digital archives from falling prey to 'link-rot' themselves. And funding continues to be a source of anxiety and tension within the multiple communities of users, developers and reviewers.

Role of 'federation'

'So I did a search in MERLOT, and I found a few things that I think might be useful for developing the content that we're putting together; but, for the most part, I'm hoping that our institution will be a provider of information.' (MERLOT)

'...but there's a lot of null searches that should be avoided, because we need to populate the library...' (DLESE)

'I'm on the editorial board and spend a lot of my time on MERLOT building the archive.' (MERLOT)

'[Populating] means identifying areas that are being asked for that we're not able to come up with.' (MERLOT)

'That populating means also identifying an individual or set of individuals who can make it richer and richer in terms of the material that are there...' (DLESE)

'So, people that have been or were already on board are thinking "contribute!" So ... if "oceans" are weak, you call NOAA or somebody to get them on board.' (DLESE)

'In a similar situation, I'm on the editorial board of History and spend a lot of time just cruising history sites to fill in the gaps....' (MERLOT)

'One of the things is to populate the library. Right now, we can tell you what resources are in the library, and we have someone who is doing collection assessment so that we can. And so we're identifying that these resources should be increased in the library before asking for them.' (DLESE)

'Collection building ... we will forever be in a collection-building phase as far as I can tell.' (DLESE)

'It was previously in its rapid growth stage and trying to figure out who we are and how to tell it to people. And now we're into what don't we have and why can't people find what they want.' (DLESE)

'So, the collection is uneven, and it's not clear to begin with to the user that it's uneven.' (DLESE)

'Collections can come into the library with a reviewed status if they choose to. In order to do that, they have to create this very rigorous review program that they have to outline and adopt, and they came forth with their collection and review document. And they have to say how they reviewed all the resources in their library for scientific accuracy, for use in a classroom, for standards…' (DLESE)

'That's why we have to start looking at the collection and say, "OK, guys, we need to go out and to collect in these [low-density collections] areas" – and that's happened.' (DLESE)

The possibilities of federation

'We heard this morning at the general session about a federated search, and I really resonated with that because as good as MERLOT is, it's not going to be able to solve it on its own. It's got to be part of a federation … But that could help, if the digital libraries framework could in some way support a federated search so that you could have the same good feelings in a federated search that you have in the search that you do with MERLOT, it would be wonderful.' (MERLOT)

'And you can tell they're starting to fuse and they're mingling. It's, like, my collection is already in two of the digital libraries. I'm sure that there are others that are in more than one. And so the issue is that they can federate between them. The more they can interchange what they have inside them, the more it will become like one digital library.' (DLESE)

With respect to this last comment, it is becoming clear that that there are many, many digital libraries out there, slowly becoming integrated (federated) such that it is difficult to tell just how many digital libraries actually exist, or how they might be accessed. As better and more comprehensive metadata are created, the possibilities for federation seem likelier.

Problems particular to libraries and digital libraries

Librarians everywhere struggle with the question of metadata. Even as new metadata archives are being built, knowledge is expanding so rapidly that even the newest metadata databases are struggling to keep up.

The role of metadata

Metadata may be a subset of the category above, just as it is likely a subset of the category 'community'. Many of the items here relate to the use of metadata across collections, for instance, which apparently becomes a problem when collections and libraries are being/becoming 'federated'.

> 'So, we've actually felt the need for a discipline-specific page that introduces information for the first time about how things are structured, why we've made certain choices, how they might find things within history.' (MERLOT)
>
> 'The way around metadata issues, it is "cross-walking".' (DLESE)
>
> 'Basically, if I've got a metadata standard, and someone else has a metadata standard, you can map onto them. It may not be perfect mapping, but [cross-walking means, for example, that you can move one collection into the format of another collection] … And so, the question then is, how to federate all these digital libraries so material usually can be discovered through all of them.' (DLESE)

Please notice the whole idea of metadata just transposed itself into the federation issue here. Mapping knowledge is a project which is not likely to be complete in our lifetimes, and metadata will continue to be both the salvation and the nemesis of digital libraries and their users for the foreseeable future.

> 'My impression is that users want to have resources described in a way that anticipated the things that they want in that resources, whether it is a website or a learning object, how granular it is [that is, is it an image, or is it an entire website].' (MERLOT)
>
> 'I think that it is worth the investment of putting educational descriptors on the resources and getting educational description of the resources that help end users find and use the learning objects or resources.' (MERLOT)
>
> 'I want the user in a seamless sort of way to be able to find [what they need], and in order for them to find that, that resource has to be described on the back end with those kinds of things [descriptors].' (MERLOT)
>
> '…and the critical thing is we're still developing a control vocabulary, a vocabulary for the library.' (DLESE)

Copyright issues; ownership of materials

Plagiarism and the digital libraries

Just as plagiarism has remained a persistent issue with other forms of intellectual property, plagiarism has been an even more difficult issue with digital materials, particularly those which are unsigned and unattributed. Frequently, the creators of pages and objects are credited, but occasionally, individuals create materials which are unsigned. What counts as plagiarism in this context? That is a question which has yet to be settled, although the comments below suggest some answers:

> 'Who owns the content? Who owns what's up on MERLOT? Ans: People who created their pages.' (MERLOT)
>
> 'The people who create it … have the ownership.' (MERLOT)
>
> 'Very early on, people said MERLOT wouldn't work because of the copyright issue, and MERLOT said, we're not even going to deal with it; we're just going to refer to it, we're never going to have it ourselves.' (MERLOT)
>
> 'Just like the Smithsonian, we own it, it's ours, belongs to the users.' (DLESE)
>
> 'I think in terms of ownership, I think it's very difficult. Certainly, if there are copyright statements available, there is clear ownership. But oftentimes, there is not any copyright statement. Then we have things like images from NASA that are public domain. So, I don't think that we should assume that it belongs to the authors. I think those things are out there to access and use.' (MERLOT)
>
> 'But it [the copyright/ownership issue] does suggest something about ownership and about the way we now view knowledge as a multi-person constructed set of instructions.' (MERLOT)

This issue seems important to us. We perhaps should especially look at users' views of what knowledge is, given the 'community' nature of knowledge-building that is going on, and the multi-site construction of that knowledge.

Issues with submissions to digital libraries (especially of 'learning objects') and how faculty members get credit in the promotion and tenure process

'Who owns the content? You own your own content, but we own the metadata. I mean, we can have the metadata ... The metadata can be harvested by NSF.' (DLESE)

'...let's say you have a TT plan, you have to provide us the metadata for that resource.' (DLESE)

'Or you can provide a resource and ask DLESE to do the metadata link to a single resource.' (DLESE)

'[Or] you can create your own metadata record, a cataloguing tool.' (DLESE)

How digital library resources are used

It is worth noting that this section of data units is the second largest in the analyses. While sheer numbers do not 'count' in the same way as they might in more experimental inquiry, nevertheless, data unit count is one measure of salience in interviewing and other kinds of data collection which lead to content analyses. There are, of course, analytic and conceptual problems with this significance estimate; for example, unsophisticated questioning or inadequate or inept analysis. Nonetheless, we feel relatively confident when the transcripts are compared with the notes taken in the various focus group sessions by professional ARL staff.

'It's also an easy way for me to send people to those sites without my having to remember what the URL is.' (MERLOT)

'I may not use a particular site the way it was constructed as an assignment in class; but I get ideas of how I might work an assignment on a topic...' (DLESE)

'And what I found is that they [teachers] really sought the animations, the quick things that they could take into the classrooms 10 minutes before class.' (DLESE)

'Their [the teachers] feedback – and I can identify with this – was quick and easy – the search engines helped them find information they could use.' (MERLOT)

'I have the most cluttered desk that you can imagine, and this is a hell of a good way to keep it organized and simply in one spot [putting the URLs and materials on MERLOT] so that I can do exactly the same thing...' (MERLOT)

'...if a faculty member realizes that stuff is going to come down and they still want to have it, they can negotiate to have that put somewhere else to have some permanency.' (MERLOT)

'So I use both a search and a harvest. I have to tell you that I also harvest stuff. There are tools out there – some of them very specialized, some of them not so specialized ... And I must tell you that I shamelessly harvest stuff, and I'm sure I'm committing all kinds of copyright violations on a daily basis – I'll confess to doing that! But I do that because I'm fearful that the stuff will sometimes disappear and go away, and so I harvest that. So I'm both a searcher and a harvester. And that's how I use MERLOT.' (MERLOT)

'It has some levels of cumbersomeness in getting to the subject matter.' (MERLOT)

'Rabbit trails are easy with MERLOT.' (MERLOT)

'I don't think MERLOT ever thought it was their responsibility to create and develop the learning objects. It simply wanted to make available the learning objects and to give credit – scholarly and academic credit – to the developers, the authors.' (MERLOT)

'But my point is that's why we're so often looking for those delightful learning objects that are – and you heard me say it before we started – the "sweet spot"... The shorter ones that you pick to plug in? Yeah, the "sweet spot".' (MERLOT)

'My collection has 75 different countries ... and 11,000 users over the last year. And I'd say a good 15 per cent of them are foreign users, at least.' (DLESE)

'Like, I know the San Diego super computer has 20 per cent of our users, and I have no clue what they're using it for yet.' (DLESE)

'I use MERLOT basically to show all my faculty how to find online course objects that they can use in conjunction with their regular classroom instruction.' (MERLOT)

'I have used, searched it for information.' (DLESE)

As readers can see, the digital libraries are used for all the purposes originally planned for them, and more. Some appear to contain quite active, dynamic data bases which are being created daily (daily atmospheric data, for instance, as a cumulative record), other things are mobile but not dynamic (simulations), and still others are fairly static, but nevertheless, extremely useful to some groups (e.g. middle school teachers).

Evaluating the digital library collections

This is a set of suggestions from the focus groups members (both DLESE and MERLOT) about what should be evaluated, who should evaluate, how it should be evaluated, how and who should be vetting the collection, and the like. Below are some representative comments. This was by far the largest subset of categories, although in the analysis, we have the set divided into this one (front of the stack), and what seemed to us to be a subset, 'Intellectual issues with digital libraries (Teaching)'.

> 'If you're wanting general advice about evaluating, I'd say, first is, what's your policies and all that stuff. 'Cause there's a lot of policy issues that go into this.' (DLESE)

Some comment needs to be made about the comment above, because it has become clear that each of the NSDL digital libraries is governed by its own set of user and developer-created policies. The policies for usage, contributions, refereeing and other matters will clearly affect the manner in which the individual libraries are evaluated. This may be less true when the evaluating individual was a contributor to policy development, but more true when the end user had no role in developing policies which now govern the individual library.

> 'Issue of "dead links", "link rot", or "site decay" – who's responsible for cleaning that up?' (MERLOT)
>
> '...If I'm translating you right, there are really two levels at which stuff gets reviewed. One is for the accuracy of the data that are on there, for the actual scientific information. The other [level at which materials on DLESE get reviewed] is pedagogical utility and facility.' (DLESE)
>
> 'You figure that in a peer-reviewed process, if the image were bad science, that the image wouldn't get up there. So that, I think the values of being able to see the review is that you can have things that can be useful but that still do have some limitations. I mean, you may be more aware of what those limitations are.' (MERLOT)
>
> 'But there are things where people have put a page and they haven't touched that page in three or four years to review it, and it just sits

there. Some decision about when do you revisit these things to see how current they are...' (MERLOT)

'We don't have enough in some areas.' (MERLOT)

'From users, you would want to go ahead and ask – user testing, what kind of user testing do they do.' (DLESE)

'How do they gain their quality of material, the pedagogical quality?' (DLESE)

Problems

'Mainly, the broken links are the problem for me...' (MERLOT)

'These teachers are desperate for this ... not just [high-quality] teaching material, they want data – scientific data. They way, they say it's more exciting if it's real-time...' (DLESE)

'The one thing I've discovered with mine, just having real-time data isn't enough ... It's not just the data, you have to have the documentation; and it doesn't have to be a full lesson plan. It's just enough so they can know the lesson plan.' (DLESE)

'I guess because there's so much information there, it wasn't as intuitive as a lot of websites that I've been to before, and I went to a lot...' (DLESE)

'I went to a lot of websites looking for things to engage the students, and I guess I had a problem just figuring out how to narrow and search it.' (DLESE)

'But I have a frustration with the website. Giving feedback is limited; it's limited to the front page.' (DLESE)

'But honestly that is an issue with me. I think it's a quality issue within the library ... when you like put up your list and you think you are getting all the right stuff and it puts you on a bad site, you want to be able to say, "I really question this site. Could you check it out and make sure that it meets the criteria for DLESE?"' (DLESE)

Sustainability of digital libraries; issues of whether or not they will continue to be funded, and related concerns

Users, developers, contributors and other interested parties are deeply concerned regarding whether or not NSF will continue to fund the national science digital libraries. The tone in which focus group members spoke of this issue suggests it is a grave one for them. Indeed, many have apparently come to believe the digital libraries are a critical national resource in the information age, and cannot imagine what their scientific life would be like without them. Other members of the focus groups point to the knowledge that a portion of usage comes from international parties, and they construct this usage as a critical effort for scientific sharing within the international scientific communities that are utilising the resources, especially the real-time data.

Members of the focus groups were quite intense as regards querying whether or not members of the research and evaluation team would learn of the NSF's strategy for sustaining and maintaining these libraries over the long haul, and many expressed concern that there might be no other agency, corporation or body which could or would assume responsibility were the federal government to cease its funding. Although none of the interviewees said so directly, they want NSF to understand that these critical resources must remain a priority if the nation is to remain scientifically competitive, and retain its scientific leadership in the larger international community.

> 'I would ask [NSF] for the strategy of sustainability ... because when it comes down to it, if it can't be sustained, then it really doesn't matter.' (DLESE)

> 'When you talk about sustainability ... are you talking about how are we going to keep the federal government funding it? Or are you talking about how do we keep growing the collection and the community?' 'Both.' (DLESE)

> 'And so, it was part of the proposal process you write in, what's your sustainability path? We get enough users, DOE wants to fund it then. We have probably 8 to 10 times the number of users that DOE has for its data, and we are having trouble getting funded by it.' (DLESE)

> 'There's a reason ... it's partially because of goodwill, good financial politics. If people know about it, people like it, they're interested, it's more likely you'll get money from Congress.' (DLESE)

> 'What about leisure use? What about wanting just to know something – instead of being the Monday *New York Times*, you go to DLESE to find out something cool and new about what's going on. So, I really – I mean, it may link to sustainability as you

mentioned – but really make it a tool that every person … And that would help in sustainability…' (DLESE)

'…and, you know, I'm not so sure how long MERLOT is going to be able to sustain itself.' (MERLOT)

Other themes that emerged, which appeared to possess less salience for interviewees, included student experiences with and in libraries and digital libraries; and the use of textbooks versus use of digital libraries. Two other categories also emerged in the categorisation process: 'scientific literacy', which refers to the role of the digital libraries in creating scientific literacy, and in creating a 'market' for scientific data, and 'the nature of MERLOT: referatory rather than repository'. The first of these might be 'recognisable' as something which should be included in the new web LibQUAL+® for digital libraries, but we are not certain the second will.

Scientific literacy as a category seemed powerful to some interviewees. As some of the foregoing data points have indicated, some users and developers seem to feel that having the digital libraries open to anyone with curiosity means that individuals might find their appetites whetted for more scientific information – genuine data from scientific findings. Several participants commented that creating scientific literacy in ordinary people was a way of increasing general sophistication and the desire for more scientific exploration; in other words, the digital libraries might help to create a more powerful market for scientific work itself.

The research and evaluation team took a first shot at 'mapping' the concepts to try to understand how the topical and category areas related to each other. Doing so, we felt, would create a more integrated sense of what concerns we should focus on in the evaluation effort for NSF. The category map, in slightly different terms, appears below, showing some of the implied relationships between categories in respondents' minds.

Clearly, while we believe we received valid and robust data from focus group respondents, we will be attempting to refine, clarify and augment those data as we refine DigiQUAL® for the online survey of users, developers, contributors and reviewers for the digital libraries, and thus we also seek input from audiences in venues in addition to the focus groups. Attendees at presentation sessions, readers of this chapter, and other interested parties who have substantive comments to make on categories, potential items for a web-based survey, and/or issues and concerns surrounding the services which digital libraries offer are invited to submit comments, suggestions or other helpful inputs to the authors.

Developing survey items

Using the actual wording of the users in the focus groups we constructed survey items from a grounded theory perspective. After identifying survey items and mapping them to themes of digital library service, we reduced the number of items to 180 based on perceived relevancy to the NSDL digital libraries profiled in earlier activities. The items were then tested in a pilot study of eight digital libraries during 2004–05 and we confirmed the emerging model of a digital library (as depicted in Figure 10.1) and its evaluation components.

The following digital libraries had tested DigiQUAL® by August 2005: CSERD, Illumina, Math Forum @ Drexel, MERLOT, NEEDS, NSDL Core Integration, and Utopia. Math Forum @ Drexel collected the largest number of surveys (775 completed surveys) (Kyrillidou and Giersch, 2005). The rest of the sites had only a very small number of surveys returned. We are trying to understand how we can increase response rates to a total market survey like DigiQUAL® in the web environment. It seems that an optional survey link is not working very well in this environment and that more compelling reasons need to be implemented for collecting robust and meaningful data. Based on the pilot implementation, we can draw some conclusions about issues to consider when conducting evaluations across digital libraries, specifically in the context of NSDL. Our major findings address those lessons learned.

Figure 10.1 The digital library environment

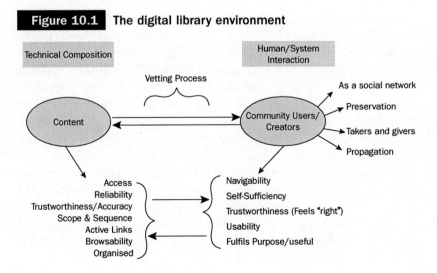

Findings

Defining the dimensions of service quality from a user perspective

While some of the items from the user focus groups overlap with items that are used in the LibQUAL+® protocol, the 12 themes are sufficiently different that the research team recommends that the DigiQUAL® protocol continue to be developed in the context of digital libraries. A question for further study is whether there will be any difference in the relevance of themes, if they are applied to digital collections developed in academic libraries, rather than collections of born-digital items and services.

Creating a tool for measuring user perceptions and expectations of service quality across contexts

The vocabulary and content of the items developed during the focus group had some interesting differences across the pilot sites. The 180 items are not all applicable across all sites. To address this during pilot testing, several pilot sites were consulted to provide input about the items. Of the 180 items that were tested, sites only selected those that were applicable.

During the pilot testing of the survey form, participating sites requested that more, rather than fewer, demographic items should be included as this was often the first opportunity sites had to gather feedback about and from their users. The researchers had to balance this request with developing a survey form of appropriate length. However, this, along with other findings below, suggests that a qualifying process may need to precede application of the DigiQUAL® protocol at a site. For example, a qualifying process might first identify the users and their demographics and then approach them to ask questions about digital library service quality.

DigiQUAL® is technically scalable. Having a centralised, secure website where participants can manage how their site's surveys are developed and modified frees ARL's developer from having to create a customised survey for every digital library, and it reduces technical and organisational barriers to digital library developers deploying DigiQUAL®.

Establishing a digital library service quality assessment programme as part of ARL's library service quality assessment programme

ARL member libraries are receptive to the idea of using DigiQUAL® in the context of their locally-created digital collections. Implementing DigiQUAL® in additional digital environments provides opportunities for further validating the survey items. This work is closely linked with the MINES for Libraries® and linkages are explored (see Chapter 2). It also relates to efforts to develop e-metrics for libraries (Kyrillidou and Giersch, 2004; Shim et al., 2001).

Identifying 'best practices' that permit generalisations across operations and development platforms

Digital libraries must have a critical mass of users committed and willing to fill in survey data before conducting evaluation activities such as a total market survey. In the meantime, they will have to rely on contextualised methods for actionable results. Conducting evaluations with digital libraries was challenging because most sites do not know who their users are or how to contact them directly. The researchers attribute this to the short-term, project-based nature of digital library development (e.g. little time or budget to conduct extensive demographic evaluations) and to the education and research focus of many sites, especially those developed for users under 18 (e.g. no login required). Not knowing approximate demographics for sites' user groups made it impossible to gauge response rates and to assess whether notification measures worked. In most cases during pilot testing, the survey response rate was low due to a lack of a critical mass of users, so the DigiQUAL® survey yielded little actionable data. In all cases, it was difficult to interpret survey responses as representative of a site's user base because there was no indication that all users had been notified of the survey. For subsequent DigiQUAL® implementations, the researchers recommend developing a profile of a digital library that would, among other things, identify if there are enough users to provide a significant number of responses. For evaluating digital libraries, the researchers recommend applying a mixed-methods approach that combines quantitative and qualitative (interviews, focus groups) methods.

Institutionalising continuous product and process evaluation efforts directed toward positive and timely management of outcomes

Digital libraries are reluctant to share the results of individual evaluation efforts. During the process of implementing the NSF-funded DigiQUAL® study, researchers learned that participants were not interested in sharing results about their sites. While the digital library community values a collaborative approach towards accomplishing project work, projects are faced with a competitive funding structure that provides no incentive for sharing data.

The depth and breadth of commitment by research libraries is indicative of the urgent need for outcome evaluation in libraries and is a reflection of the enthusiasm of the postsecondary library community for alternative measures. Adapting the LibQUAL+® for the digital library community remains a necessary and important next step. The digital library environment continues to morph, and developments such as cyberinfrastructure, cyberlearning and e-science (Association of Research Libraries/Coalition for Networked Information, 2008; Borgman, 2007; Tenopir and King, 2004) will influence further our notions of what constitutes a digital library.

There is a danger of allowing the means to become the end in the form of a technological determinism – rigorous understanding of the disciplinary transformations and the challenges of transitioning into digital and reducing print resources is helping libraries engage in systematic assessment methods. Assessment and evaluation coupled with responsible development will help libraries survive and thrive into the new century.

Bibliography

Association of Research Libraries/Coalition for Networked Information (2008) 'Reinventing science librarianship: Models for the future', paper presented at the ARL/CNI Fall 2008 Forum, Arlington, VA, 16–17 October, available at: *http://www.arl.org/resources/pubs/fallforumproceedings/forum08proceedings.shtml* (accessed 27 November 2008).

Borgman, C. (2007) *Scholarship in the Digital Age*, Boston, MA: MIT Press.

Cook, C. (ed.) (2002a) 'The maturation of assessment in academic libraries: The role of LibQUAL+™', *Performance Measurement and Metrics* 3(2): 40–107.

Cook, C. C. (2002b) 'A mixed-methods approach to the identification and measurement of academic library service quality constructs: LibQUAL+™', unpublished PhD dissertation, Texas A&M University.

Cook, C. and Heath, F. (2001) 'Users' perceptions of library service quality: A LibQUAL+™ qualitative study', *Library Trends* 49(4): 548–84.

Cook, C. and Thompson, B. (2001) 'Psychometric properties of scores from the web-based LibQUAL+™ study of perceptions of library service quality', *Library Trends* 49(4): 585–604.

Cook, C., Heath, F. and Thompson, B. (2001a) 'Users' hierarchical perspectives on library service quality: A LibQUAL+™ study', *College and Research Libraries* 62(2): 147–53.

Cook, C., Heath, F., Thompson, R. L. and Thompson, B. (2001b) 'Score reliability in web- or internet-based surveys: Unnumbered graphic rating scales versus Likert-type scales', *Educational and Psychological Measurement* 61(4): 697–706.

Cook, C., Heath, F. and Thompson, B. (2002) 'Score norms for improving library service quality: A LibQUAL+™ study', *portal: Libraries and the Academy* 2(1): 13–26.

Cook, C., Heath, F. and Thompson, B. (2003) '"Zones of tolerance" in perceptions of library service quality: A LibQUAL+™ study', *portal: Libraries and the Academy* 3(1): 113–23.

Heath, F., Cook, C., Kyrillidou, M. and Thompson, B. (2002) 'ARL Index and other validity correlates of LibQUAL+™ scores', *portal: Libraries and the Academy* 2(1): 27–42.

Heath, F., Kyrillidou, M. and Askew, C. (eds) (2004) 'Libraries act on their LibQUAL+™ findings: From data to action', *Journal of Library Administration* 40(3–4): 1–241.

Kyrillidou, M. (2006) 'Service quality: A perceived outcome for libraries', in P. Hernon, R. E. Dungan and C. Schwartz (eds) *Revisiting Outcomes Assessment in Higher Education*, Westport, CT: Libraries Unlimited, pp. 331–66.

Kyrillidou, M. and Giersch, S. (2004) 'Qualitative analysis of ARL E-metrics participant feedback about the evolution of measures for networked electronic resources', *Library Quarterly* 74(4): 423–40.

Kyrillidou, M. and Giersch, S. (2005) 'The DigiQUAL protocol for digital library evaluation', in *Proceedings of the 5th ACM/IEEE-CS*

Joint Conference on Digital Libraries, New York: ACM Press, pp. 172–3.

Kyrillidou, M. and Heath, F. (2004) 'The starving research library user: Relationships between library institutional characteristics and Spring 2002 LibQUAL+™ scores', in *Libraries Act on Their LibQUAL+™ Findings: From Data to Action*, New York: Haworth Press, pp. 1–11.

Kyrillidou, M. and Persson, A. (2006) 'The new library user in Sweden: A LibQUAL+™ study at Lund University', *Performance Measurement and Metrics* 7(1): 45–53.

Kyrillidou, M. and Young, M. (2008) *ARL Statistics 2005–06*, Washington DC: ARL.

Kyrillidou, M., Olshen, T., Heath, F., Bonnelly, C. and Côte, J. (2005) 'La mise en œuvre interculturelle de LibQUAL+MC Le cas du français', *BBF Paris* 50(5): 48–55.

Kyrillidou, M., Cook, C. and Rao, S. S. (2008) 'Measuring library service quality and LibQUAL+®', in *Academic Libraries Research Perspectives, Vol. 2*. Chicago, IL: ALA/ACRL: 253–301.

Lincoln, Y. (2002) 'Insights into library services and users from qualitative research', *Library and Information Science Research* 24(1): 3–16.

Lincoln, Y., Cook, C. and Kyrillidou, M. (2004) 'Evaluating the NSF National Science Digital Library Collections', available at: *http://www.libqual.org/documents/admin/merlot%20paper2_final.pdf* (accessed 26 November 2008).

Lincoln, Y., Cook, C. and Kyrillidou, M. (2005) 'User perspectives into designs for both physical and digital libraries: New insights on commonalities/similarities and differences from the NDSL digital libraries and LibQUAL+™ data bases', paper presented at 7th ISKO-Spain Conference: The Human Dimension of Knowledge Organization, Barcelona, 6–8 July, available at: *http://bd.ub.es/isko2005/lincoln.pdf* (accessed 26 November 2008).

Tenopir, C. and King, D. W. (2004) *Communication Patterns of Engineers*, Hoboken, NJ: John Wiley and Sons.

Thompson, B. and Cook, C. (2002) 'Stability of the reliability of LibQUAL+™ scores: A "reliability generalization" meta-analysis study', *Educational and Psychological Measurement* 62(4): 735–43.

Thompson, B., Cook, C. and Heath, F. (2000) 'The LibQUAL+™ gap measurement model: The bad, the ugly, and the good of gap measurement', *Performance Measurement and Metrics* 1(3): 165–78.

Thompson, B., Cook, C. and Heath, F. (2001) 'How many dimensions does it take to measure users' perceptions of libraries?: A

LibQUAL+™ study', *portal: Libraries and the Academy* 1(2): 129–38.

Thompson, B., Cook, C. and Thompson, R. L. (2002) 'Reliability and structure of LibQUAL+™ scores: Measuring perceived library service quality', *portal: Libraries and the Academy* 2(1): 3–12.

Thompson, B., Cook, C. and Heath, F. (2003a) 'Structure of perceptions of service quality in libraries: A LibQUAL+™ study', *Structural Equation Modeling* 10(3): 456–64.

Thompson, B., Cook, C. and Heath, F. (2003b) 'Two short forms of the LibQUAL+™ survey assessing users' perceptions of library service quality', *Library Quarterly* 73(4): 453–65.

Thompson, B., Cook, C. and Kyrillidou, M. (2005) Concurrent validity of LibQUAL+™ scores: What do LibQUAL+™ scores measure? *Journal of Academic Librarianship* 31(6): 517–22.

Thompson, B., Cook, C. and Kyrillidou, M. (2006a) 'Stability of library service quality benchmarking norms across time and cohorts: A LibQUAL+™ study', paper presented at the Asia-Pacific Conference of Library and Information Education and Practice, Singapore, 4–7 April, available at: *http://www.coe.tamu.edu/~bthompson/libq2005 .htm* (accessed 28 November 2008).

Thompson, B., Cook, C. and Kyrillidou, M. (2006b) 'Using localized survey items to augment standardized benchmarking measures: A LibQUAL+™ study', *portal: Libraries and the Academy* i(2): 219–30.

Thompson, B., Kyrillidou, M. and Cook, C. (2007a) 'On-premises library versus Google™-like information gateway usage patterns: A LibQUAL+® study', *portal: Libraries and the Academy* 7(4): 463–80.

Thompson, B., Kyrillidou, M. and Cook, C. (2007b) 'User library service expectations in health science versus other settings: A LibQUAL+® study', *Health Information and Libraries Journal* 24(Suppl. 1): 38–45.

Thompson, B., Kyrillidou, M. and Cook, C. (2008) 'Library users' service desires: A LibQUAL+® study', *Library Quarterly* 78(1): 1–18.

Torgovnik, M. (2008) 'File under fleeting: Archives are more ephemeral than they seem', *The Chronicle Review*, 5 September, B14–B16.

Shim, W., McClure, C. R., Fraser, B. and Bertot, J. C. (2001) *Data Collection Manual for Academic and Research Library Network Statistics and Performance Measures*, Washington, DC: ARL.

Zeithaml, V. A., Parasuraman, A. and Berry, L. L. (1990) *Delivering Quality Service: Balancing Customer Perceptions and Expectations*, New York: Free Press.

Part 4
How to conduct an evaluation activity

11

Planning digital library evaluation with logic models

Michael Khoo and Sarah Giersch

Introduction

Effective digital library evaluation integrates a wide range of organisational, methodological and technical factors. At the same time, evaluation work can be constrained by such factors as limited funds, limited time and limited access to users. How can evaluators work within these parameters to produce a realistic evaluation work plan that yields actionable results? This chapter introduces a checklist that outlines some key practical steps associated with planning for digital library evaluation, with particular emphasis on developing a logic model. The checklist places evaluation planning at the intersection of four activities: identifying strategic evaluation questions, selecting appropriate evaluation methods, negotiating stakeholder buy-in and obtaining adequate resources to support the evaluation. We will focus on the process of using strategic evaluation questions to develop a logic model and then identify the synergies between this activity and the other three activities (some of which are covered in more detail elsewhere in this book).

An underlying assumption of the checklist is that digital library evaluation consists of a series of longitudinally linked activities, in which the success of later evaluation activities depends significantly on the preparation that went into the earlier activities. Paying close attention to evaluation during the planning stages – including identifying evaluation questions, and specifying an evaluation budget – can be crucial to supporting substantive evaluation efforts later in the life of the digital library. This chapter introduces two logic model-based evaluation methods that can be useful in planning formative and summative digital library evaluation, especially during the initial stages of planning a digital library. The methods are presented within the context of our own digital library evaluation experiences, and draw upon a number of existing online evaluation guides (e.g. Frechtling, 2002; Reeves et al., 2006).

Digital libraries are complex systems, and planning a digital library evaluation is a complex activity

Digital libraries are composed of a wide range of social, technological, organisational and other phenomena, embedded in a variety of external contexts (e.g. social, political, economic, organisational, etc.). They can be modelled as sociotechnical systems, comprised of many components linked in complex and mutually constitutive ways (Bishop et al., 2003). The external contexts in which they are embedded also interact in mutually constitutive ways, both with each other and with digital libraries. For example, factors such as a school's bandwidth, the number and age of its computers, the presence or absence of technological support staff, and the availability of professional development, can all affect educational technology use in ways that have nothing to do with the technology itself (National Education Association, 2008).

As sociotechnical systems, digital libraries exhibit many of the properties of complex adaptive systems, including unpredictable development and emergent properties (Marchionini, 2000). While new digital libraries may begin with broadly similar aims and activities – such as developing resources, collections, metadata, catalogues, search engines and web interfaces – the complex local conditions in which they are situated shape their growth and development in unpredictable and unique ways. With the recent development of a range of web-based tools that support personalised services, seamless content creation and publication, and reuse and re-combination of multiple data formats, which are now being offered through digital libraries, there is no longer a 'one size fits all' version of the digital library (Lagoze et al., 2005; McArthur and Zia, 2008; Miller, 2006).

The complexity of digital library evaluation work is illustrated by an example from the National Science Digital Library (NSDL). Funded by the National Science Foundation (NSF), the NSDL is a series of distributed projects engaged in a number of digital library building activities, such as developing online science, technology, engineering and mathematics

(STEM) resources, technology architecture and web-based services (NSDL, year unknown). One of the conditions for receiving NSF funding is that NSDL projects are expected to conduct evaluation work and to report the data to NSF via annual reports. A 2006 survey of evaluation practices among NSDL projects (Bartolo et al., 2006) asked the projects about their engagement with a range of evaluation activities, from developing evaluation questions, metrics and instruments, and identifying evaluators, to collecting and analysing evaluation data, and disseminating evaluation reports and sending findings to NSF. The survey assumed that evaluation activities occurred as part of an integrated workflow, with each stage of the workflow generating a foundation upon which the next stage can be developed. For example, the drafting of evaluation questions supports the development of measures for project success; project metrics support the design of data collection methods; methods enable data collection; and data collection supplies material for analysis, reports and articles. In the case of NSDL, the survey data revealed that as projects moved along this evaluation workflow, the likelihood that they would abandon their evaluation work increased, and the implementation of evaluation activities exhibited a downward attrition trend along the evaluation workflow. While almost all projects started out with an evaluation plan, fewer projects completed evaluation and reported data to NSF or to professional audiences (see Table 11.1, Figure 11.1). This decline occurred both with completed projects and also with projects that were still being funded and which had yet to complete their work. The survey also identified a number of resource barriers to carrying out evaluation, including lack of budget, lack of staff, lack of evaluation capacity (including difficulties in hiring external evaluators appropriately qualified in either evaluation and/or digital library expertise), and lack of time. Each of these constraints could act on each of the evaluation stages, causing activities to stall at that particular stage.

The example of NSDL projects' experience with completing integrated evaluation activities illustrates the importance of some of the longitudinal factors that can affect digital library evaluation. Sufficient resources are required to support each stage of the digital library evaluation workflow, and lack of resources at one workflow stage will affect not just that stage of the workflow, but also subsequent stages. Given the complexity of digital libraries, evaluation works best when implemented as a holistic and integrated activity that extends throughout the duration of digital library development. While this work requires a larger initial amount of effort to prepare, a well-planned, longitudinal evaluation strategy has the potential to yield more useful data for the

Table 11.1 Percentage reported types of evaluation practices in NSDL

Evaluation activity	% Respondents reporting activity
Planning activities	
Evaluation plan included in NSF proposal	89
Designated internal/external evaluator(s)	83
Developed formal metrics of project success	46
Developed formal methods and instruments	71
Implementation activities	
Implemented evaluation plan and collected data	75
Analysed evaluation data	75
Dissemination activities	
Presented findings at workshops	70
Made findings available in internal report	64
Presented or published findings at conferences	62
Sent evaluation findings to NSF	48
Published findings in journals	23

same amount of resource expenditure than an unplanned, ad hoc and non-integrated approach.

An evaluation planning checklist

The rest of this chapter outlines a checklist of four key activities involved in planning and organising a digital library evaluation initiative, both during proposal writing to fund the digital library project, and in the context of conducting evaluations of already-funded digital libraries. More broadly, the checklist is both a model of what digital libraries are, and also a model of what evaluators often do. Specifically, it is based on the assumption that evaluation consists not just of the evaluation requirements outlined in programme solicitations, but also of a series of integrated sets of practices that support the development and implementation of a holistic model of the system under evaluation. An underlying assumption of the checklist is that later evaluation work

Figure 11.1 Percentage reported types of evaluation practices in NSDL

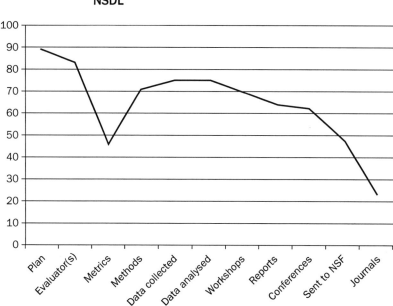

needs to be supported by the earlier identification of strategic evaluation questions, and by the pre-allocation of resources to address those questions.

The components of the checklist are:

- identifying key formative and summative evaluation *questions* (this will be the main focus of the discussion, and will include a discussion of logic models);

- selecting appropriate *methods* (such as web metrics, usability and human-computer interaction (HCI) work, surveys interviews and focus groups, ethnography, etc.);

- identifying important *stakeholders* (funders, managers, developers, users, etc.) and establishing stakeholder buy-in;

- *budgeting* for evaluation work in the initial project proposal.

These four early-stage evaluation planning activities are represented in Figure 11.2 as a series of overlapping circles, intended to convey the fact that while these activities involve separate considerations and tasks, they

Figure 11.2 Four key activities involved in planning and organising a digital library evaluation initiative

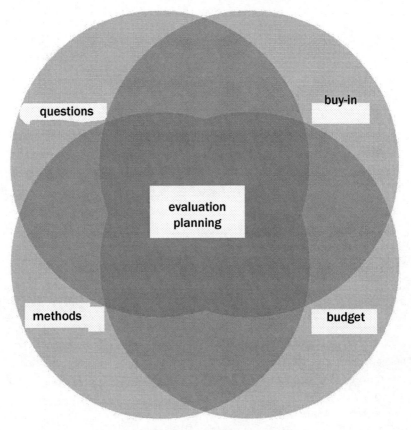

are closely linked and interdependent. For example, the drafting of strategic evaluation questions is closely related to stakeholder buy-in, shapes the methods chosen, and is affected by the budget available for evaluation activities. Again, stakeholder buy-in has a close relationship both with shaping the strategic questions, and setting an evaluation budget. Taken together, the areas of activity in Figure 11.2 can provide substantial support for the evaluation work carried out during the actual project, and it will be harder for projects to begin implementation of an evaluation plan late in the life of a project without having addressed these activities (although this does not mean that commencing evaluation during the latter stages of a project is impossible).

Planning for summative and formative evaluation

In the rest of this chapter we expand upon the four evaluation planning activities outlined in Figure 11.2, focusing mainly on the identification of strategic summative and formative evaluation goals. In the following section we also briefly cover some of the linkages between this activity and selecting methods, obtaining buy-in, and setting a budget.

Planning summative evaluation questions and goals

Evaluation resources are used most efficiently when formative and summative questions address specific strategic issues for a project, with the outcomes from these evaluation questions being used to guide project development in useful ways (Reeves et al., 2006). The development of strategic evaluation questions can be supported by integrating evaluation planning into the overall project research plan during the early stages of the project. Proposal writing and evaluation planning can be mutually supporting activities, with the description of the proposed work shaping the development of the evaluation plan, and the evaluation plan providing useful feedback on the feasibility of the project proposal. In practice, this means working with the emerging research proposal, maintaining communication with managers, developers and other project members, and eliciting from project members clear descriptions of what they are planning to do.

Using logic models to plan summative evaluation

The identification of summative evaluation questions can be supported through the use of logic models: graphical, high-level, system-based conceptual models of a project (such as a digital library) that describe how that project is funded, what it does, and what it hopes to achieve. A logic model does this principally by linking project inputs to activities, and then to project outcomes (Morge et al., 2008; Renger and Hurley, 2006).

Logic models generally describe four high-level sets of project activities: (a) project inputs, that is, the various funding sources and revenue streams that support project activity; (b) project activities, that is, the processes that the project engages in on a day-to-day level;

(c) short-term outputs, that is, the immediate results; and (d) long-term project outcomes, 'broader and more enduring impacts on the system' (Frechtling, 2002: 17). These activities are longitudinally articulated; for instance, project inputs support the project activities, and the project activities generate the short-term and long-term outcomes (however, there are a number of variations on these themes, e.g. Centers for Disease Control and Prevention, 2008; Frechtling, 2002; Taylor-Powell and Henert, 2008; W. K. Kellogg Foundation, 2004).

As a hypothetical example, Figure 11.3 presents a possible outline of a logic model for an educational digital library project. Here, the input is NSF funding; the project's activities include creating exemplary resources and metadata, developing a web interface, carrying out comprehensive outreach activities, and building strategic partnerships with educational institutions. Expected short-term outputs include the development of themed collections, public awareness of the library, and growing numbers of satisfied users of the library and its website. Long-term outputs include the successful incorporation of library materials into school curricula, and an increase in students' knowledge of the library's subject domain.

Figure 11.3 A basic logic model for evaluating an educational digital library

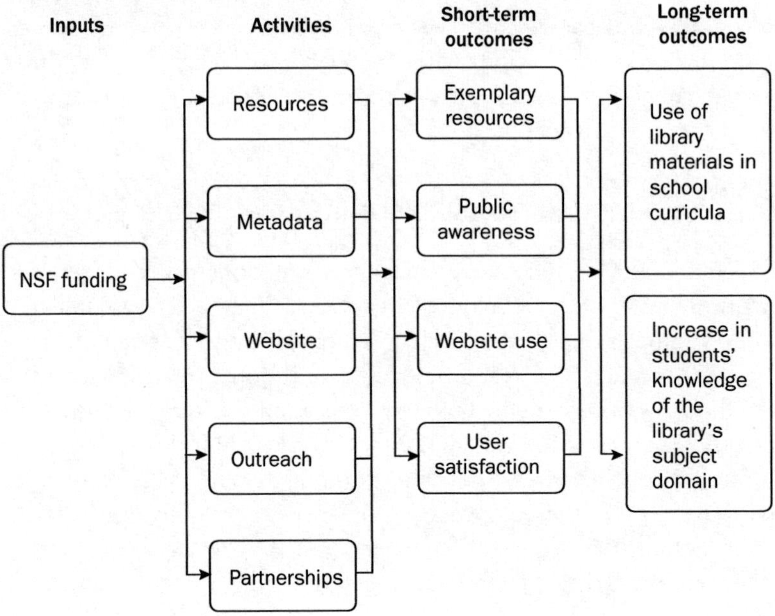

A major benefit of a logic model approach, if it is used in conjunction with discussions with project managers and developers, especially at the beginning of a project, is that it supports stakeholders to identify and articulate some of the basic components, linkages and aims of a project. In particular, by prompting a project to clearly define goals and outcomes, it helps stakeholders to begin defining exactly how they would like to achieve those outcomes using the available resources (such as project funds and available skills and expertise). For example, Frechtling (2002) suggests using the logic model approach to work backwards from the expected outcomes, as a way of determining what activities would need to take place in order to achieve theses outcomes.

Planning formative evaluation questions and goals

Evaluation planning should also include a number of formative evaluation measures – for instance, the number of resources generated, the quality of those resources, the quality of metadata, web interface usability, and so on – which can both produce useful data for the ongoing iterative improvement of a digital library and can provide a solid foundations upon which to build summative evaluation. While logic models do identify inputs, activities and outputs at the overall project level, they do not necessarily offer support for understanding how the internal linkages in a project support project activities in converting these inputs into outcomes. In a summative logic model, the internal functions of a project are often 'black boxed' and obscured from view. How, therefore, can evaluators identify suitable library components for formative evaluation (especially given the internal complexity of digital libraries)? This section describes how the logic model approach can also be adapted to guide the planning of formative evaluation questions, and as an example, describes how such an approach was implemented with the NSDL.

Using logic models to plan NSDL evaluation

As described above, the NSDL consists of a series of distributed projects engaged in a number of digital library building activities, such as developing online science, technology, engineering and mathematics (STEM) resources, technology architecture and web-based services. Selecting common formative metrics for evaluation across this heterogeneous mix of components was not easy. One common unit that did link many NSDL projects across the context of the NSDL programme was that of the digital, or online, resource. Specifically, many NSDL project activities were involved with creating resources, adding them to collections and cataloguing them, making them available on the web, or supporting their use in the classroom. The NSDL therefore developed a logic model-based formative evaluation approach – the model was called the 'resource lifecycle' – which focused on the production of digital library resources in the NSDL as a way of identifying internal NSDL components and linkages for formative evaluation (e.g. Khoo, 2006a, 2006b). Having defined digital resources as the unit of analysis, the model tracked resources through various stages of NSDL operations, from creation to the moment of use, and then beyond to the moment of redesign and improvement. Overall, the model identified several basic sequential areas of activity in which various NSDL projects acted on or modified digital resources, including:

- resource creation;
- collection creation;
- resource retrieval;
- resource use and reuse.

Each of these stages was then modelled as a simple logic model in itself, with inputs, activities and outputs, and the stages were joined, with the outcome from one stage forming the input of the next stage (two example stages of the model are shown in Figure 11.4).

Taken together, these stages constitute a 'production line' model, each stage of which involves transforming digital resources, in the process adding value and utility to those resources. For example, a resource that has been reviewed for pedagogical effectiveness, scientific accuracy, and technological functionality is more valuable than a resource that has not; a resource described by accurate metadata is more valuable than a resource that is not; a resource embedded within a powerful search and discovery tool is more valuable than one that is not; and so on. It is the cumulative outcome of all stages of the model that ensures the development of exemplary resources for NSDL; conversely, poor-quality operations at any one stage of the cycle can have adverse effects downstream in the workflow. For instance, poor metadata quality affects search and retrieval; poor resource quality affects classroom use; poor usability affects the user experience (and presumably adversely affects repeat visits); and so on.

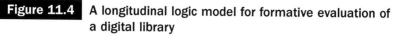

Figure 11.4 A longitudinal logic model for formative evaluation of a digital library

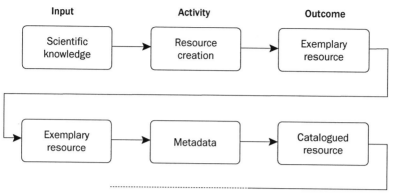

The resource lifecycle model had several advantages for the NSDL evaluation work. The model provided a unifying narrative within which to begin examining the wide range of disparate projects within NSDL. Components of the model's stages – such as resource quality, website usability, etc. – identified strategically useful places at which to carry out formative evaluation of individual project components, and also provided a coherent overview of how different evaluation activities at different parts of NSDL – such as webmetrics and user interviews – might be related. In the form of documentation (in the case of NSDL, a white paper by Khoo, 2006c), the model provided a useful 'boundary object' (Star and Griesemer, 1989) that could be used to explain the rationale for evaluation work to various stakeholders, including NSDL managers, individual NSDL projects, and the NSF (as well as to obtain buy-in and support from those groups – see below).

One disadvantage of the approach was that it could be resource-intensive, and required expertise in a wide range of digital library areas. Further, some of the potential formative evaluation areas identified were difficult to investigate, for a variety of reasons, including access to database systems (e.g. in the case of metadata), access to servers (in the case of web metrics), access to users (in the case of classroom use), etc. Finally, as noted above, many digital libraries are now introducing services that are not resource-centric and are therefore more difficult to model using this approach and which may require newer logic models to describe them. Despite these limitations, however, the model clarified and organised some of the disparate dimensions of NSDL in a useful way, provided coherence and focus for a range of formative evaluation concepts and practices, and helped in the identification of important internal linkages within NSDL where formative evaluation resources could be targeted.

In summary, logic models are useful tools, which support planning at the earliest phases of a digital library project, while also providing a means of integrating evaluation activities into the project plan. They provide a framework for identifying summative evaluation questions that are tied to project outcomes and also for identifying formative evaluation questions that are linked to digital library development activities throughout the life of the project. The planning of formative and summative evaluation questions does not take place in the abstract, however, and the following section describes how the development of logic model-based evaluation questions during the project proposal stage is closely linked with the activities of identifying data collection methods, promoting buy-in among stakeholders, and developing an evaluation budget for a project.

Relationship to methods, buy-in and budget

This section briefly examines the relationship between identifying evaluation questions, and the three other areas of evaluation planning outlined above: selecting data collection methods, negotiating buy-in and budgeting for evaluation activities.

Methods

Developing formative and summative evaluation questions supports the selection of appropriate tools and techniques for subsequent evaluation activities (a range of different quantitative and qualitative methodologies is discussed in the following chapters). If multiple questions have been identified, a project will ideally be able to deploy several ongoing evaluation methods in a 'mixed methods' approach (Ryan et al., 2001), or what Marchionini et al. (2003) refer to as an iterative and 'multifaceted' approach to digital library evaluation and development, in which 'multiple data views are essential to guide design and to help us to understand the impact of digital libraries'. If one or more evaluation approaches are used to address the same question(s), confidence in evaluation data will be increased if the methods can be triangulated.

Logistical factors for methods (often related to budget issues – see below) include the presence of evaluation skills on the project team, and whether or not to hire an external evaluator (for a task such as usability this may be expensive, but probably cheaper in the long run than paying project staff to become familiar with a new evaluation technique); comparing the types of tools to be used (for instance, choosing free web metrics tools, or more expensive but also more powerful proprietary tools); choosing the mix of laboratory and naturalistic studies of users (laboratory studies can be easier and quicker to organise, however, they may miss some of the more subtle data that can be obtained from observing digital library users 'in the wild', e.g. Khoo and Ribes, 2005); and comparing time scales and cost (different methods, such as surveys and ethnography, can differ significantly in resource requirements in terms of time and money).

Buy-in

As the formal evaluation plan proceeds, it is useful to begin obtaining buy-in for the proposed work from stakeholders, such as project members, funding agencies, users and others who may have an interest in the outcome(s) of the project. Buy-in can be supported by eliciting and addressing stakeholders' models of and expectations for a project. Note that different stakeholders may have different priorities for a project, and may advocate for different evaluation metrics and measurements; for instance, funding agencies may have different evaluation priorities than the projects they fund. (Agencies' general requirements, which can be used to help frame strategic evaluation goals, are usually described in programme solicitations, and agencies may make other evaluation materials available elsewhere on their website (e.g. see Chapter 3, this volume; Frechtling, 2002).

As was also noted in Chapter 3, there is a danger that projects may see evaluation as a burden imposed by funding agencies, in which evaluation data and outcomes may be unwelcome or threatening to a project (e.g. as evidence that a project is 'not succeeding'); and the evaluation relationship can potentially become adversarial (Frechtling, 2002; Reeves et al., 2006). Buy-in can be supported by drafting and circulating proposals for discussion, for instance in memo or white paper form, and by having stakeholders discuss the proposed plan. Documents generated at this stage can also be used to support the description of the evaluation in the project proposal, and also serve as the basis for discussion of ongoing evaluation as the project progresses.

Canvassing various stakeholders' conceptions of the proposed project goals and outcomes can require significant effort, for several reasons. A project's aims can remain in flux until the submission of the proposal (or even after). There may be different stakeholder (e.g. agency, developer and user) understandings of a project, or no commonly articulated overall goals for the project, or disagreement among project members regarding the key strategic goals of a project, or differences between projects and funding agencies with regard to appropriate evaluation measures, or insufficient clarity on the role or purpose of evaluation for a project. Different stakeholder groups may also hold (often without realising it) different mental models of the project's goals, and these differences need to be untangled and reconciled (Khoo, 2005). Even in these circumstances, it is still useful to continue to identify preliminary questions from various stakeholders to use as the basis for beginning the evaluation activities.

Budget

Evaluation is 'a people-intensive process, and therefore, most of the money spent on evaluation usually will be for dedicated evaluation personnel and/or external consultant costs' (Reeves et al., 2006: 21). The proposed evaluation work must be included in the budget (and not borrowed from 'leftover' funds) or else it will be difficult to complete. The planning stages of a project proposal are a good point at which to start developing an appropriate evaluation budget as it may become harder later in the project's life to request funds for evaluation. Opinions differ as to how much should be included in a budget for evaluation; for instance, Reeves et al. (2006) recommend 5–10 per cent of the overall budget, while some government agencies recommend that 10–15 per cent of the overall budget should be spent.

An evaluation budget is often a miniature version of the full proposal budget, and should be accompanied by a detailed budget justification that includes (where appropriate) items such as staff time, external consultants' fees, participant stipends for laboratory studies, evaluation hardware and software costs, and travel (both for any evaluation work and also for the presentation of results), etc. (Horn, 2001). The availability of evaluation budget resources can influence the selection of different types of evaluation methods (e.g. one-shot quantitative versus longitudinal qualitative evaluation), and different types of evaluation tools (such as web metrics packages).

If evaluation planning is left to the end of the proposal writing, the evaluation budget runs the risk of being minimised at the expense of other project components, or reduced as final adjustments are made to the full budget proposal. Lack of funding at this stage of the evaluation work could generate problems later in the life of the project, when it may prove difficult or impractical either to carry out the required work, or to request additional funding. On the other hand, there are useful synergies between formulating the evaluation questions as part of a logic model (see previous section) and creating the evaluation budget. Having a sense of what is realistically achievable for evaluation in terms of the entire project's resources can help to guide the discussion on the research questions and what is hoped to be achieved overall by the project.

Summary

Digital libraries are complex phenomena, and the evaluation of digital libraries is a complex activity that requires considerable planning if it is to be accomplished successfully. We have argued in this chapter for the importance of including digital library evaluation planning at the very earliest stages of a project, as a way of supporting the overall development of the project proposal, establishing the evaluation questions, and making the case for an appropriate allocation of resources to support the investigation of these questions. To help frame this work, we identified four key interrelated areas of evaluation planning: (a) formative and summative evaluation questions, (b) suitable methods for investigating these questions, (c) stakeholder buy-in for the proposed work, and (d) a suitable budget to support the work. We have also discussed the application of a logic model approach to the identification of strategic formative and summative evaluation questions. Logic models analyse digital libraries as systems of coordinated activities, with specified inputs, goals and outcomes, in which each activity incrementally adds value and utility, and in which the output of any one activity forms the input of one or more succeeding stages. Logic models can also be used to identify key strategic linkages within a project and their upstream and downstream dependencies, which can then be used as loci for focused and coordinated evaluation activities.

Bibliography

Bartolo, L., Diekema, A., Khoo, M. and McMartin, F. (2006) 'Evaluation practices in NSDL', available at: *http://eval.comm.nsdl .org/docs/06_evaluation_practices.pdf* (accessed 1 June 2008).

Bishop, A., Van House, N. and Buttenfield, B. (2003) 'Introduction: Digital libraries as sociotechnical systems', in A. Bishop, N. Van House and B. Buttenfield (eds) *Digital Library Use: Social Practice in Design and Evaluation*, Cambridge, MA: MIT Press, pp. 1–21.

Centers for Disease Control and Prevention (2008) 'Introduction to process evaluation in tobacco use prevention and control', available at: *http://www.cdc.gov/tobacco/publications/index.htm* (accessed 1 June 2008).

Frechtling, J. (2002) 'The 2002 user-friendly handbook for project evaluation', available at: *http://www.nsf.gov/pubs/2002/nsf02057/ start.htm* (accessed 1 June 2008).

Horn, J. (2001) 'A checklist for developing and evaluating evaluation budgets', available at: *http://www.wmich.edu/evalctr/checklists/ evaluationbudgets.htm* (accessed 1 June 2008).

Khoo, M. (2005) 'The tacit dimensions of user behavior: The case of the digital water education library', in *Proceedings of the 5th ACM/IEEE Joint Conference on Digital Libraries, Denver, CO, 7–11 June*, New York: ACM Press, pp. 213–22.

Khoo, M. (2006a) 'Evaluating the National Science Digital Library', in *Proceedings of the 6th ACM/IEEE Joint Conference on Digital Libraries, Chapel Hill, NC, 11–15 June*, New York: ACM Press, p. 342.

Khoo, M. (2006b) 'A sociotechnical framework for evaluating a large-scale distributed educational digital library', in *Proceedings of the 10th European Conference on Digital Libraries, Alicante, 17–22 September*, Berlin: Springer-Verlag, pp. 449–52.

Khoo, M. (2006c) 'The "resource lifecycle": A sociotechnical framework for evaluating NSDL', available at: *http://eval.comm.nsdl.org/docs/ whitepaper.pdf* (accessed 1 June 2008).

Khoo, M. and Ribes, D. (2005) 'Studying digital library users in the wild, JCDL 2005 (Denver, CO): Workshop report', *D-Lib Magazine* 11(7–8), available at: *http://dlib.org/dlib/july05/khoo/07khoo.html* (accessed 1 June 2008).

Lagoze, C., Krafft, D., Payette, S. and Jesuroga, S. (2005) 'What is a digital library anymore, anyway?' *D-Lib Magazine* 11(11), available at: *http://www.dlib.org/dlib/november05/lagoze/11lagoze.html* (accessed 1 June 2008).

Marchionini, G. (2000) 'Evaluating digital libraries: A longitudinal and multifaceted view', *Library Trends* 49(2): 304–33.

Marchionini, G., Plaisant, C. and Komlodi, A. (2003) 'The people in digital libraries: Multifaceted approaches to assessing needs and impact', in A. Bishop, N. Van House and B. Buttenfield (eds) *Digital Library Use: Social Practice in Design and Evaluation*, Cambridge, MA: MIT Press, pp. 119–60.

McArthur, D. and Zia, L. (2008) 'From NSDL 1.0 to NSDL 2.0: Towards a comprehensive cyberinfrastructure for teaching and learning', in *Proceedings of the 8th ACM/IEEE Joint Conference on Digital Libraries, Pittsburgh, PA, 16–20 June*, New York: ACM Press, pp. 66–9.

Miller, P. (2006) 'Coming together around Library 2.0: A focus for discussion and a call to arms', *D-Lib Magazine* 12(4), available at: *http://www.dlib.org/dlib/april06/miller/04miller.html* (accessed 1 June 2008).

Morge, S., Hill, K., Tagliarini, G. and Sridhar, N. (2008) 'USeIT and the logic model', in *Proceedings of Society for Information Technology and Teacher Education International Conference 2008, Las Vegas, NV, 3–7 March*, Chesapeake, VA: AACE, pp. 4249–55.

National Education Association (2008) 'Access, adequacy, and equity in education technology: Results of a survey of America's teachers and support professionals on technology in public schools and classrooms', available at: *http://www.nea.org/research/images/08gainsandgapsedtech.pdf* (accessed 1 June 2008).

National Science Digital Library (year unknown) 'About NSDL', available at: *http://nsdl.org/about/* (accessed 1 June 2008).

Reeves, T., Apedoe, X. and Woo, Y. (2006) 'Evaluating digital libraries: A user-friendly guide (revised version)', available at: *http://www.dpc.ucar.edu/projects/evalbook/index.html* (accessed 1 June 2008).

Renger, R. and Hurley, C. (2006) 'From theory to practice: Lessons learned in the application of the ATM approach to developing logic models', *Evaluation and Program Planning* 29(2): 106–19.

Ryan, J., McClure, C. and Bertot, J. C. (2001) 'Choosing measures to evaluate networked information resources and services: Selected issues', in C. McClure and J. Bertot (eds) *Evaluating networked information services*, Medford, NJ: ASIST, pp. 111–35.

Star, S. and Griesemer, J. (1989) 'Institutional ecology, "translations", and boundary objects: Amateurs and professionals in Berkeley's

Museum of Vertebrate Zoology, 1907–1939', *Social Studies of Science* 19(3): 387–420.

Taylor-Powell, E. and Henert, E. (2008) 'Developing a logic model: Teaching and training guide', available at: *http://www.uwex.edu/ces/pdande* (accessed 1 June 2008).

W. K. Kellogg Foundation (2004) 'Logic model development guide: Using logic models to bring together planning, evaluation and action', available at: *http://www.wkkf.org/Pubs/Tools/Evaluation/Pub3669.pdf* (accessed 1 June 2008).

12

Examining how end users use and perceive digital libraries: a qualitative approach

Maria Monopoli

Introduction

This chapter focuses on the user-centred evaluation of digital libraries. This means that the outcomes of this type of evaluations are mainly based on users' opinions, actions, feelings and perceptions. Users become the centre of attention and reveal the extent to which a digital library supports their needs and demands, their roles and practices. If analysed in a proper and creative way, their feedback can lead to the implementation of user-centred systems. Norman and Draper (1986) define the user-centred system as a design based on the user's point of view, thus emphasising people rather than technologies. This concept refers to the implementation of systems focusing on users' necessities, perceptions, mental models and information-processing structures.

According to Saracevic (2000), the user-centred approach focuses not only on the individual user, but also at the social ('how well does a library support the needs of a society or a community?') and institutional level ('how well does a library support the institutional or organisational objectives?'). He refers to the digital library interface and whether or not a given interface is able to provide and support user searching, browsing and interaction with an information system.

According to Van House et al.:

> For digital libraries to be truly useful, designers need to first understand the larger context that determines their [users] information needs and purposes for using the DL, that is, the

context of the users' work; the individual user's specific work and tasks; his or her information acts, and, finally his or her DL use. (Van House et al., 1996)

In addition, according to Ferreira and Pithan (2005) 'the conception, planning and implementation of digital libraries, in any area of knowledge, demands innumerable studies in order to verify and guarantee the final product adequacy to the users' necessities'.

Qualitative research – a rich definition

The *Third New International Dictionary of the English Language* (1993: 1858) defines the term *qualitative* as 'relating to or involving quality or kind'. Consequently, qualitative data are associated with data expressed in terms of quality or kind, providing empirical information about the world in the form of words. Neuman (1997: 328) gives a richer picture of the meaning and significance of qualitative research, specifying that it involves the activity of documenting real events, recording what people say, observing specific behaviours, studying written documents, or examining visual images. This valuable qualitative data can be used to better understand any phenomenon. Alternatively, the data can also be used to gain new perspectives on issues about which much is already known, or to gain more in-depth data that may be difficult to convey quantitatively. Qualitative analysis is also appropriate in situations where one needs to first identify the variables that might later be tested quantitatively, or where the researcher has determined that quantitative measures cannot adequately describe or interpret a situation.

In other words, someone could recognise that there are many valid reasons for doing qualitative research. Strauss and Corbin (1990: 19) specify that one reason is the validity of research based on qualitative research approach – the conviction of the researcher based upon research experience. They continue by emphasising that 'some researchers are also come from a scientific discipline, such as anthropology, both of which traditionally advocate the use of qualitative methods for data gathering and analysis, whose use has given satisfactory results'.

Strauss and Corbin (1990) also emphasise the nature of the research problem, arguing that 'some areas of study naturally lend themselves more qualitative types of research, for instance, research that attempts to uncover the nature of persons' experiences with a phenomenon'.

According to Hannabuss (1995), quantitative research is associated with measurement and numbers used to express quantity. These numbers are used to give some information about the world. On the other hand, Hannabuss supports that the role of qualitative research is to identify and examine variables. Therefore, participants are asked to respond to a number of questions and the interviewers probe and explore their responses. The goal of the interviewers is to identify and define participants' perceptions, opinions and feelings about the topic or idea being discussed and to determine the degree of agreement that exists in the group. This type of research is much more subjective than quantitative research and the quality of the findings is directly dependent upon the skill, experience and sensitivity of the interviewers.

Qualitative research in the area of library and information science

Library and information science (LIS) is an emerging discipline which is becoming increasingly important for those who are willing to find information in order to satisfy their (or others) information needs. Afzal (2006: 22) holds that the primary reason that the role of LIS has changed in the last decade is the ever-increasing informatisation of society. He explains that:

> the advent of information technology (IT) has changed the global horizons forever and created an enormous change in the way in which people acquire information and knowledge. Though libraries are changing with these times, there will be tremendous pressure on librarians and information scientists to cater to the needs of people and organizations in a most effective and efficient way. (Afzal, 2006: 22)

As regards a solution to how LIS should deal with this situation, Afzal (2006) argues that this demands 'a better understanding of many information phenomena not currently well understood, and qualitative research can play an important role in furthering that understanding'.

Qualitative research was limited in the area of LIS until the early 1980s. However, this attitude gradually started to change from the late 1980s and the use of qualitative research and methods has been on the increase in LIS (Afzal, 2006). Initially, LIS researchers showed a greater interest in systems rather than the humans using these systems, and therefore the research methods selected seemed to be inclined towards more quantitative methods (Tenopir, 2003). When later researchers understood the need for a more qualitative approach, they started to show greater interest in investigating user needs and information-seeking behaviour.

An examination of more recent published literature shows that the qualitative evaluation of libraries is a vital issue for their implementation. They contribute to identifying and addressing specific issues and requirements for immediate or future action in order to create libraries that are useful and effective (Van House et al., 1996). In particular, evaluations are able to provide ideas regarding the services that new types of libraries, such as digital libraries should offer to their end users. For example, they provide information for searching or browsing facilities, for support services, for reading information in electronic format, for storing information for future use or for communicating with information scientists or other users who share the same interests. For this purpose, end users have been identified as playing a vital role in these qualitative evaluations providing their personal experience and opinion on digital libraries. They are able to inform those who are responsible for creating digital libraries about a variety of issues, such as the searching and/or methods that users should be provided with, the type of information that users expect to find in a digital library, the support services they prefer to have or the preferred method of storing information for future use.

The Electronic Library Programme (eLib) and the Digital Library Initiative (DLI), which are two leading research programmes in the implementation of digital libraries for the academic community in the UK and the USA respectively, have both shown an early interest in users (Kelleher et al., 1996). In 1996, the eLib study published a paper describing a number of guidelines for the evaluation planning of the eLib programme. Specifically, the paper suggested that the contribution of users is essential to the development of digital libraries. Their help is centred on a variety of issues, such as indicating their preference from among given design alternatives, testing the usability of a system, testing versions of systems which reveal major problems, and suggesting improvements that a system might offer in order to satisfy the information needs of its customers.

On behalf of the DLI, Bishop – one of the leading members – states that:

> Results from user studies can help digital libraries designers and policymakers formulate appropriate goals, arrive at a more complete

understanding of costs and benefits, design and allocate resources to both technologies and programmes that offer the best means of achieving goals, and assess the degree to which network policies and programmes have achieved their stated goals. (Bishop, 1995)

Similarly, an earlier but prominent piece of research in the area of digital libraries was the ELINOR project of De Montfort University (Ramsden, 1998). It was the first project to build a working electronic library for use by students in a UK university. The ELINOR project also showed a great interest in users and evaluations based on their experience. It was an attempt to fill some gaps in knowledge regarding the attitudes, activities and problems of users. The data would then indicate priorities for improvements to digital libraries and/or for incorporation in libraries.

Some years later there has been a great body of literature describing the absence of digital library evaluations and the need for this kind of research. Characteristically, in a paper submitted to the Annual Meeting of the American Society for Information Science in 2000, Saracevic (2000) commented that while many interesting things have been explored in the area of digital libraries, the research on evaluations (especially user evaluations) is absent from the published work. Saracevic (2004) attempts to explain this lack of research and concludes that evaluation of digital libraries is likely to be very difficult to accomplish due to its complexity (evaluation is a complex process that demands patience and insistence from evaluators), prematurity (it may be too early in the evolution of digital libraries for evaluation), interest levels (there is probably insufficient interest in the evaluation of digital libraries), funding (evaluation is time-consuming, expensive and most importantly requires commitment), culture (evaluation means very different things to different constituencies) and cynicism (who actually wants to know what people say about a product or service?).

Kani-Zabihi et al. (2006) go a step further and express their worries about two key issues. They comment that it is a common and disappointing situation that users are seldom involved in the implementation of digital libraries. This means that they are not invited to express their opinions on either the types of services that should be provided to users or on the collection of information that should be included in the digital library. They continue by emphasising the second issue, suggesting that this situation has led to the design and implementation of digital libraries that are not user-friendly and that demand users to have sophisticated information skills in order to use them successfully.

Nonetheless, the fact that there are researchers like Branford and Buchanan (2003) and Kani-Zabihi et al. (2006), who believe that the future of digital libraries is very much dependent on their users, is very encouraging. These authors maintain that having a better understanding of user behaviours, needs and beliefs can enable those responsible for creating digital libraries to make the appropriate changes – changes which are essential for libraries to satisfy user needs.

Finally, Wilson (2000) comments that qualitative research is appropriate to the study of the needs underlying information-seeking behaviour because researchers' concern is centred on:

- uncovering the everyday life of the people they are studying;
- using this knowledge to understand the needs driving individuals' information-seeking behaviour;
- using this understanding to appreciate the meaning of information in people's everyday life; and
- gaining a better understanding of the user and being able to design more effective information services and create useful theories of information-seeking behaviour and information use.

User-based qualitative evaluation of digital libraries

How can users be useful in the implementation of digital libraries? Would it be possible for users to provide qualitative data in terms of helping designers to create more user-friendly and widely accepted digital libraries?

Generally, the value of user-based qualitative data is that it is (mostly) based on the opinions of actual users. Users become the focus of attention, revealing their feelings and perceptions on various issues related to digital libraries and then researchers have to explore their views.

Previous literature on the involvement of users in the evaluation of digital libraries has shown that they can provide valuable data. Their contribution is focused on the selection of information or/and services provided by a digital library. Specifically, various studies have shown users to have considerable involvement in usability studies. Chowdhury et al. (2006) provide a comprehensive paper on the concept of usability and its impact on digital libraries, concluding that although there have been relatively few evaluation studies during the first period of digital libraries implementation, the usability area of research has attracted significant attention. Briefly, usability assessment, a term most common in the area of HCI, addresses primarily the capabilities of the interface and the possibilities of users to interact with it. However, this approach seems to be too narrow in terms of evaluating something as complex as a digital library. According to Chowdhury and Chowdhury:

> Usability can be defined as a system's capability in human functional terms to be used easily and effectively by the specified range of users, given specified training and support, to fulfil a specified range of tasks, within the specified range of environmental scenarios. (Chowdhury and Chowdhury, 1999)

Reeves et al. (2003) define usability, in the context of digital libraries, as the effectiveness, efficiency, and – most importantly – personal satisfaction with which users can access and make productive use of the resources in a digital library. Nielsen (2003) simply identifies usability as a quality attribute that assesses how easy user interfaces are to use. In his attempt to shed light on the significance of usability studies, he specifies that the meaning of 'usability' is defined by the following five quality components:

- *Learnability*: How easy is it for users to accomplish basic tasks the first time they encounter the design?
- *Efficiency*: Once users have learned the design, how quickly can they perform tasks?
- *Memorability*: When users return to the design after a period of not using it, how easily can they re-establish proficiency?
- *Errors*: How many errors do users make, how severe are these errors, and how easily can they recover from the errors?
- *Satisfaction*: How pleasant is it to use the design?

Although usability studies have become one of the most popular ways to approach digital library evaluation (Buttenfield, 1999), usability is only one of the possible and needed criteria for qualitative evaluation. Others include the content and quality of information provided to users and the performance of the system. The concept of the content and quality of information is most commonly known as usefulness. To be more specific about the meaning of usefulness, Tsakonas and Papatheodorou (2006) identify five usefulness criteria:

- *relevance*: refers to the content of the information and how close it comes to the user's real need;
- *format*: investigates the way that information is presented;
- *reliability*: is focused on the credibility of the information;
- *level*: the various possible ways that data can be presented;
- *timeliness*: analyses how current the information is in order to satisfy the user's information need.

Finally, to evaluate the perceived performance of the system, precision, recall and response time remain principal evaluation criteria.

Qualitative research methods

There is an extensive range of research methods concerning the qualitative analysis of end users' use and perceptions of digital libraries. These methods include questionnaires, observations, interviews, focus groups, transaction logs, diary studies, usability testing, documents and texts, and the researcher's impressions and reactions (Myers, 2004). Based on the research methods provided by Marchionini (2000) and Reeves et al. (2003), Chowdhury et al. (2006) categorise them into four main groups:

- *Observations*: These may be baseline observations, structured observations, participants' observations, think-aloud observations and transaction log analyses. Baseline observations aim to get first-hand data; observers have to take notes of activities accomplished by users in a semi-structured form. The purpose is to help evaluators to become situated within the setting and to become familiar with the subjects. Structured observations aim to systematically observe and record the behaviour of users. Participant observations allow evaluators to interact with the subjects being observed in a semi-structured way. This interaction might be in the form of asking and/or answering questions. Think-aloud observation is a method of investigating the cognitive behaviour of users while they are working on specific tasks. Finally, transaction log analysis aims to automatically capture and analyse the users' actions during specific tasks.

- *Interviews*: These may be structured, semi-structured or unstructured. Although structured interviews are relatively quick and easy to conduct and the data easy to analyse, semi-structured interviews allow the evaluator to probe and gather more detailed information.

- *Document analysis*: This involves critical analysis of the documents produced by the users with a view to accessing the resources used, such as personal diaries, e-mails or transcripts of conversations that describe users' impressions and reactions regarding digital libraries.

- *Task/job analysis*: This has a focus on identifying the tasks performed by the users and the information resources used in order to accomplish each task.

Most recent studies have identified user-logging data as an important method of qualitative evaluation. According to Nicholas (2000), transaction log analysis is the automatic monitoring activity of a computer system. Peters et al. (1993) provide a more detailed definition, specifying that a transaction log analysis contains three elements based on the etymology of the term:

- A *transaction* which is 'a sequence of communicative acts between a human and a computer system. Typically, the end-user constructs a search argument, and the computer system responds.'

- A *transaction log* which 'must contain at least basic information about the search argument as input by the end-user, the system response, the date and time of the transaction, and the location or virtual location of the activity. TLA captures a sequence of events in time and space.'

- A *transaction log analysis* which 'involves the gathering of transaction data, coupled with a purposeful effort to analyze the data, either quantitatively or qualitatively, in order to generate new knowledge. Gathering and analyzing are the two essential activities. The ease with which the data are gathered belies (and perhaps contributes to) the travails of analysis.'

Often, the same computer that stores and delivers information to humans also captures, stores and perhaps analyses data about interactions between itself and human beings. These logs then can be conceptualised both as a form of system monitoring and as a way of observing the information-seeking of end users and making some statements about their information needs. Normally, a transaction log record includes character input by end users when the return/enter key or function key is activated together with other aspects of that moment of input, including the date and time, terminal identifier, and search command identifier, followed by selected aspects of the response from the computer system such as the number of 'hits' (Peters et al., 1993).

Peters et al. (1993) mention that the primary objective of researchers using transaction log data is to improve the computer system, human utilisation of the system, and human understanding of how the system is used by information seekers. This information can provide system designers and managers with valuable data about how the system is being used by actual end users. It also can be used to study prototype systems and potential system improvements.

For the purposes of library and information science research, Peters et al. (1993) narrowly define transaction log analysis as the study of electronically recorded interactions between online information retrieval systems and the persons who search for the information found in those systems. The initial pioneers in the area of information science were people who realised that the computer catalogues (OPACs) could do more than just retrieve information quickly. These systems were also capable of capturing data and monitoring their use. This data could then be analysed in order to refine and design information systems and to provide insights into the information-seeking processes of end users. Previously these insights would be obtained by questioning a number of end users (Nicholas et al., 1999).

The great advantages of transaction logs are not simply their size and reach, but also the fact that they are direct and immediately available records of what users have actually done and not what they say they might or would do. Most importantly, however, user-logging data can be used for much more than generating usage statistics. For example, Reeves et al. specify that:

> information about users' navigation choices could be used to inform decisions about page design and layout. Or error rates and user actions to recover from errors may provide useful information about the skill level of typical users, and this information might influence future decisions about interface design and help features of the library. (Reeves et al., 2003: 49)

Additionally, determining the structure of relations among documents retrieved from users and analysing these relationships might give valuable data about the usefulness of digital libraries or the structure of the digital library user community.

For example, Bysouth (1990) found that the search terms recorded in the logs were very useful for analysis because they revealed information about which search options were selected, which types of Boolean operators were actually used and how many terms were used. When all the information is pieced together, an idea of 'how' the search is carried out by the user emerges. However, it is worth mentioning that transaction log analysis falls short of providing an understanding of user perceptions of their searches. Although logs provide highly-detailed data about how users actually interact with a digital library, they do not reveal users' thoughts and intentions or whether users are satisfied or dissatisfied with the results (Griffiths et al., 2002). Similarly, Nicholas et al. (2000) mention that although logs can provide a significant volume of data, that data can be fuzzy. They continue:

> To get a much clearer picture, it is necessary to find out why people search in the ways described by the logs, how satisfied are they with what they have found and how accurate a portrayal are the maps drawn by the logs. (Nicholas et al., 2000)

Selecting evaluation methods

The choice and implementation of research methods impose intellectual and practical constraints on the researcher, not least of which is the extent to which the validity of the method can be explained. The major debate is centred on which method is best. However, it is not just a case of choosing the best one, as each category has its own advantages and disadvantages. Nevertheless, a researcher must take a number of factors into consideration before choosing the research method.

Nicholas (2000) points out that data collection methods require long and hard consideration. This is due to the fact that data does not come cheap and an evaluation can cost a lot of money. In addition, the credibility and validity of a study can be informed by the method chosen. Thus, a meticulous investigation into which method can give the most desirable results is essential. However, certain factors can guide researchers to choose the appropriate research methods to help them obtain the desirable results for their study.

The primary reason is to specify the research problem, which involves representing what you want to know – the reasons for carrying out the research (Hannabus, 1995). Nicholas (2000) then suggests three factors that should be identified. The first issue is associated with the type and quality of data required to be collected. Great thought must be given to whether researchers want to obtain quantitative and/or qualitative data. Regarding their origin, quantitative research methods were developed in the natural sciences in order to study natural phenomena, while qualitative research methods were developed in the social sciences to enable researchers to investigate social and cultural phenomena. Social scientists realised that for their specific subject area, there was a need to move beyond enumeration towards understanding. In addition, their theories can only be measured qualitatively rather than quantitatively (Bains, 1997).

The second factor refers to a belief that it is necessary to select methods with care and, most importantly, to adopt as wide a range of methods as possible. Although there have been researchers who prefer either quantitative or qualitative research work, some other researchers suggest the combination of quantitative and qualitative research methods in one study. At a general level, these methods have the advantage that researchers are able to capitalise on the strengths of more than one approach, and to compensate for the weaknesses of each approach (Punch, 1998). Summarising, using multiple types of data analysis techniques first provides more data and different types of data. Second, multiple types of data analysis techniques can be used on the different types of data with the goal of gaining a more comprehensive and valid understanding of human information behaviour. However, it is essential to mention that using multiple methods increases the resources and time needed to collect and analyse data (Sonnewald et al., 2001).

Finally, the third factor is the information community being investigated. The target group sometimes dictates the type of research that needs to be chosen in order to carry out a study. According to Nicholas (2000), there is little chance of investigating practitioners, such as journalists, politicians and lawyers, who are busy and self-important. On the other hand, academics are generally a captive audience, whereas practitioners and the general public certainly are not.

Combining evaluation methods

Researchers have begun to use two or more research methods within a study or across a series of studies in order to gain a more complete understanding of human information behaviour. For example, researchers at City University, London have been particularly concerned with the combination of quantitative and qualitative data. In one important piece of research, Hancock-Beaulieu (1993) employed interviews, questionnaires, observations, think-aloud observations and transaction log analyses in order to obtain a comprehensive picture of users' searching behaviour. The authors argued that a basic logging facility providing both qualitative and quantitative data could only be used as an effective evaluative method with the support of other means of eliciting information from users. This recent trend of supplementing transaction log analysis with other research methods is defined by Kurth (1993) as an encouraging attitude. He believes that this method contributes to counteracting two serious limitations in transaction log analysis. The first limitation is associated with the description-only part of the story of online systems use, while the second concerns the description of an even smaller part of the story of users' information-seeking behaviour.

To illustrate further the need for both qualitative and quantitative methods, Kaske (1993) describes the following simple example of a log that showed a number of subject searches made on two very different topics. The log also showed that these two topics were not searched in an efficient way, suggesting that the user failed to find all the items available under the first topic and then moved to the second topic. However, the log indicated that the user searched each topic one step at a time, alternating between the two topics. Had the researchers not interviewed the patrons when they completed their searching, there would have been no way to determine whether the searching had been conducted by a single person or a couple taking turns to search their different term paper topics on the same terminal.

Another quite early survey that used a combination of methodologies is by East et al. (1995). The authors used transaction logs, interviews and questionnaires to gain a holistic picture of the use of Bath Information Data Services (BIDS) by British universities from 1988 to 1994. BIDS provides direct end-user access to four databases supplied by the Institute of Scientific Information, namely Science Citation Index, Social Sciences Citation Index, Arts and Humanities Citation Index and the Index to Science and Technical Proceedings. The service allows academic staff, research staff and students at subscribing institutions to search these databases from any terminal with a network connection and search and retrieve bibliographical references (East et al., 1995). Researchers who were responsible for carrying out this study brought together three research methods. First, they analysed the transaction logs providing quantitative data. Their goal was to indicate the number of end users who accessed the specific service, providing their profile concerning their subject area (e.g. natural or social sciences), and occupation (e.g. research staff or student). Second, they carried out a number of in-depth interviews with users. Third, they continued with a detailed questionnaire distributed to a wide range of users. Their purpose was to collect quantitative and qualitative data which would provide an insight into how BIDS was used and how users perceived the benefits that the service provided.

More recently, Ferreira and Pithan (2005) illustrated the use of multiple research methods, but with the main purpose of gaining qualitative data. The aim of this usability study was to integrate concepts and techniques from the fields of information science and HCI. For the purpose of this study, the authors used the InfoHab – the Center of Reference and Information in Habitation – which offers researchers, professionals and companies a free digital databank on Brazilian technical and academic production in the construction field. Based on qualitative empirical research methods, the authors analysed the interaction and use made by a specific group of users of the InfoHab digital library, and specifically considered the affective and cognitive aspects found and the actions the users took in order to accomplish their tasks. The data collection was divided in three phases: random exploration of the new interface of InfoHab, performance of a predefined task given by the research team, and an interview at the end of the meeting. The main research method was direct observation, including think-aloud technique and semi-structured interviews. The advantage of the think-aloud technique was the fact that users were free to voice their thoughts and actions during the experiment. Kvale (1996) emphasises that although at the most basic level, interviews are just conversations, qualitative research interviews can contribute to understanding the world from the subjects' point of view, unfold the meaning of peoples' experiences and uncover their lived world prior to scientific explanations. Patton (1987) notes that quotations are a valuable source of information, revealing respondents' levels of emotion, their thoughts about what is happening, their experiences, and their basic perceptions.

Results showed that users faced some difficulties during the accomplishment of the tasks; however they felt satisfied at the end, partly because of the interview process. During the semi-structured interviews, users had the opportunity to become aware of other services or search techniques provided by the specific digital library which they had not noticed before. This finding illustrates the advantage of qualitative evaluation and confirms Dervin's (1984) comment that qualitative studies that make the user remember and speak out his/her thoughts and experiences help his/her learning.

An even more recent study is described by Apedoe (2007). He carried out a qualitative research study designed mainly to investigate the opportunities and obstacles presented by a digital library for supporting teaching and learning in an undergraduate geology course. The qualitative research methods employed were direct observation, document analysis and interviews. Participants were invited to evaluate the usability and usefulness of the specific digital library, providing their perceptions and opinions on its advantages and disadvantages.

Concluding, it is worth mentioning the suggestion of a sociologist called Lofland (1971) who has identified four important, but simple elements in collecting qualitative data. First, the qualitative evaluator must *get close enough to* the people and situation being studied in order to be able to understand the depth and details of what occurs. Second, the qualitative evaluator must aim at capturing *what actually happens and what people actually say*. Third, qualitative data are focused on collecting a *pure description* of people, activities, perceptions and interpretations. Fourth, qualitative data consist of direct *quotations* from people.

Bibliography

Afzal, W. (2006) 'An argument for the increased use of qualitative research in LIS', *Emporia State Research Studies* 43(1): 22–5.

Apedoe, X. S. (2007) 'Investigating the use of digital library in an inquiry-based undergraduate geology course', *Canadian Journal of Learning and Technology* 33(2), available at: *http://www.cjlt.ca/index .php/cjlt/article/view/18/16* (accessed 2 December 2007).

Bains, S. (1997) 'End-use searching behavior: considering methodologies', *The Katharine Sharp Review*, 4(Winter), available at: *http://mirrored.ukoln.ac.uk/lis-journals/review/review/winter1997/ bains.pdf* (accessed 10 March 2009).

Bishop, A. P. (1995) 'User research and the NSF/ARPA/NASA Digital Library Initiative (DLI) projects: capsule descriptions of work in progress', available at: *http://forseti.grainger.uiuc.edu/dlisoc/socsci_ site/user-research-paper-ann.html* (accessed 25 March 2008).

Blandford, A. and Buchanan, G. (2003) 'Usability of digital libraries: a source of creative tensions with technical developments', *IEEE-CS TC Bulletin* 1(1), available at: *http://www.ieee-tcdl.org/Bulletin/v1n1/blandford/blandford.html* (accessed 20 May 2007).

Buttenfield, B. (1999) 'Usability evaluation of digital libraries', *Science and Technology Libraries* 17(3/4): 39–59.

Bysouth, P. T. (1990) 'Evaluating the use of several approaches to online literature retrieval by research scientists', in P. T. Bysouth (ed.) *End-User Searching: The Effective Gateway to Published Information*, London: Association for Information Management, pp. 105–23.

Chowdhury, G. G. and Chowdhury, S. (1999) 'Digital library research: major issues and trends', *Journal of Documentation* 55(4): 409–48.

Chowdhury, S., Landoni, M. and Gibb, F. (2006) 'Usability and impact of digital libraries: a review', *Online Information Review* 30(6): 656–80.

Dervin, B. (1984) 'A theoric perspective and research approach for generating research helpful to communication practice', *Public Relations Research and Education* 1(1): 30–45.

East, H., Sheppard, E. and Jeal, Y. (1995) *A Huge Leap Forward: A Quantitative and Qualitative Examination of the Development of Access to Database Services by British Universities, 1998–1994*, British Library R&D Report No. 6202, London: BLRIC.

Ferreira, S. M. and Pithan, D. N. (2005) 'Usability of digital libraries: A study based on the areas of information science and human-computer-interaction', *OCLC Systems and Services* 21(4): 311–23.

Fidel, R. and Green, M. (2004) 'The many faces of accessibility: engineers' perceptions of information sources', *Information and Processing Management* 40(3): 563–81.

Griffiths, J. R., Hartley, R. J. and Wilson, J. P. (2002) 'An improved method of studying use-system interaction by combining transaction log analysis and protocol analysis', *Information Research* 7(4): 2008, available at: *http://Informationr.net/ir/7-4/paper139.html* (accessed 2 May 2008).

Hancock-Beaulieu, M. (1993) 'A comparative transaction log analysis of browsing and search formulation in online catalogues', *Program* 27(3): 269–80.

Hannabuss, S. (1995) 'Approaches to research', *Aslib Proceedings* 47(1): 3–11.

Kani-Zabihi, E, Ghinea, G. and Chen, S. Y. (2006) 'Digital libraries: what do users want?' *Online Information Review* 30(4): 395–412.

Kaske, N. K. (1993) 'Research methodologies and transaction log analysis: issues, questions, and a proposed model', *Library Hi-Tech* 11(2): 79–86.

Kelleher, J. Sommerlad, E. and Stern, E. (1996) 'Evaluation of the Electronic Libraries programme: Guidelines for eLib project evaluation', available at: *http://www.ukoln.ac.uk/services/elib/papers/tavistock/evaluation-guide/intro.html* (accessed 11 April 2007).

Kurth, M. (1993) 'The limits and limitations of transaction log analysis', *Library Hi-Tech* 11(2): 98–104.

Kvale, S. (1996) *Inter Views: An Introduction to Qualitative Research Interviewing*, Thousand Oaks, CA: Sage.

Lofland, J. (1971) *Analysing Social Settings*, Belmont: Wadsworth.

Marchionini, G. (2000) 'Evaluating digital libraries: a longitudinal and multifaceted view', *Library Trends* 49(2): 304–33.

Myers, M. D. (2004) 'Qualitative research in information systems', available at: *http://www.qual.auckland.ac.nz* (accessed 1 February 2007).

Neuman, L. W. (1997) *Social Research Methods: Qualitative and Quantitative Approaches*, Boston, MA: Allyn and Bacon.

Nicholas, D. (2000) *Assessing Information Needs: Tools, Techniques and Concepts for the Internet Age*, London: Aslib.

Nicholas, D., Huntington, P. and Lievesley, N. (1999) 'Cracking the code: web log analysis', *Online and CD-ROM Review* 23(5): 263–5.

Nicholas, D., Huntington, P., Lievesley, N. and Wasti, A. (2000) 'Evaluating consumer website logs: a case study of The Times/The Sunday Times website', *Journal of Information Science* 26(6): 399–411.

Nielsen, J. (2003) 'Usability 101: introduction to usability', available at: *http://www.useit.com/alertbox/20030825.html* (accessed 1 February 2008).

Norman, D. A. and Draper, S. W. (1986) 'Cognitive engineering', in D. A. Norman and S. W. Draper (eds) *User-Centered-System Design: New Perspective on Human-Computer-Interaction*, Hillsdale, NJ: Lawrence Erlbaum Associates, pp. 31–61.

Patton, M. Q. (1987) *How to use Qualitative Methods in Evaluation*, Newbury Park, CA: Sage.

Peters, T. A. (1993) 'The history and development of transaction log analysis', *Library Hi-Tech* 11(2): 41–66.

Peters, T. A., Kurth, M., Flaherty, P., Sandore, B. and Kaske, N. K. (1993) 'An introduction to the special section on transaction log analysis', *Library Hi-Tech* 11(2): 38–40.

Punch, K. F. (1998) *Introduction to Social Research: Quantitative and Qualitative Approach*, London: Sage.

Ramsden, A. (1998) *ELINOR – Electronic Library Project*, London: Bowker-Saur.

Reeves, T., Apedoe, X. and Woo, Y. (2003) 'Evaluating digital libraries: a user-friendly guide', available at: *http://eduimpact.comm.nsdl.org/ evalworkshop/UserGuideOct20.doc* (accessed 4 March 2008).

Sarasevic, T. (2000) 'Digital library evaluation: toward and evolution of concepts', *Library Trends* 49(3): 350–69.

Sarasevic, T. (2004) 'Evaluation of digital libraries: an overview', paper presented at the DELOS WP7 Workshop on the Evaluation of Digital Libraries, Padua, 4–5 October, available at: *http://www.scils.rutgers.edu/ ~tefko/DL_evaluation_Delos.pdf* (accessed 23 April 2008).

Sonnenwald, D. H., Wildermuth, A. and Harmon, G. L. (2001) 'A research method to investigate information seeking using the concept of information horizons: an example from a study of lower socio-economic students' information seeking behaviour', *The New Review of Information Behaviour Research* 2: 65–86.

Strauss, A. and Corbin, J. (1990) *Basics of Qualitative Research: Grounded Theory Procedures and Techniques,* Newbury Park, CA: Sage.

Tenopir, C. (2003) 'Information metrics and user studies', *Aslib Proceedings: New Information Perspectives* 55(1/2): 13–17.

Third New International Dictionary of the English Language [Unabridged] (1993) Springfield, MA: Merriam-Webster.

Tsakonas, G. and Papatheodorou, C. (2006) 'Analysing and evaluating usefulness and usability in electronic information services', *Journal of Information Science* 32(5): 400–19.

Van House, N. A., Butler, M. H., Ogle, V. and Schiff, L. (1996) 'User-centered iterative design for digital libraries: the Cypress experience', *D-Lib Magazine*, February, available at: *http://www.dlib.org/dlib/ february96/02vanhouse.html* (accessed 4 March 2008).

Wilson, T. D. (2000) 'Recent trends in user studies: action research and qualitative methods', *Information Research* 5(3), available at: *http:// informationr.net/ir/5-3/paper76.html* (accessed 2 February 2008).

13

Investigating users' perceptions and acceptance of digital libraries: a quantitative approach

Yin-Leng Theng

Introduction

Even though empirical evaluation is essential to the design of good digital libraries, it can be difficult and expensive to recruit real users to test all aspects of several versions of a system. Further, there is a limited number of practical evaluation techniques that designers can use to design and build more usable digital libraries while meeting the time constraints of the design process (Theng, 2005). Many have argued that it can be too slow and costly for the financial and time constraints of the design process. Landauer (1995) points out that it is not good enough to design an interactive system without subjecting it to some form of evaluation, because it is impossible to design an optimal user interface at the first attempt. Dix et al. (1997) argue that even if one has used the best methodology and model in the design of the interactive system, one still needs to assess the design and test the system to ensure that it behaves as expected and meets end users' requirements. With respect to interface evaluation, Nielsen (1993) simply advises that designers should conduct some form of testing.

Insights from qualitative evaluations are beneficial in helping us to understand the reasons why problems occur. However, using established qualitative usability techniques requires a competent level of 'craft skills', even with the most commonly used techniques of discount usability engineering. On the other hand, as designers need robust, quantifiable metrics, quantitative evaluations can be designed to help designers compare and evaluate the effectiveness of systems. Triangulation of findings from different perspectives using a combination of qualitative and quantitative evaluation techniques provides a more holistic assessment of the usability and usefulness of interactive systems.

Digital library evaluation and two studies

Many digital library programmes have been driven by technology-related initiatives (Führ et al., 2001). As noted by Bollen and Luce (2002), the evaluation of the effectiveness of digital libraries and the extent to which they address user needs has commonly been accorded less importance than the development and implementation of novel applications. Digital library evaluation is considered a multifaceted problem that cuts across a wide range of systems, interfaces, user communities as well as human–computer interaction issues. Hong et al. (2002) have called attention to the lack of evaluations from the user perspective. Previous research has shown that digital libraries can easily remain unnoticed and under-utilised in spite of their availability. There is now a call for user-focused research and interest in user behaviour studies as an essential part of digital library development. Barry and Squires' study (as cited in Hong et al., 2002) has supported a shift from evaluating how useful a piece of technology is by itself, towards evaluating its usefulness from the user's perspective.

While usability criteria represent one of the more popular ways to approach digital library evaluations from the user's perspective, Saracevic (2000) has recognised that usability is only one of the many possible criteria. Hong et al. (2002) have reiterated this point, emphasising the need to understand users' acceptance of digital libraries and to identify the factors that can influence their decision to use digital libraries. Choudhury et al. (2002) have also listed well-known examples of evaluation studies that have focused on user satisfaction with library services. Various methods have been utilised in the studies, including surveys, ethnographic studies and focus groups.

Saracevic and Kantor (1997a, 1997b) have conducted a long-term study to develop a taxonomy of user values for library and information services. The central premise of their study was to assume that value was related to use. It was suggested that in the study of value, the message should not be treated in isolation, and information should be considered in its cognitive and contextual sense. The approach to the study was a perceived value approach. Perceived value was defined as the information users' subjective valuation of the benefits of the given information. It was assumed that users could recognise the value of information, and either rank its value if given an appropriate scale, or translate the value into monetary value if monetary terms were used. It was acknowledged that this approach could lack rigour and precision, and that there would be difficulties in dealing with the different attributes. However, the gain would be in recognising the judgment of the users, who are the immediate beneficiaries of the services.

In another study by Hong et al. (2002), the technology acceptance model (TAM) was used as a theoretical framework to investigate the effect of a set of individual differences (computer self-efficacy and knowledge of search domain) and system characteristics (relevance, terminology and screen design) on perception and intention to use digital libraries. According to TAM, adoption behaviour is determined by the intention to use a particular system, which in turn is determined by perceived usefulness and perceived ease of use of the system. Hong et al. (2002) defined perceived usefulness as 'the extent to which a person believes that using the system will enhance his job performance', and perceived ease of use as 'the extent to which a person believes that using the system will be free of effort'. These perceptions fall in line with the dimensions of results discussed in the Reasons-Interaction-Results (R-I-R) model by Saracevic and Kantor (1997a).

This chapter focuses on quantitative usability evaluations of digital libraries and related environments such as online communities and mobile devices. Underlying theories and models, inspired from computer science and social science, underpinning user interactions have been used in the design of the four studies. Two studies are described to illustrate quantitative techniques to investigate users' perceptions regarding the usability and usefulness of these systems conducted at appropriate stages of the software development cycle, as shown in Figure 13.1:

- *Study 1* investigates users' acceptance of weblogs and explores implications for the design of educational digital libraries incorporating online community-enhanced features conducted during the *feasibility phase* (Theng and Lew, 2006).

- *Study 2* focuses on a study conducted during the *design* and *prototyping phases* of the Mobile G-Portal project for refinement (Theng et al., 2007).

Figure 13.1 Two studies at different stages in the software lifecycle

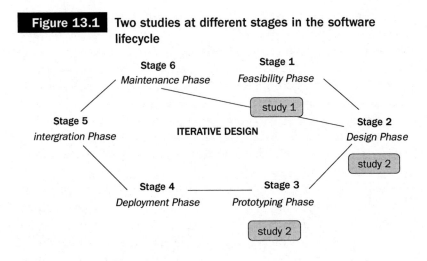

Study 1: Users' acceptance of weblogs for educational digital libraries during the feasibility phase

Adapting The TAM of Davis (1989), Study 1 investigated factors that might influence the acceptance of weblogs as a tool for teaching and learning in higher education, as perceived by university students (Theng and Lew, 2006). It aimed to determine how usefulness perceptions were affected by students' awareness of weblog technology and the benefits of blogging for educational purposes, instructor and peer support, and student readiness for student-centred learning. It also determined how perceptions regarding ease of use were influenced by feelings of weblog self-efficacy, prior computing and IT experience, and availability of resources and support, or facilitating conditions. Three research questions were posed to answer the above objectives:

- *RQ1*: To what extent are students' perceptions of weblog usefulness influenced by awareness of weblog technology and weblog capabilities, peer and tutor support, and readiness for student-centred learning?

- *RQ2*: To what extent are students' perceptions of the ease of use of weblogs influenced by feelings of weblog self-efficacy, prior computing and IT experience and facilitating conditions?

- *RQ3*: In the context of the use of weblogs in higher education, what is the relationship between students' perceptions of weblog usefulness, weblog ease of use and their intentions to use weblogs?

Three main constructs of TAM examining students' acceptance of the use of technology for teaching and learning purposes were incorporated into the theoretical model: perceived usefulness (PU); perceived ease of use (PEOU) and behavioural intention to use (BI). PU and PEOU were each proposed as determinants of BI. PEOU was also retained as a determinant of PU. Based on TAM, a set of hypotheses was generated to answer the research questions posed above. A theoretical model was proposed, the structural paths of which represented the hypotheses generated. Students' awareness of weblogs, peer and tutor support and readiness for student-centred learning were conceptualised as external variables affecting PU. Weblog self-efficacy, prior computing and IT experience and self-reported facilitating conditions were conceptualised as external variables affecting PEOU. In addition, the model did not measure actual use, as the study was not designed to explain the actual use of weblogs, but rather to predict the *likelihood* of usage in the event of weblogs being implemented in university courses.

The structural paths of the model representing the hypotheses generated to address RQ1 were defined by Hypotheses 1a, 1b and 1c (see Table 13.1. RQ2 and RQ3 were defined by Hypotheses 2a, 2b and 2c (see Table 13.2), and Hypotheses 3a, 3b and 3c (see Table 13.3) respectively.

Methodology

A questionnaire instrument was designed to obtain inputs on the eight variables comprised in the model, namely PU, PEOU, BI and the external

Table 13.1   Hypotheses 1a, 1b and 1c for RQ1

Hypothesis 1a	Students' awareness of weblogs and their capabilities has a significant effect on the PU of weblogs as learning tools
Hypothesis 1b	Peer support and tutor support have a significant effect on PU
Hypothesis 1c	Readiness for student-centred learning has a significant effect on PU

Table 13.2 Hypotheses 2a, 2b and 2c for RQ2

Hypothesis 2a	Students' weblog self-efficacy significantly affects the PEOU of weblogs as a learning tool
Hypothesis 2b	Prior computing and IT experience has a significant effect on PEOU
Hypothesis 2c	Facilitating conditions have a significant effect on PEOU

Table 13.3 Hypotheses 3a, 3b and 3c for RQ3

Hypothesis 3a	PEOU has a significant effect on PU
Hypothesis 3b	PU has a significant effect on the BI to use weblogs as a learning tool
Hypothesis 3c	PEOU has a significant effect on BI

variables of PU and PEOU. Respondents were asked to indicate the extent of their agreement with the survey questions using a seven-point Likert-type scale. The items were modified to make them relevant to the context of education and weblogs. Also measured were demographic variables, such as gender, age and educational level, and weblog, computer and internet experience. The study sought to revalidate these relationships in the context of weblogs as learning tools in higher education with Hypotheses 3a, 3b and 3c. The PU and PEOU of weblogs for learning in higher education were measured using five items each. These were scales developed by Davis (1989) and validated in numerous studies on TAM such as Moore and Benbasat (1991). As with other studies on instructional technology (e.g. Davis, 1993; Theng et al., 2005), the questions were modified to suit the educational setting.

Figure 13.2 shows the modified model to examine students' acceptance of weblogs as learning tools in higher education. To ascertain each variable, it also includes references to the questions posed.

Protocol

Five participants were selected for pre-testing as a means of obtaining feedback on the questions. They were requested to review the questionnaire for ambiguity, repetition, inconsistency, incorrect grammar

Figure 13.2 Theoretical model addressing the three research questions on perceived usefulness, perceived ease of use and behavioural intention to use

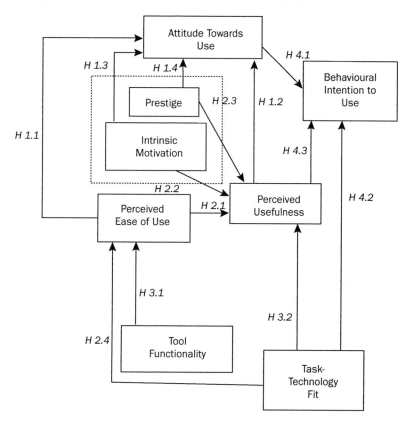

and any other problems there might be in providing responses to the questions. They were also asked to evaluate the visual appearance of the questionnaire. The questionnaire was revised accordingly.

As Study 1 was concerned with the perceptions and intentions of university students regarding weblogs, undergraduate and postgraduate students of a local university were selected to participate in the study. The questionnaire was administered by hand or as an attachment to e-mail messages sent to students on the Master of Information Science degree mailing list maintained by the university. Responses were collected over a period of three weeks from 30 September to 21 October 2005. A total of 68 students participated in the study.

Findings and analysis

Space constraints do not permit us to provide detailed analysis. Here, we report overall analysis of respondents' feedback under the following subsections:

- profiles of respondents and usage patterns of computers/internet/ weblogs;
- perceptions of weblog usefulness: Hypotheses 1a, 1b and 1c;
- perceptions of ease of use: Hypotheses 2a, 2b and 2c; and
- behavioural intention to use: Hypotheses 3a, 3b and 3c.

Hypothesis 1a: weblog awareness

The relationship between overall weblog awareness and PU is statistically significant (χ^2 = 14.2, p = 0.007). Table 13.4 summarises the effect of awareness of specific weblog uses and functions on perceptions of weblog usefulness as a learning tool.

Hypothesis 1b: Peer and tutor support

Table 13.5 summarises the results of the test on the hypothesis that peer and tutor support affect perceptions of weblog usefulness as a learning tool. The findings seemed to suggest that support from persons most closely connected with the student in the educational process, namely his or her peers and tutors, had a significant effect on the student's perception of weblog usefulness for learning purposes.

Table 13.4   Perceived usefulness and weblog awareness

Weblog awareness	χ^2	p	df	Significant?
Minimise information overload	18.967	0.001	4	Yes
Independent learning	18.654	0.001	4	Yes
Networking	15.098	0.005	4	Yes
Critical thinking	11.238	0.024	4	Yes
Know about weblog use	10.265	0.036	4	Yes
Know how to use blogs	7.204	0.125	4	No
Interdisciplinary learning	8.003	0.091	4	No
Knowledge sharing	6.435	0.169	4	No

Table 13.5   Perceived usefulness and overall support

Overall support	χ^2	p	df	Significant?
Overall peer and tutor support	9.771	0.044	4	Yes
Overall peer support	11.523	0.021	4	Yes
Overall tutor support	10.981	0.027	4	Yes

Looking at the effect of peer and tutor support separately, it was further revealed that students' perceptions of weblog usefulness would more likely be influenced by tutor support than peer support. There were statistically significant relationships between students' perceptions of weblog usefulness and tutor support for such use ($\chi^2 = 32.4$, $df = 4$, $p < 0.001$), or the use of computer-mediated communication in general ($\chi^2 = 12.4$, $df = 4$, $p = 0.014$), or if there was tutor support for class participation ($\chi^2 = 0.046$, $df = 4$, $p = 0.046$). In contrast, students' perceptions of weblog usefulness were only affected by peer support of use ($\chi^2 = 21.655$, $df = 4$, $p < 0.001$).

Hypothesis 1c: Readiness for student-centred learning

The survey on the interactive aspect of student-centred learning quizzed students on their motivations to participate in interactive learning activities, such as the discussion of course topics with classmates and tutors, peer review of coursework and group-work conducted online. It also queried their comfort with interacting with classmates in an online written forum.

Overall readiness for student-centred learning ($\chi^2 = 5.254$, $df = 4$, $p = 0.262$) was not significantly related to PU of weblogs as learning tools. The relationship between PU and a student's inclination towards interactive learning was statistically significant ($\chi^2 = 10.827$, $df = 4$, $p = 0.029$). The findings suggested that students who were motivated towards interactive learning and comfortable with online interaction would likely find weblogs to be useful for learning.

Hypothesis 2a: Self-efficacy

Computer self-efficacy is defined as one's beliefs about the ability to use computers effectively. Students' feelings of weblog self-efficacy significantly influenced ($\chi^2 = 21.348$, $df = 4$, $p = 0.001$) their PEOU for learning purposes. Weblogs were thus perceived as easier to use by students with higher levels of self-efficacy.

Hypothesis 2b: Prior experience

Overall, prior computing and IT experience had significant influence on PEOU (χ^2 = 15.925, df = 4, p = 0.003). However, prior experience with personal computers (p = 0.081) and the internet (p = 0.323) did not affect perceptions of weblog ease of use. The following prior experiences gave significant results: weblogs (χ^2 = 20.187, df = 4, p < 0.001); HTML (χ^2 = 13.949, df = 4, p = 0.007), discussion threads (χ^2 = 18.778, df = 4, p = 0.001), wikis (χ^2 = 11.401, df = 4, p = 0.022) and e-mail (χ^2 = 13.737, df = 4, p = 0.008).

Hypothesis 2c: Facilitating conditions

Facilitating conditions had a significant effect on students' PEOU for learning purposes (χ^2 = 13.184, df = 4, p < 0.05). Thus, students were likely to consider weblogs easy to use if the necessary infrastructure and technical support were available.

Hypothesis 3a: Effect of PEOU on PU

PEOU had no significant effect on students' PU for learning purposes. The Chi-square value (χ^2 = 7.244) had p = 0.124. In other words, even if students found weblogs easy to use, they might not necessarily consider them a useful learning tool.

Hypothesis 3b: Effect of PU on BI

It was found that PU of weblogs for learning significantly influenced overall intention to use weblogs as a learning tool in higher education (χ^2 = 30.839, df = 4, p < 0.001). Table 13.6 illustrates the effect of

| Table 13.6 | Perceived usefulness and behavioural intention to use for learning activities |

Effect of PU on BI (learning activities)	χ^2	p	df	Significant?
Organise/manage web links	23.400	< 0.001	4	Yes
Discuss with classmates	21.717	< 0.001	4	Yes
Self-directed learning	18.418	0.001	4	Yes
Discuss with tutors	16.644	0.002	4	Yes
Submit coursework	15.969	0.003	4	Yes
Work on group projects	14.401	0.006	4	Yes

perceptions of weblog usefulness on intentions to use weblogs for a variety of specific learning activities.

Hypothesis 3c: Effect of PEOU on BI

PEOU of weblogs for learning had no significant influence on overall intention to use weblogs as a learning tool in higher education (χ^2 = 1.108, df = 4, p = 0.893). No significant results support Hypothesis 3c in relation to the intention to use weblogs for a variety of specific learning activities, even if the weblogs were perceived to be easy to use.

Implications and summary

The findings suggested that students would likely accept weblog use as a course requirement if they perceived the activity to be useful for learning. We suggest that designers of educational digital libraries can learn from the growing success of weblogs.

If educational digital libraries were to be truly dynamic (Theng et al., 2001), allowing user-initiated actions with a social space for collaborative and individual practices, it might be useful for digital library designers/developers to learn from the design of weblogs when creating a dynamic, collaborative, socially-trusted environment in educational digital libraries, hence exploiting the current trend of involving the design of community-focused consumer technology, such as Wikipedia, to promote the growth in popularity and use of digital libraries for education.

Study 2: Field testing of the mobile G-Portal prototype

In Study 2, we extended G-Portal's web platform to a mobile PDA prototype (Theng et al., 2007). Integrated with G-Portal, a web-based geospatial digital library of geography resources, Study 2 describes the implementation of Mobile G-Portal, a group of mobile devices as learning tools to support collaborative sharing and learning for geography fieldwork. Based on a modified TAM (Davis et al., 1989) and a task-technology fit (TTF) model (Dishaw and Strong, 1999), an initial study with Mobile G-Portal was conducted involving two teacher design partners and 39 students in a local secondary school.

Methodology

Study 2 aimed to investigate the use of PDAs in learning and teaching geography. Specifically, we wanted to investigate the degree of acceptance of the Mobile G-Portal for geography fieldwork among secondary school students in Singapore. Our study, applying the integrated TAM/TTF model, aimed to achieve two objectives:

- to investigate students' attitudes and behavioural intentions regarding the use of Mobile G-Portal for geography fieldwork by considering the factors of perceived usefulness, perceived ease of use, intrinsic motivation, prestige, tool functionality and task-technology fit; and

- to examine the suitability of the PDA as the client application for the Mobile G-Portal in supporting data collection for geography fieldwork.

To address the two objectives, four hypotheses were generated to investigate the students' acceptance of the PDA for use in geography fieldwork:

- *Hypothesis 1*: Students' attitude towards the use of the PDA is significantly affected by PU, PEOU, intrinsic motivation and prestige.

- *Hypothesis 2*: This hypothesis postulates that the perceived usefulness of the PDA is significantly affected by perceived ease of use, intrinsic motivation, prestige and TTF (Dishaw and Strong, 1999). It aims to find out how factors of PEOU, intrinsic motivation, prestige and TTF could influence PU. Students who perceived the PDA as easy to use may think that it is useful. Similarly, students might find the PDA useful for geography fieldwork as they were already intrinsically motivated to use it. The prestige gained from using the PDA may influence the perception that the PDA was useful for fieldwork. TTF was proposed to influence PU as if the students felt that the PDA fitted the tasks given during fieldwork, they might conclude that the PDA is a useful tool.

- *Hypothesis 3*: Students' perceived ease of use of the PDA is significantly affected by tool functionality and TTF. There could be a relationship between PEOU, tool functionality and TTF. A PDA with good tool functionality might result in greater ease of use of the tool, enabling smooth completion of tasks.

- *Hypothesis 4*: Students' behavioural intention to use a PDA for future fieldwork is significantly affected by their attitude towards its use, TTF and perceived usefulness. In Hypothesis 4, three constructs were identified to explain students' behavioural intention to use a PDA for future geography fieldwork. A good attitude or feeling about the PDA might result in an intention to use it in the future. A good match between the tool and the associated fieldwork would result in future intention to use the tool. A perception that the PDA is useful would strongly explain for behavioural intention to use. The constructs that individually relate to behavioural intention are shown in three sub-hypotheses.

Students' acceptance of the PDA was examined using the constructs of perceived usefulness, perceived ease of use and TTF. Figure 13.3 shows the research model.

The study consisted of two parts, gathering both quantitative and qualitative feedback on the Mobile G-Portal: (i) Part I – the questionnaire survey testing hypotheses to understand subjects' perceived acceptance of the Mobile G-Portal for geography fieldwork; and (ii) Part II – the interview with students regarding suggested improvements.

Findings and analysis

Data from the 39 respondents were analysed using SPSS. Responses to five-point Likert-type scale questions were entered as ordinal data with an

---

Figure 13.3 Research model

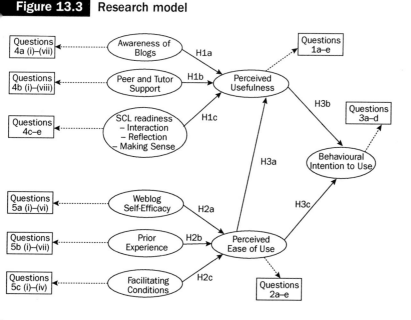

absolute value (strongly disagree = 1, disagree = 2, neutral = 3, agree = 4, strongly agree = 5). In the questionnaire, several items were used to measure each variable except for two variables on prestige and behavioural intention to use. Thus, a mean value for each variable was derived by summing the absolute value of each response to the question and dividing it by the number of the responses. A study on the distribution of each measurable variable showed that normality was not compromised. A reliability analysis using Cronbach's α to measure the reliability of each measurable variable with more than one item was carried out. Table 13.7 shows that the Cronbach's α for this questionnaire instrument exceeded the recommended 0.60 (Nunnally and Bernstein, 1994), indicating good reliability of the survey items.

Multiple regression analysis was used to determine if each independent variable was significant in explaining for the dependent variable. All proposed relationships were assumed to be linear. The dependent variables were normally distributed which satisfied the assumptions required for regression analysis. A 0.05 significance level or 95 per cent confidence interval was used to determine the best fit for the research model.

Owing to space constraints, we will discuss only the results from the multiple regression analysis and hypotheses testing:

- *Determinants of attitude towards use*: PU ($p = 0.007$) significantly and positively explained for attitude. PEOU ($p = 0.147$), intrinsic motivation ($p = 0.135$) and prestige ($p = 0.681$) were not significant determinants of attitude. The model was not due to chance because of the significant F-value ($F = 14.038$, $df = 4$, $p = 0.001$). A large R-value of 0.798 indicated a strong relationship. The R-square value of 0.637 implied that 63.7 per cent of the variance was explained by the model.

Table 13.7 Reliability analysis for variables with more than one item

Measurable variable	No. of items	Cronbach's α
Intrinsic motivations	4	0.845
Tool functionality	8	0.755
Task-technology fit	2	0.807
Perceived usefulness	4	0.836
Perceived ease of use	5	0.857
Attitude towards use	2	0.835

- *Determinants of PU*: PEOU ($p = 0.003$) and TTF ($p = 0.001$) were the strongest determinants of PU ($F = 17.283$, $df = 4$, $p = 0.001$). Intrinsic motivation and prestige did not significantly influence students' PU of the PDA.

- *Determinants of PEOU*: Hypothesis 3 was supported as tool functionality ($p = 0.019$) and TTF ($p = 0.046$) were both positive and significant determinants in explaining for students' PEOU ($F = 7.837$, $df = 4$, $p = 0.001$). There was a moderately strong relationship in this regression mode ($R = 0.703$). The *R*-square result also showed that 40.4 per cent of the variation in PEOU was explained for by tool functionality and TTF.

- *Determinants of behavioural intention*: Attitude ($p = 0.001$), PU ($p = 0.001$) and TTF ($p = 0.019$) significantly explained for students' behavioural intention to use PDA. The high *F*-statistics ($F = 31.579$, $df = 3$, $p = 0.001$) showed that the variation explained for by the regression model was not due to chance. The high *R*-value of 0.861 indicated a strong relationship between the dependent variable and independent variables. The model explained 74.2 per cent of the variation in attitude. However, TTF had a negative non-standardised and standardised coefficient,l which implied a negative relationship with intention to use PDA.

- *Determinants of task-technology fit*: Only appropriate tool functionality ($p = 0.001$) shows significance in determining if PDA was fit to support geography fieldwork ($F = 7.544$, $df = 2$, $p = 0.002$). The low *R*-value of 0.307 indicated a moderately weak relationship between the dependent variables and independent variables.

Consistent with many studies (Davis, 1992; Davis et al., 1989; Dishaw and Strong, 1999), students seemed more positive in their attitude if they perceived that the device was useful in helping them complete their tasks during fieldwork.

Both TTF and tool functionality of the PDA significantly explained for the students' perception on the ease of use of the device. When the fit between the tasks and the tool was high, it meant that the students were able to complete their tasks with ease. Similarly, more tool functionality that could support the tasks would increase the ease of use of the device. Thus, this research had again emphasised the need for more robustness in the hardware and software functionalities of the PDA to support the tasks of reading, recording, saving and storing information during fieldwork.

Implications and summary

Findings from regression analysis and initial feedback on the prototype in Study 2 show the subjects seemed to accord more value to the functionality of the device and its usefulness in helping them complete tasks during geography fieldwork. PU of the mobile device was most significant in influencing its acceptance as compared with intrinsic motivation, prestige and perceived ease of use. On the other hand, perception regarding ease of use and TTF influenced perception of the usefulness of the PDA. Both TTF and tool functionality also significantly affected the perceived ease of use of the PDA. Their attitude affected their intention to use the PDA for future fieldwork. Lastly, tool functionality also determined the match of the technology to the fieldwork tasks.

Discussion and conclusion

The classroom of today is constantly undergoing changes. Instead of traditional methods of chalk and talk and teaching from textbooks, educationalists are exploring ways in which information and communication technology can be used to support experiential and student-centred learning, allowing students to construct their knowledge more competently, independently and in an enjoyable way. Information and communication technology has changed the way teaching and learning is taking place in local classrooms. Presently, the internet, educational multimedia software and presentation applications have become common teaching and learning resources in the classroom.

Expensive computer laboratories have been built to support the use of these resources for learning. Desktop computers are common tools that students use for learning and completing assignments. For example, in many schools, notebooks serving similar functions and purposes as desktops are now easily available for students and teachers. Handheld computers are mobile, flexible devices that can provide real-time one-to-one support for students from within the context of their learning activities.

This chapter describes two case studies to illustrate the need to make conscious efforts to evaluate new devices and systems, and investigate learners' acceptance and adoption of such systems in making learning more effective, efficient and enjoyable. In contrast with traditional e-learning systems focusing on content delivery and progress monitoring, the new digital landscape promises learning which emphasises a wider range of tasks (including outdoor activities away from the classrooms) supporting collaborative, participatory learning (Study 1), or 'on-the-move' learning (Study 2). Underlying theories and models underpinning user interactions were used in the design of the studies and the construction of the survey instruments. Hypotheses testing and advanced statistics were employed in the analysis of findings applied in identifying factors affecting users' perceptions and acceptance of these systems conducted at appropriate stages of the software development cycle.

However, conducting quantitative usability studies can be cumbersome and expensive. To reduce the use of extensive and time-consuming testing by real users, ongoing work includes exploring research in executable user models. The idea is to automatically generate executable cognitive user models to simulate a real user's behaviour as a cost-effective means to rapidly iterate and test design, without the attendance of real users, to enable designers to detect usability problems in their systems more quickly than is currently possible with traditional user modelling techniques. Executable cognitive user models are software agents that simulate real end-user behaviour, as well as predict end-user performance (Miao et al., 2002). They can embed multidisciplinary knowledge that most designers and end users would not be expected to know or be able to verbalise in their accounts of interaction. They are able to do more exhaustive checking of prototypes, long before they have reached a stage where actual human-user interaction would be practicable. Because user models are reusable, it is possible to simulate rapidly large groups of end users and obtain useful statistical information. The idea in using executable models achieves a two-fold purpose in rapidly iterating the design process and avoiding many design blunders. However, the reliability and efficiency of the executable cognitive user models are very much dependent on the cognitive theories used to generate them (Barnard and May, 1993). Thus, for the results obtained from simulating executable user models to be reliable, it is therefore important for them to be sufficiently tested (Wilson and Clarke, 1993).

Acknowledgments

This work is partially funded by Nanyang Technological University (RG8/03), and the Centre for Research in Pedagogy and Practice

(CRP 40/03 LEP). I would like to thank Elaine and Kuah Li who conducted Studies 1 and 2. I also thank the students at Nanyang Technological University, and teachers and students from Serangoon Secondary School for their participation and feedback in the studies.

Bibliography

Barnard, P. J. and May, J. (1993) 'Cognitive modelling for user requirements', in P. F. Byerley, P. J. Barnard and J. May (eds) *Computers, Communication and Usability: Design Issues, Research and Methods for Integrated Services*, Amsterdam, New York: North-Holland, pp. 101–45.

Bollen, J. and Luce, R. (2002) 'Evaluation of digital library impact and user communities by analysis of data patterns', *D-Lib Magazine* 8(6), available at: *http://www.dlib.org/dlib/june02/bollen/06bollen.html* (accessed 3 November 2002).

Choudhury, S., Hobbs, B., Lorie, M. and Flores, N. (2002) 'A framework for evaluating digital library services', *D-Lib Magazine* 8(7/8), available at: *http://www.dlib.org/dlib/july02/choudhury/07choudhury.html* (accessed 15 October 2002).

Davis, F. D., Bagozzi, R. P. and Warshaw, P. R. (1989) 'User acceptance of computer technology: a comparison of two theoretical models', *Management Science* 35(8): 982–1003.

Davis, F. D., Bagozzi, R. P. and Warshaw, P. R. (1992) 'Extrinsic and intrinsic motivation to use computers in the workplace', *Journal of Applied Psychology* 22(14): 1111–32.

Davis, F. (1989) 'Perceived usefulness, perceived ease of use, and user acceptance of information technology', *MIS Quarterly* 13(3): 319–40.

Davis, F. D. (1993) 'User acceptance of information technology: system characteristics, user perceptions and behavioral impacts', *International Journal of Man-Machines Studies* 38(3): 475–87.

Dishaw, T. D. and Strong, D. M. (1999) 'Extending the technology acceptance model with task-technology fit constructs', *Information and Management* 36(1): 9–21.

Dix, A., Finlay, J., Abowd, G. and Beale, R. (1997) *Human–Computer Interaction* (2nd edn), New York: Prentice-Hall.

Fishben, M. and Ajzen, I. (1975) 'Belief, attitude, intention, and behaviour: An introduction to theory and research', available at: *http://people.umass.edu/aizen/f&a1975.html* (accessed 12 May 2006).

Fuhr, N., Hansen, P., Mabe, M., Micsik, A. and Sølvberg, I. (2001) 'Digital libraries: A generic classification and evaluation scheme', in *Proceedings of the 5th European Conference on Digital Libraries, Darmstadt, 4– 9 September, LNCS Vol. 2163*, Berlin: Springer-Verlag, pp. 187–99.

Goodhue, D. L. and Thompson, R. L. (1995) 'Task-technology fit and individual performance', *MIS Quarterly* 19(2): 213–236.

Hong, W., Thong, J. Y. L., Wong, W. and Tam, K. (2002) 'Determinants of user acceptance of digital libraries: An empirical examination of individual differences and system characteristics', *Journal of Management Information Systems* 18(3): 97–124.

Hu, P. J., Hu, Clark, T. H. K. and Ma, W. W. (2003) 'Examining technology acceptance by school teachers: a longitudinal study', *Information and Management* 41(2): 227–41.

Klopping, I. M. and McKinney, E. (2004) 'Extending the technology acceptance model and the task-technology fit model to consumer e-commerce', *Information Technology, Learning, and Performance Journal* 22(1): 35–48.

Lam, T., Cho, V. and Qu, H. (2007) 'A study of hotel employee behavioral intentions towards adoption of information technology', *International Journal of Hospitality Management* 26(1): 49–65.

Landauer, T. (1995) *The Trouble with Computers: Usefulness, Usability and Productivity*, Cambridge, MA: MIT Press.

Levy, D. and Marshall, C. (1994) 'What color was George Washington's white horse? A look at the assumptions underlying digital libraries', in *Proceedings of the 4th ACM/IEEE-CS Joint Conference on Digital Libraries, Tucson, AZ, 7–11 June*, New York: ACM, pp. 163–9.

Moore, G. C. and Benbasat, I. (1991) 'Development of an instrument to measure the perceptions of adopting an information technology innovation', *Information Systems Research* 2(3): 192–222.

Nielsen, J. (1993) *Usability Engineering*, Boston, MA: Academic Press

Nunnally, J. C. and Bernstein, I. H. (1994) *Psychometric Theory* (3rd edn), New York: McGraw-Hill.

Saracevic, T. (2000) 'Digital library evaluation: Toward an evolution of concepts', *Library Trends* 49(2): 350–69.

Saracevic, T. and Kantor, P. B. (1997a) 'Studying the value of library and information services: Part I – Establishing a theoretical framework', *Journal of the American Society for Information Science* 48(6): 527–42.

Saracevic, T. and Kantor, P. B. (1997b) 'Studying the value of library and information services: Part II – Methodology and taxonomy', *Journal of the American Society for Information Science* 48(6): 543–63.

Theng, Y. L. (2005) 'Designing hypertext and the web', in *Encyclopedia of Information Science and Technology* (Vol I-V), Hershey, PA: Idea Group Reference, pp. 822–6.

Theng, Y. L. and Lew, Y. W. (2006) 'Weblogs for higher education: Implications for educational digital libraries', in *Proceedings of the 10th European Conference on Digital Libraries, Alicante, 17–22 September, LNCS Vol. 4172*, Berlin: Springer-Verlag, pp. 559–62.

Theng, Y. L., Goh, D., Lim, E. P., Liu, Z. H., Ming, Y., Pang, L. S. and Wong, P. B.-B. (2005) 'Applying scenario-based design and claims analysis on the design of a digital library of geography examination resources', *Information Processing and Management* 41(1): 23–40.

Theng, Y. L., Mohd-Nasir, N., Buchanan, G., Fields, B., Thimbleby, H. and Cassidy, N. (2001) 'Dynamic digital libraries for children', in *Proceedings of the 1st ACM/IEEE-CS Joint Conference on Digital Libraries, Roanoke, VA, June 24–28*, New York: ACM, pp. 406–15.

Theng, Y. L., Tan, K. L., Lim, E. P., Zhang J., Goh, D., Chatterjea, K., Chang, C. H., Sun, A., Hu, H., Dang, N. H., Li, Y. and Vo, M. C. (2007) 'Mobile G-Portal supporting collaborative sharing and learning in geography fieldwork: An empirical study', in *Proceedings of the 7th ACM/IEEE-CS Joint Conference on Digital Libraries, Vancouver, BC, 17–23 June*, New York: ACM, pp. 462–71.

Venkatesh, V. (2000) 'Determinants of perceived ease of use: integrating control, intrinsic motivation, and emotion into the technology acceptance model', *Information Systems Research* 11(4): 342–65.

Venkatesh, V. and Davis, F. D. (2000) 'A theoretical extension of the technology acceptance model: four longitudinal studies', *Management Science* 46(2): 186–204.

Index